Slavery and African Ethnicities
in the Americas

Slavery and African Ethnicities in the Americas: Restoring the Links

by Gwendolyn Midlo Hall

The University of North Carolina Press

Chapel Hill

Set in Minion with Syntax display
by Tseng Information Systems, Inc.
Manufactured in the United States of America
⊗ The paper in this book meets the guidelines for permanence
and durability of the Committee on Production Guidelines for
Book Longevity of the Council on Library Resources.

Grateful acknowledgment is made to Jerome S. Handler for facilitating the use
of illustrations from the website "The Atlantic Slave Trade and Slave Life in the Americas,"
<http://hitchcock.itc.virginia.edu/Slavery>, sponsored by the Virginia Foundation
for the Humanities and the University of Virginia Library.

Library of Congress Cataloging-in-Publication Data
Hall, Gwendolyn Midlo.
Slavery and African ethnicities in the Americas : restoring the links /
by Gwendolyn Midlo Hall.
p. cm.
Includes bibliographical references and index.
ISBN 0-8078-2973-0 (cloth : alk. paper)
1. Africans — America — Ethnic identity. 2. Slavery — America — History.
3. Slaves — America — History. I. Title.
E29.N3H35 2005
305.896′01812 — dc22
2005005917
09 08 07 06 05 5 4 3 2 1

To my daughter, Rebecca L. Hall,
and my granddaughter, Sajia I. Hall:
the next two generations of women historians
        among my descendants.

Contents

Illustrations, Figures, Maps, and Tables

FIGURES

MAPS

TABLES

Truth and Reconciliation

> This slave trade and slavery spread more human misery, inculcated more dis-
> respect for and neglect of humanity, a greater callousness to suffering, and
> more petty, cruel, human hatred than can well be calculated. We may excuse
> and palliate it, and write history so as to let men forget it; it remains the most
> inexcusable and despicable blot on modern human history.
> — W. E. B. Du Bois, *The Negro* (1915)

Americans throughout the Western Hemisphere owe a vast, but rarely acknowledged debt to Africa. Our national and regional cultures arose from the
process of creolization: the cross-fertilization of the most adaptive aspects of
the knowledge and traditions of the diverse peoples who met and mingled
here. Throughout the Americas, Africans and their descendants played a
major role in this process. Much of the wealth of the major nations of Europe
and America was built on the labor and the suffering of many millions of
Africans. Nevertheless, Africa remains the Dark Continent. Its peoples are
largely invisible as concrete human beings. Its descendants in the Americas
are almost invariably referred to as blacks and/or slaves or former slaves or
at best as generic Africans. This book seeks to go beyond these abstract concepts and make those Africans who played a crucial role in the formation of
cultures throughout the Americas more visible. It takes only a few steps in
this vast and complex task.

The Atlantic slave trade from sub-Saharan Africa began in 1444, more than
half a century before Columbus "discovered" the Americas. These early Portuguese voyages down the Atlantic coast of West Africa were motivated above
all by the search for gold. The Atlantic slave trade began almost incidentally
when free Africans were attacked, kidnapped, put aboard a Portuguese ship,
dragged to Portugal in chains, and sold. Enslaved Africans quickly increased
in value, and the market for them grew.

After the conquest and colonization of the Americas, the demand for
enslaved Africans intensified, and the transatlantic slave trade escalated. It
brought many millions of Africans to the Americas. Although the numbers

of Africans who arrived in the Western Hemisphere has been hotly debated among scholars for many years, we cannot come up with more than a minimum figure. W. E. B. Du Bois estimated that about 100 million Africans lost their lives as a result of the maritime slave trades. He assumed that 15 million Africans reached American shores and left five corpses behind in Africa or at sea for each African landed alive; and that nearly as many Africans died during the trans-Saharan and Indian Ocean slave trades.[1] This traffic in human beings started centuries before the Atlantic slave trade began, continued long after it ended, and still exists in Sudan and in Mauritania. Before the twentieth century, the world population was much smaller than it is today, making these losses even more staggering. The estimated 100 million dead were an important part of the productive population of Africa.[2]

During the first half of the nineteenth century, almost 400 years after it began, the Atlantic slave trade was gradually outlawed. Efforts to suppress it developed slowly over time and with limited success. The illegal slave trade proceeded apace.[3] To avoid the cost and trouble of returning them to Africa, many Africans seized by British antislave trade patrols from ships captured on their way to Cuba were brought to Cuba and kept there under the euphemism of *emancipados*.[4] Yankee ships and ships of other nations under Yankee flags operated freely, protected by the U.S. government from search and seizure until Abraham Lincoln stopped them during the Civil War in the United States. Even after the Atlantic slave trade actually ended (in 1850 in Brazil, in 1866 in Cuba), so-called contract laborers continued to be seized and exported to various regions of Africa, to islands off its coasts, as well as to the Caribbean. These "contract" laborers were certainly misnamed. They did not and could not voluntarily agree to or sign contracts. They were free people captured in warfare or kidnapped in order to sell them abroad.[5] Suppression of the slave trade and slavery within Africa became a pretext for penetration and colonization of the continent by the major European powers. The Berlin Conference of 1885, while carving up Africa to create colonies for the major European powers, passed a declaration against slave trading.[6] King Leopold of Belgium's "Congo Free State" was created under the ideological flag of fighting against slave traders. The tropical forest population of this and other rubber-producing areas of Africa was halved within a decade by terror to force Africans to engage in brutal work in return for starvation wages. The workers were beaten with whips to force them to work beyond their capacity. Their wives and children were kidnapped and held to force the men to provide their quota of rubber. European rulers and investors made huge fortunes. After the Hereros revolted in German Southwest Africa (now Namibia), their German rulers carried out a deliberate, publicly announced policy of genocide against them. In European colonies in Africa, communal lands were privatized, taxed, and seized. Head taxes in cash were imposed to force Africans to work for Europeans.[7] Escalating numbers of slaves within Africa produced "legitimate" products traded to Europe and the Americas. Thus the Atlantic slave trade lasted for over 400 years, and slavery and forced labor in Africa intensified as the Atlantic slave trade ended.[8]

We cannot ignore, dismiss, or rationalize the four terrible centuries of the Atlantic slave trade, the staggering number of its victims on both sides of the Atlantic and at sea, the fabulous wealth it created in Europe, Brazil, the United States, the Caribbean, and Spanish America. It paved the way for the European colonization of Africa, which sometimes proved to be even more destructive of human life than the Atlantic slave trade itself. This history is much more than a burden of the past. It has mutated into the present in new forms. Its victims cannot be blamed or ignored.

In South Africa, Nelson Mandela proclaimed and practiced the principle of truth and reconciliation. There can be no reconciliation without truth. History is a story told by historians. Although it is partially based on fact, it is neither fact nor fiction. A good historian is a detective who asks important questions, seeks out collections of documents and other evidence, selects what she/he considers important, and subjects it to careful evaluation and interpretation. This entire process is a judgment call in which rationalization and denial loom large. No matter how sophisticated and abstract the methodology, history is telling a story that is more or less true. Some of these stories conform to short-lived fads. The greatest challenge to historians is to seek out and approximate the truth as closely as possible, avoiding rationalizations and denials, which serve to dress up the behavior of particular nations and cast them in a benign light. Historians need to communicate their findings to the widest possible audience in order to help transcend narrow national identities. Meeting this challenge requires courage and fair-mindedness and the highest level of competence, skill, and hard work.

This book challenges the still widely held belief among scholars as well as the general public that Africans were so fragmented when they arrived in the Western Hemisphere that specific African regions and ethnicities had little influence on particular regions in the Americas. In most places, the pattern of introduction of Africans does not support this belief. The impact of specific African regions and ethnicities on particular places in the Americas emerges from this study. Specific groups of Africans made major contributions to the formation of the new cultures developing throughout the Americas. This process is called creolization. The diverse peoples who met and mingled in the Americas all made major contributions to its economy, culture, esthetics, language, and survival skills. Africans and their descendants have received very little recognition for their contributions and sacrifices and very few of the benefits. It is time to make the invisible Africans visible.

I hope the reader will not mind if I explain my experiences with this very challenging task. In 1984, I entered the courthouse of Pointe Coupée Parish in New Roads, Louisiana, to do research for my book *Africans in Colonial Louisiana*. The clerk of court asked me what I was looking for. I told him I was studying slaves and slavery and asked to see documents dating from the eighteenth century. He informed me very politely that there were no slaves in Pointe Coupée during the eighteenth century. To prove his point, and with great confidence, he got a copy of a census dating from the mid-eighteenth century. We looked at it together, and he was shocked to discover that the population listed in that census was overwhelmingly enslaved. After studying various kinds of documents housed in this courthouse, I realized that they were extraordinary. They described the slaves in great detail and, most surprising of all, included a lot of information about their African ethnicities. Further research has indicated that these ethnic designations in Louisiana documents were most likely self-identifications and, more rarely, identifications by other Africans.

The information contained in these documents was so dense and complex that I created a database to record and analyze it. A decade later, a few years after my book *Africans in Colonial Louisiana* was published, I returned to the Pointe Coupée Courthouse with two other researchers working under a National Endowment for the Humanities contract to extend the databases to all documents describing slaves in all of Louisiana through 1820. We were told that the Pointe Coupée documents could no longer be consulted because they had been badly scorched during an arson fire aimed at the colonial documents. Fortunately, the Mormons had microfilmed them before they were torched. The Louisiana Endowment for the Humanities, with support from the National Endowment for the Humanities, has now restored the most valuable volume.

The present book was inspired by speaking to audiences throughout the United States as well as in Canada, Cuba, Jamaica, Martinique, Costa Rica, France, Spain, Burkina Faso, Morocco, and Senegal. Strangely, the first public lectures I ever gave were in Francophone Africa in French. This experience gave me confidence that I could lecture in English and Spanish as well.

This is an ambitious, but a short book. As its title implies, it seeks ways to restore the links among Africans throughout the Americas with Africans in Africa. It is not simple. It discusses 400 years of the Atlantic slave trade. Research for this book has required knowledge of changes among peoples and changing conditions in major regions of Africa and the Americas as well as changing patterns in the transatlantic slave trade and the transshipment slave trade in the Americas. Its methodology is comparative. The work of historians is often very specialized. Their information and understanding of their specialty, a particular place and time, is of course superior. But sometimes when they try to be global, they tend to generalize by projecting what they know about their areas of specialization onto other times and places. This methodology is flawed. Nothing in the realm of slavery stood still. Patterns changed over time and place in both Africa and the Americas.

It is unclear to me why some scholars of the African diaspora have become so enamored with theories of boundaries and identity formation that they apply them to all black Africans and use these theories to deny the existence of self-conscious groups among any Africans on either side of the Atlantic. Modern nations as we now know them did not exist in sub-Saharan Africa throughout the Atlantic slave trade. But they did not exist in Europe or the Americas either. It is only for Africans that complex, varied, unclear and changing ethnonyms and typonyms are invoked to avoid studying them as concrete human groups. Neither Europeans nor Native Americans are lumped together as abstractions and made invisible. The meanings of African ethnic names changed over time and place. In order to understand the meanings of these designations recorded in documents, we have to cross the Atlantic and compare them in regions in Africa and America over time. Once these ethnicities have been reasonably confidently identified for a particular time and place, we need to study the existing conditions when they arrived at their final destinations and how they interacted with other peoples: red, black, brown, white, and mixed blood. This difficult, complex, but fascinating task has only just begun. Thanks to the foresight and support of Dr. Leon R. Tarver II, president of the Southern University System, a firm foundation for substantial future progress is already under way. Southern has established a project to create a master African ethnicities database with standardized fields to be published on a website with a complete search engine. It will be developed in collaboration with scholars carrying out research throughout the Americas. I am very happy to say that I will direct this project and teach students how to work with and contribute to it.

Acknowledgments

My life and career as a historian has been troubled by a combination of great faith in the social impact of history, growing confidence in the concrete and distrust of the abstract, lack of deference to changing fads in methodology and interpretation, self-assurance in my ability to do original and important work, and the desire to communicate my findings to the vast world beyond professional scholarship. When I was young, women were not taken seriously as historians. The history of slavery has remained a jealously guarded male bastion much longer than have other specialties in history. The more I learned and matured, the more confident I became that my work was at least as good as anyone else's. My nonconformist attitudes along with difficulties in traveling to professional meetings because of heavy, unshared family responsibilities kept me isolated.

Researching and writing this book and speaking about it at various stages of its development have been very rewarding experiences. It started out as one aspect of a research and writing project under contract with the National Endowment for the Humanities involving collaboration between Patrick Manning as an Africanist and me as a Latin Americanist. The databases about Louisiana slaves that I had created for my book *Africans in Colonial Louisiana* were extended under that contract and developed a life of their own. I was particularly surprised by the keen interest that my databases inspired. They were first published on compact disk in 2000. They were discussed with great insight and in some detail with key illustrations in David Firestone's article "Anonymous Louisiana Slaves Regain their Identity," published on the front page of the Sunday *New York Times* on July 30, 2000. (The article is available at <http://www.nytimes.com/library/national/073000la-slaves.html>.) After much media coverage, my databases were mounted on websites with search engines. The once invisible Louisiana slaves are now out in cyberspace. The data about them can be downloaded in several software packages free of charge (see the listings for the databases in the bibliography). People all over the world are now becoming acquainted with these previously anonymous Louisiana slaves.

This book is the result of the past twenty years of creating databases, studying and databasing documents in three languages, using databases created by other historians, studying books and articles published in four languages, asking many questions via email to scholars living and working in several continents, attending and presenting papers at a few conferences and seminars, and getting feedback about my draft manuscripts from expert readers, mainly specialists in African history. It was inspired by speaking to both scholars and community audiences in several countries. Most community people who attended my lectures were undaunted by the novelty and complexity of the ideas presented or by my at times imperfect grasp of their languages.

Patrick Manning was my first teacher of African history. But our plans for a collaborative book did not materialize. He went on to focus on his very important projects of teaching and program development in world history. I had to continue to learn what I could about African history on my own. During this process, I came into contact with some of the best and most generous of scholars: Joseph E. Inikori, Robin Law, Paul E. Lovejoy, and Joseph C. Miller. They have devoted the most time and attention to answering my many questions, reading some or all of my manuscript and sending me detailed comments. These scholars sometimes disagree among themselves as well as with me. But I am confident that we all believe in the importance of each other's work. Paul Lovejoy has given me the only intellectual home I have ever known. His enthusiasm and energy are boundless. As director of the Harriet Tubman Resource Centre on the African Diaspora at York University in Toronto, he brings out the best in the exciting international community of scholars and graduate students he has attracted there. I owe a deep debt to my colleagues with ties to the Tubman Center: Catherine Coquery-Vidrovitch, José Curto, David Eltis, Manolo Garcia Florentino, Rina Cáceres Gómez, Jane Landers, Carlos Liberato, Ugo Nwokeji, João José Reis, David Richardson, Marisa Soares, Renée Soulodre–La France, and David V. Trotman. Their fine writings and publications speak for themselves. Other colleagues have read parts of my manuscript at various stages and given me very helpful feedback and help. They include Douglas B. Chambers, Michael A. Gomez, my daughter Rebecca L. Hall, Ibrahima Seck, and Lorena Walsh. My debts to Cuban colleagues, my old friend Fé Iglesias García and my new friend Olga Portuando Zúñiga, run deep.

Many other colleagues and friends have appreciated my work and given me great help and encouragement. They include Joe Lewis Caldwell, Rafael

Casimir, John and Donna Cummings, David Hackett Fischer, Sylvia Frey, Jerome S. Handler, John Holmes, Martin A. Klein, Virginia Gould, Kathe Hambrick, Linda Heywood, Maureen Hewitt, Lance Hill, Joyce Marie Jackson, Eileen Julien, Mary Karesch, Joyce King, Paul LaChance, Hassimi Maiga, Steven H. Miles, Rhonda Miller, Steven Mintz, Andres Perez y Mena, Hyman Samuelson, Michael Sartisky, Charles Siler, Ibrahim K. Sundiata, Leon R. Tarver II, John K. Thornton, Timothy Tyson, Michael G. White, and Mabel Robinson Williams. Lucy Dunderdale helped me prepare the bibliography under great time pressure.

My recently deceased sister Razele Lehmann gave me uniquely kind and bottomless moral support. She is sorely missed. Her husband, René Lehmann, has taken up some of the slack. My son Leo Yuspeh keeps trying despite his devastating illness. Special thanks are extended to my old friend Henry Austin, who over the years has helped me locate books and carry them back and forth to the Howard Tilton Memorial Library of Tulane University and its splendid Latin American Library. He has kept the home fires burning during my many long absences from New Orleans and has looked after me as best he can whenever I return. Last but far from least is my son, Dr. Haywood Hall, who has taken time out from his demanding projects helping to develop international emergency medicine in Mexico and Latin America. He has shared with me some of the triumphs of my old age.

This book covers a lot of ground. Much of it is fairly recent knowledge to me. I have tried to be as accurate as possible in my presentations, discussions, and interpretations of African history. But I know that at times I have failed. I hope those who are better informed will correct my mistakes and that some of the questions raised will continue to be discussed within the framework of broad comparisons over time and place on both sides of the Atlantic. Inevitably, it is highly political. That is why I have challenged some of the ideas of eminent scholars whose work I deeply appreciate and respect and have relied on heavily in other contexts. These scholars include David Eltis, David Northrup, Richard Price, and John K. Thornton, all towering figures in African diaspora studies. I hope they will understand that my criticisms of some of their arguments stem from my deep belief in the power of history to mold the perceptions of people all over the world and create and enhance universal consciousness as our world shrinks and ethnic and religious conflicts escalate.

Methodologically speaking, the study of the modern African diaspora should, in my opinion, begin with Africa. The African continent—the ancestral homeland—must be central to any informed analysis and understanding of the dispersal of its peoples. . . . Scholars, arguably, cannot and should not define themselves as diaspora specialists if their area of expertise is confined to one society, or worse, to one small corner of that society.

—Colin Palmer, "Defining and Studying the Modern African Diaspora" (1998)

CHAPTER ONE

Gold, God, Race, and Slaves

Slavery in the Americas was justified by racist ideology. Many scholars as well as the wider public believe that black Africans were enslaved because they were viewed by whites as inferiors. But the identification of race with slavery is largely a projection backward in time of beliefs and ideologies that intensified during the four centuries of the Atlantic slave trade, the direct European occupation and colonization of Africa during the late nineteenth century and into the second half of the twentieth, and the brutal exploitation of Africa's labor and natural resources ever since.

Before the Atlantic slave trade began, racism justifying slavery in medieval Spain and Portugal was aimed at people with light skin. Although there were some enslaved blacks there, slave status was identified with whites. The very word "slave" is derived from "Slav": whites who were captured in Eastern Europe and shipped into medieval Spain in large numbers. Racist ideology was based on climatic determinism, but it was the Slavs who were considered natural slaves. A scholar who lived in Spain during the eleventh century wrote:

> All the peoples of this category who have not cultivated the sciences are more like animals than men. . . . They live very far from southern countries . . . in glacial temperatures with cloudy skies. . . . As a result, their temperament has become indifferent and their moods crude; their stomachs have become enlarged, their skins pale and their hair long. The finesse of their minds, the perspicacity of their intelligence is null. Ignorance and indolence dominate them. Absence of judgment and grossness are general among them. Thus are the Slavs, the Bulgarians, and neighboring peoples.[1]

In medieval Spain and Portugal, dark-skinned people were often identified as conquerors and rulers rather than as slaves. The Islamic conquest of Spain began in 711 under Arab leadership. The Moorish conquest began in 1085.

1

Moors ruled in the Iberian Peninsula for almost 400 years before the Atlantic slave trade began. The trans-Saharan trade linking sub-Saharan Africa with the Mediterranean world predated the birth of Islam. Pure, unadulterated gold arrived via the ancient camel caravan trade across the Sahara Desert. The purity and reliable weight of the coins minted in medieval Spain stimulated trade throughout the Mediterranean world. D. T. Niane has written:

> In the tenth century the king of Ghana was, in the eyes of Ibn Ḥawḳal, "the richest sovereign on earth . . . he possesses great wealth and reserves the gold that have been extracted since early times to the advantage of former kings and his own." In the Sudan it was a long-standing tradition to hoard gold, whereas in Ghana the king held a monopoly over the nuggets of gold found in the mines: "If gold nuggets are discovered in the country's mines, the king reserves them for himself and leaves the gold dust for his subjects. If he did not do this, gold would become very plentiful and would fall in value . . . The king is said to possess a nugget as big as a large stone." However, the Sudanese always kept the Arabs in the most complete ignorance regarding the location of the gold mines and how they were worked.

Salt, silver, copper, and kola nuts were also used as trading currencies. Ivory, skins, onyx, leather, and grain were important export items. The black slaves exported were mainly female domestics in demand by the Berber Arab aristocracy. Niane states that the numbers of black male slaves exported in medieval times for labor across the Sahara to Egypt and the Mediterranean has been exaggerated.[2]

As the Reconquest advanced, the Iberian Christian kingdoms sought to bypass the trans-Saharan trade controlled by the Moors, sail down the West African coast, and exploit the sub-Saharan gold deposits directly. Rather than slaves, gold was the main concern of the Portuguese rulers, merchants, and explorers who first sailed down the Atlantic coast of West Africa. Black slaves, initially a byproduct of the search for gold, became an increasing source of wealth in the Iberian Christian kingdoms.

The Senegal River Valley had deep, sustained economic, technological, cultural, religious, and political ties with Spain and Portugal. These contacts began very early. Jewish trading communities in sub-Saharan West Africa evidently preceded Islam. As early as the eighth and ninth centuries, Arab chronicles report Jewish farmers in the Tendirma region on the Niger River. A Portuguese chronicle dating from the early sixteenth century speaks of very rich but oppressed "Jews" in Walata.[3]

The Almoravids, a puritanical religious movement, were the first Islamic

Nok-Sokoto Culture, Nigeria, "Head of Court Figure," terra cotta, ca. 300 B.C.–A.D. 200. This piece is among the oldest sculptures found in sub-Saharan West Africa. (New Orleans Museum of Art: Gift of Mrs. Françoise Billion Richardson, 95.357.)

conquerors in sub-Saharan Africa. Established by Ibn Yasin among the Sanhaja Berbers, they moved south across the Sahara Desert to control the gold
trade of Galam and the gold mines of Bambuk and Buré along the upper
Senegal River. Wardjabi, king of Takrur, was an early convert. He and his
son Labi allied themselves with the Almoravids and began to attack Godala,
king of Ghana, in 1056. They captured Koumbi Saleh, the capital of the ancient kingdom of Ghana, in 1076. The kingdom of Takrur then controlled
the Senegal River and its basin and monopolized the famous gold trade of
Galam. The Almoravids had almost simultaneously moved north across the
Sahara, founded Marrakech, and established their capital there in about 1060.
In Spain, Toledo fell to the Christians in 1085. The Islamic Taïfa kingdoms had
allowed the Christians to advance by intriguing and fighting among themselves. They invited the Almoravids in to protect them. The Almoravids defeated the Christians, withdrew, and then were reinvited in after the Taïfa
kingdoms had failed again to stop the Christian advance. This time the Almoravids remained as rulers. By 1090, they had taken back much of the Iberian
Peninsula from the Christians, stopped the gold payments made to the Christian kingdoms by the Taïfas, and created the first Moorish dynasty in Spain.
This dynasty merged Western Islam into a huge state stretching from the
Senegal River Valley, Mauritania and the western Sudan, Morocco, and most
of what is now Spain and Portugal.

Thus four centuries before the Atlantic slave trade began, black Africans
from the Senegal region were quite familiar in the Iberian Peninsula. Many
dark-skinned peoples appeared in the late eleventh century not as slaves but
as warriors, conquerors, rulers, bards, and musicians. In paintings portraying
meetings and negotiations among Christians and Moors during the Spanish
Reconquest, the Moorish generals, negotiators, and rulers were often por-
trayed as blacks.[4] The Almoravids recruited black mercenaries as soldiers. In
Seville during the first half of the twelfth century, officials tried to make distinctions between the Almoravids rulers and their black mercenary troops,
requiring them to wear masks (*abid*) different from those worn by the Almoravids rulers (*litām*).[5]

The rule of the Almoravids in Spain was given an unjustifiably bad reputation by two nineteenth-century Northern European historians: Philip K.
Hitte and Reinhart Dozy.[6] These eminent founders of the European history
of the Islamic world did not escape from the intense, overt racism of their
times. They sometimes relied uncritically on sources of questionable ob-
jectivity. Resentful apologists for the Taïfa Kingdoms wrote some of these
sources. Other sources derived from apologists for the Almohads Dynasty,
which overthrew the Almoravids. The Almoravids are rarely discussed in his-

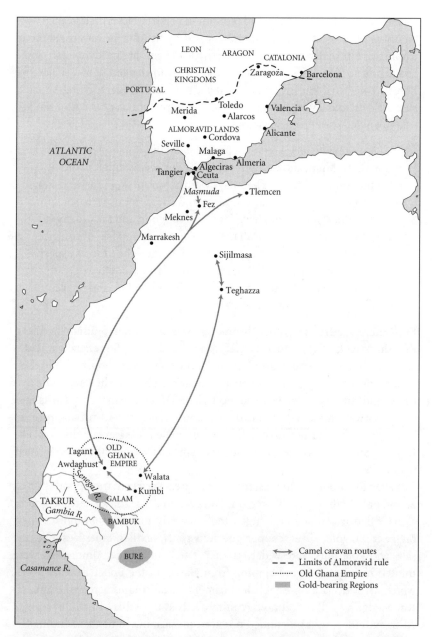

Map 1.1.   Almoravid Dynasty, 1090–1146. Adapted from maps by O. Saidi and
P. Ndiaye, in *UNESCO General History of Africa*, vol. 4, ed. D. T. Niane, and
vol. 5, ed. B. A. Ogot (Berkeley: University of California Press, 1984 and
1992); copyright © 1984 and 1992 UNESCO.

tory, and when they are, their bad reputation persists. Nevertheless, they were highly praised by their contemporaries and by Spanish historians, some of whom have proudly proclaimed that Africa began at the Pyrenees.[7] Some Spanish historians have emphasized the unacknowledged debt Renaissance Europe owed to Moorish Spain. In 1899, Francisco Codera, citing an early chronicle in Arabic, argued against racist interpretations of the Almoravids' rule in Spain. The chronicler wrote:

> The Almoravids were a country people, religious and honest. . . . Their reign was tranquil, and was untroubled by any revolt, either in the cities, or in the countryside. . . . Their days were happy, prosperous, and tranquil, and during their time, abundant and cheap goods were such that for a half-ducat, one could have four loads of flour, and the other grains were neither bought nor sold. There was no tribute, no tax, or contribution for the government except the charity tax and the tithe. Prosperity constantly grew; the population rose, and everyone could freely attend to their own affairs. Their reign was free of deceit, fraud, and revolt, and they were loved by everyone.

Even after its overthrow, other chroniclers of Islamic Spain praised the rule of the Almoravids. They wrote that learning was cherished, literacy was widespread, scholars were subsidized, capital punishment was abolished, and their gold coins were so pure and of such reliable weight that they assured prosperity and stimulated trade throughout the Mediterranean world. Christians and Jews were tolerated within their realms. When the Christians rose up in revolt, they were not executed but were exiled to Morocco instead. The Almoravids were criticized, however, for being excessively influenced by their women.[8]

When the Moors ruled Western Islam, a great variety of trade goods passed abundantly within this vast region. Horses and cattle, hides, leather goods, skins, dried fruits, arts and crafts, tools, swords and other weapons, ivory, onyx, grain, gold, silver, copper, precious gems, textiles, tapestries, pottery, salt, and kola nuts were widely traded. The coins of the Almoravids were minted mainly from gold coming from Galam in the upper Senegal River, which arrived via long-established camel caravan routes across the Sahara. Knowledge as well as technology moved across the Sahara in all directions.[9] Al-Ŝaqudī (d. 1231/32) identified nineteen musical instruments including the guitar found throughout Western Islam. He attributed the origin of most of these instruments to pre-Moorish Islamic Spain. The accuracy of this attribution should not be taken at face value. His book was a defense and glorification of pre-Moorish Spain.[10] Music is, of course, the most transportable cultural feature because it speaks a nonverbal, universal language. Musical style, musical instruments, and systems of musical notation traveled freely back and forth across the Sahara. Some Renaissance and post-Renaissance European music, including notation of pitch and rhythm, probably was transmitted from Moorish Spain.[11] Alonso de Sandoval, a Jesuit missionary working in Cartagena de Indias during the first half of the seventeenth century, wrote that the Guineans taught the Spanish and Portuguese a famous dance called "Canarios."[12] Transculturation of music and dance throughout Greater Senegambia, Northwest Africa, Spain, Portugal, and thence to the Americas is an open question. The origins and directions of this flow of music remain to be studied. Rhythm, singing, dance, and musical instruments demonstrate cross-culturation across the Sahara in all directions. This ancient cradle of music might help explain the universal appeal of jazz as well as what is now called World Music.

Iberian languages contain substantial vocabulary derived from Arabic words for law, administration, public offices, military and naval terms and ranks, architecture, irrigation, manufacturing, and other technologies. Spain exported principles of the Spanish Reconquest to the Americas. During its early stages, the pope justified the Atlantic slave trade as an extension of the Reconquest to sub-Saharan Africa and gave Portugal a monopoly of the maritime trade there. Christian beliefs, laws, and practices in Spain and Portugal were deeply influenced by Islamic concepts of international law, the rights and privileges of the conqueror and the conquered, the justification for enslavement, the law of slavery, and the mutual obligations and rights of masters and slaves. The concepts of just war and legal enslavement, including limitations on the right to enslave coreligionists, stemmed largely from Islamic law. Discussions about legal enslavement in early America involved mainly the mutable concept of religion rather than the immutable concept of race. When African slavery was introduced into the English colonies in the Americas during the seventeenth century, Christianity, not race, continued to dominate discussions of legal slavery, just enslavement, and whether enslaved Africans who converted to Christianity had to be freed. The link between religion and race centering on the curse of Ham played a minor role in these early discussions.[13] Racist justifications for enslavement and slavery of black Africans increased over time.

Despite the relative fluidity of color prejudice in medieval Spain and Portugal, as the Atlantic slave trade developed, slavery became associated with blacks, and antiblack racism became very powerful in Portuguese and Spanish America. Although its forms were different, racism was just as strong as in other American colonies. Corporatism was the foundation of law. The corporatist legal system was based on inequality before the law. It made legal and social distinctions among groups of people defined in accordance with comparative amounts of white blood among mixed-bloods and how many generations they were removed from slavery. Thus important distinctions were made among nonwhites, creating conflicts among them. It was a very efficient mechanism of social control for societies where the Spanish and Portuguese were a small minority ruling and exploiting a large subaltern population. It enabled the Iberian elite to exercise more effective control over all of the social layers beneath them. Thus some white blood in the lower casts carried much more weight in Latin America than it did in the British colonies. In insecure frontier societies like Spanish Florida and Louisiana and elsewhere in Latin America, military and police use of slaves and their descendants was promoted as a strategic policy. Manumission of slaves was encouraged to expand the layer of protection enjoyed by Spanish colonists and rulers against their own subjects as well as against foreign threats.[14] These more privileged, militarized population sectors were expected to keep order, chase runaway slaves, and serve as militias during the frequent wars among the European colonizers of the Americas. Purity of blood, *pureza de sangre*, was highly valued among the Latin American elite, although its Native American and African antecedents can sometimes be documented. Antiblack racism was and remains very powerful in Latin America. Some scholars from the United States, impressed by these formal contrasts with racism in their own country, have spread still widely believed myths of mild slavery and benign race relations in Latin America, making it much harder to combat racism because its existence is often denied.[15]

Not enough has changed since W. E. B. Du Bois lamented the state of denial and the high level of rationalization among historians of the Atlantic slave trade and slavery in the Americas. Some eminent historians are still excusing and rationalizing it, and their ideas are spreading in Europe and even in Africa. One popular argument is that slavery was widespread in Africa before the Atlantic slave trade began and that Africans participated in this trade on an equal basis with Europeans. Many "Western" historians deny that European and American wealth and power was built up to a great extent from the Atlantic slave trade and the unpaid labor of Africans and their descendants in the Americas.

Slave trade and slavery existed throughout the world for millennia. But it was not the same in all times and places. Slavery is a historical—not a sociological—category. The transatlantic slave trade was uniquely devastating. It was surely the most vicious, longest-lasting example of human brutality and exploitation in history. It was an intrusive, mobile, maritime activity carried out by faraway powers insulated from retaliation in kind. For over 400 years, it involved the hemorrhaging of the most productive and potentially productive age groups among the population in African regions deeply affected by it.[16]

Why was it Africans who were enslaved and dragged to the Americas to fulfill the colonists' needs for labor? Why did Europeans victimize Africans instead of sending their own people or other Europeans to the Americas either as voluntary immigrants or forced laborers? Until very recent times, when advanced technology became the primary basis for the wealth and power of nations, population was the most crucial factor. The populations of Spain, Portugal, and the Netherlands were very thin and their empires huge. France was a continental power with long, vulnerable borders. Its efforts to find significant numbers of French volunteer workers for its colonies failed. Its ministers expressed deep concern about the loss of the country's "useful" population and outlawed deportation of French men and women as forced laborers unless they were military deserters, criminals, prostitutes, or considered useless and/or troublemakers. Widespread rioting in Paris and elsewhere forced France to stop the kidnapping of French citizens for deportation to its colonies. The land of the Netherlands was tiny, and its populace commensurately small. The Dutch empire in the Americas was largely commercial. Dutch merchants supplied enslaved Africans primarily to the colonies of other European powers, bought raw sugar for their country's refineries in Amsterdam, and sold it throughout Europe.

England had a greater population surplus than the Continental powers. Located off the European coast and protected by the English Channel, she was much better placed strategically than France. Former peasants were removed from their land by sheep enclosures as the woolen industry grew. Irish war captives, English "criminals," and religious dissenters were available to send, or to go voluntarily to the Americas. David Eltis concluded that equal numbers of Europeans and Africans (about 300,000 of each) arrived in English America during the last half of the seventeenth century while African "immigrants" vastly outnumbered Europeans in Dutch, French, and Portuguese colonies.[17] But as the labor-hungry sugar plantation system developed in the Caribbean, the need of the British for labor in their own colonies and to sell elsewhere in America could not have been satisfied internally without risking labor shortages, rising labor costs, and internal rioting and disruption. The European powers avoided disorganizing their own societies and undermining their own wealth and power by sharply limiting the number of their own people sent to America. They did not engage in warfare to obtain slaves from neighboring powers, thereby avoiding retaliation in kind. Instead, they

imposed on faraway Africa the financial cost, destruction, social disorganization, demoralization, and population loss resulting from warfare and kidnapping to obtain captives for enslavement. European colonizers imported
millions of young Africans to work in their colonies in the Americas. Africa
bore the burden of nurturing and supporting the very young and the very
old. Many of the most productive Africans died in warfare connected with the
Atlantic slave trade, in famines and social disruptions, in slave coffles headed
to slave trade ports, and in filthy pens with little food and water, which was
often contaminated, while awaiting embarkation on slave trade ships; more
died during the crossing of the Atlantic on crowded, filthy, pestilent ships or
shortly after landing and as they were being transshipped to their final destinations. These are the main reasons that Africans, not Europeans, were enslaved and sent across the Atlantic.[18]

During the past decade, David Eltis has been arguing that Africans were
enslaved and shipped to the Americas because whites considered other whites
as insiders who could not be enslaved and blacks as outsiders who could. He
concludes that the Atlantic slave trade and slavery in the Americas should
be seen as an "ideological" phenomenon and not rooted in economics. He
has written that "freedom as it developed in Europe first made possible the
slavery of America and then brought about its abolition." This "ideological"
explanation for the Atlantic slave trade—and, indeed, for its abolition—is
flattering to Europeans. It dismisses economic motives and exploitation. It assumes that only whites ("Westerners") had a concept of freedom, which they
finally, magnanimously extended to blacks. According to this argument, enslaved Africans in the Americas had nothing to do with their own liberation.
The Haitian Revolution is dismissed as "arguably a Western phenomenon."[19]
David Brion Davis has commented, "In a pathbreaking exercise in counter-
factual history, David Eltis has argued that Western Europeans would have
populated the New World with white European slaves if cultural inhibitions
had not checked pure economic interest."[20]

The brutality of the ruling elite of Europe toward their own people before
the French Revolution of 1789 is worth noting. In 1760, a memorandum of
the office of the king of France stated casually that 60,000 French troops had
been executed for desertion. French colonial authorities in Louisiana proposed giving the Choctaw Indians a sum equal to what they received for the
scalps of Chickasaw Indians for the scalps of French military deserters. The
tender heart of the French crown toward the poor and unprotected of France
is well revealed by a report to the king of France: "Populating Louisiana has
been absolutely neglected since France has taken possession of the colony.
Men and women who were criminals and prostitutes whom one wished to

get rid of in Paris and throughout the kingdom were sent at various times, but the little care taken of them upon their arrival as well as their laziness and licentiousness resulted in their destruction and there are practically none of them left today. It can be regarded as fortunate for this colony that such a bad race was wiped out at its beginning and did not give birth to a vicious people with corrupt blood."[21]

There is an increasingly popular argument that Africans and Europeans shared equal responsibility for the Atlantic slave trade.[22] Unfortunately, some Africans, the vast majority of whom were the victims, not the perpetrators, are accepting the blame. There have been ceremonies in Africa where Africans accepted responsibility and apologized for the Atlantic slave trade. It is not true that African industriousness and productiveness made Africans equal, active participants in the Atlantic slave trade. Sub-Saharan Africans were indeed productive. They had to be in order to nurture the tens of millions of people destroyed and gobbled up by the Atlantic slave trade. Although European maritime traders had to negotiate as equals—and often as inferiors—with African traders along the Atlantic coast, in broad perspective over time, African power was undermined and fractionalized by the slave trade and the warfare, social disorganization, and population loss that it involved. Europe and Africa were not equal partners in this gruesome activity.

There was a vast distinction between slavery in Africa and slavery in the Americas. Many forms of labor systems existed in sub-Saharan Africa. They involved a variety of mutual obligations. Many different words were used for the various forms of slavery. In Africa, slavery was often a system of incorporation into the society. According to Robert Harms:

When a newly purchased slave arrived in a Bobangi village, he was either a *montambu*, a purchased slave, or a *montangi*, a prisoner of war. War prisoners were usually sold again to get them as far as possible from the point of capture, but purchased slaves were generally incorporated into the society[, which] would generally lead to full membership. . . . While slave status gave the dispossessed person a master to protect him from others, it provided only limited security because there was nobody to protect him from the master. . . . The main difference between a slave and a freeman was that a freeman could not be killed at the whim of his master or at the funeral of his master. This was not only a legal distinction, but also a practical one derived from the fact that a freeman's family would protect him, while a slave had nobody. A rich and powerful slave, however, had his own slaves to protect him, so there was little practical difference in legal rights. . . . The slaves defined their re-

lationship to their master and his family as well as their relationships to
each other by employing the idiom of kinship. A slave called his master
"father," and whichever of the master's wives had been chosen to take
care of him was called "mother." Slaves of the same age as well as free-
born children of the master were called "brother" and "sister." . . . A
young slave might call an older slave of the same master "uncle," even
though they both called their master "father."

During the first years of slavery, the purchased slave was in great danger of
being killed at the death of his master, so that he could accompany him to
the next world, or as part of a ritual to seal an agreement between chiefs. But
this danger diminished after he learned the language and was incorporated
into the family.[23]

Some scholars claim that before the Portuguese arrived, there was no word
for "slave" in the Bantu languages of West Central Africa. Costa e Silva describes a mild form of slavery. The children, nieces, and nephews of these
"slaves" were absorbed into the society. It was widely accepted throughout
much of Africa over the centuries that the children of slaves were free. Distinctions were made between slaves kept in Africa and those collected for
shipment into the Atlantic slave trade. They were sometimes referred to by
a different name. The military use of slaves and the use of female slaves as
concubines and sometimes co-wives and mothers of the children of elite men
continued to allow for significant upward mobility for some slaves and their
descendants in Africa. Some of them rose to the highest ranks of society.
These patterns existed long before the Atlantic slave trade began and continued well into the modern period.[24]

Distinctions made between slaves kept in Africa and slaves sold abroad
continued to be operative throughout the history of the Atlantic slave trade.
There were rules governing who could be enslaved. Slaves were often viewed
and treated as inferior members of extended families while in the process of
being absorbed by them. They or their descendants normally could not be
sold. In 1738, F. Moore wrote, "Tho' in some Parts of Africa they sell their
Slaves born in the Family, yet in the River Gambia they think it a very wicked
thing; and I never heard of but one that ever sold a Family-Slave, except
for such Crimes as would have made them to be sold had they been free. If
there are many Family-Slaves, and one of them commits a Crime, the Master cannot sell him without the joint Consent of the rest; for if he does, they
will all run away, and be protected by the next Kingdom to which they fly."
These rules were still rigorously enforced in Greater Senegambia during the
late eighteenth century. Slaves born in the master's house or whom he had

owned for more than twelve months could not be sold "unless they escaped, threatened the life of a free person, or engaged in incorrigible behavior."[25]

Robin Law has written:

> In Dahomean tradition, one of the fundamental laws attributed to the founder-king Wegbaja, in the seventeenth century, prohibited the sale as slaves of anyone born within the kingdom, contravention being a capital offence; in principle, this rule was enforced so rigorously as to prohibit the sale even of female captives who became pregnant while in transit through Dahomey. . . . Slaves in Dahomey were in principle foreigners, captives taken in war or purchased from outside the country; Dahomeans should be enslaved only in punishment for some specific and serious offence. When kings of Dahomey, in default of sufficient supplies of foreign slaves, resorted to "selling their own subjects" as was alleged both of Tegbesu in the last years of his reign and of Gezo in the early 1820s, this was considered aberrant and illegitimate, in effect an index of social breakdown.[26]

Interviews conducted as late as 1972–73 by David Northrup in southeastern Nigeria with forty informants indicate that distinctions were made between slaves destined to be retained in Africa and those to be sold into the Atlantic slave trade. The children of slaves kept in Africa became free.[27]

In the Americas, Europeans called everyone they bought by one word: "slave." Incorporation into the master's family was rarely a possibility, although there were a few exceptions for female concubines and their children during the early stages of colonization. Slavery in the Americas varied, but not by legal definition, form, and linguistic distinction as in Africa. Slavery in the Americas was no doubt more exploitative and brutal than slavery in Africa before the nineteenth century because it was geared toward maximizing the production of goods for an inexhaustible international market while minimizing costs. Slavery on plantations producing valuable, highly labor-intensive export crops, especially sugar, differed from that on plantations producing other, less demanding crops. Rural and urban slavery were substantially different. Slavery in mines where African skills were heavily relied on was different from slavery in other occupations. Mining for silver, gold, and copper was carried out under distinctive conditions. Mining for diamonds, emeralds, and other precious stones differed from mining for metals. Diving for pearls was an especially dangerous occupation. Although by definition, slaves could be bought and sold, restrictions on family breakup during sale varied over place and time in both law and practice. Enforcement

Women warriors parading before the Dahomey king and European men.
(Archibald Dalzel, *The History of Dahomey: An Inland Kingdom of
Africa*, 1793.)

was uneven. Depending on timing, demographic patterns, and varying traditions among colonists, slave concubines and children of white masters were
sometimes freed by custom if not by law. Manumission rights and regulations
varied over time and place as well. Skilled male slaves were more likely to
have wives and children than unskilled slaves did. At many times and places
in the Americas, slaves could sell products from the garden plots assigned
to them; the domestic animals they raised; the berries, herbs, and shellfish
they gathered; the fish, birds, and game they caught; the firewood and finer
woods they cut and carried to sawmills and markets; and the craft products
they made. Indeed, many American colonies and states depended almost entirely on food produced and sold by slaves in the markets of villages, towns,
and cities as well as along the roads. Domestic slaves generally ate better and
were better clothed than field slaves. Thus there was no one rigid condition
or system of slavery in America. But it differed from African patterns of in-

corporating slaves and their descendants into the families of the masters and the broader community. Although paternalism was a factor in slave control in the Americas, its possibilities were more limited. Extremely restricted social advancement for slaves in the Americas, as compared to the upward mobility of slaves in Africa, left few alternatives to brutal methods. Masters had a more limited repertoire for controlling their slaves and less to offer besides contempt and fear.

The Atlantic slave trade had a devastating impact on Africa. Escalating prices paid for millions and millions of people over the centuries transformed the methods of procuring and treating slaves and undermined productive but less profitable activities. It created a progressively increasing level of violence and disorganization in African societies. As early as 1526, Affonso, king of Kongo, a close ally of the Portuguese and a devout Christian, complained, "There are many traders in all corners of the country. They bring ruin to the country. Every day, people are enslaved and kidnapped, even nobles, even members of the king's own family."[28]

King Affonso tried to ban Portuguese traders and expel all whites except teachers and missionaries, but he failed. John K. Thornton's study of the early correspondence of West Central African rulers establishes that it was not slavery itself but the European violation of African rules limiting and controlling it that motivated their complaints.[29] Chaos, warfare, and empire building connected with the slave trade had an incalculably destructive, disruptive, and demoralizing effect. Warfare in Africa is difficult to disaggregate from the escalating Atlantic slave trade. Although it was often propelled by internal considerations, it became increasingly provoked, inspired, greased, and supported by the European demand for slaves in the Americas as the frontiers for the capture, kidnapping, and sale of Africans supplying the Atlantic slave trade expanded and moved inland. By 1650, the Gold Coast became a major market for European guns and powder. Guns were incorporated into the military by phalanxes firing from a distance before engaging in hand-to-hand combat. Akwamu and Mina mercenaries were used in the Slave Coast. One can indeed find in Lower Guinea after 1650 a proliferating slave trade driven by large-scale, escalating purchases of European arms.[30] It is hard to divorce warfare in Africa from the Atlantic slave trade. Philip D. Curtin's attempt to separate political from economic warfare in Africa has been cogently criticized by Boubacar Barry.[31] John K. Thornton is right that discussion of warfare in Africa cannot be reduced to "primitive" raiding for slaves. But he continues to defend the analytical separation of economic from political warfare in Africa—a distinction that is hard to make in regard to any place in the world—and he projects the limited usefulness of European firearms in

West Central Africa during the sixteenth and seventeenth centuries much too broadly to other times and places in Africa.[32]

Europeans did not simply tap into a preexisting supply of slaves or a slave trade in Africa. Slaves could not be easily purchased on various coasts for decades after the Europeans first arrived and began to look for human chattel. A new market in slaves had to be created. Although early chronicles by Portuguese entrepreneurs indicate that domestic slavery existed in Senegal when they arrived and that slaves were being exported into the trans-Saharan trade, there is little evidence that a major slave trade operated along the West African coast before the first Portuguese ship collected slaves in Senegambia in 1444.[33] That ship's crew attacked and kidnapped their victims.[34] It was always safer and easier to buy people who were already enslaved than to attack, kidnap, and capture them directly. Africans sold into the Atlantic slave trade were rarely slaves in African societies. They were largely free people captured to satisfy the insatiable market for slaves in the Americas. As the demand for slaves increased and prices rose, the judicial system became corrupted in order to "produce" more slaves for export to the Americas. The victims included free people as well as slaves. It was only after the Atlantic slave trade ended that internal dynamics as well as the European demand for "legal" goods produced by slaves in Africa resulted in massive enslavement, slave trading, and an increasingly brutal slave system within Africa.[35]

There was no visible slave trade in Aja/Yoruba lands of the Slave Coast when the Europeans first visited there. They described markets where many goods were bought and sold. They looked hard for and inquired about slave markets but were told that such markets only existed 800 miles inland. This was, of course, not true and might have been a means to encourage the Portuguese to move on. The earliest Portuguese slave trade from the Bight of Benin began in the kingdom of Benin not very far away, but it lasted for only a few decades before the king put a stop to it. During the eighteenth century, a group of Aja peoples told an English traveler that the root of their unhappiness was "that they were ever visited by the Europeans. They say that we Christians introduced the traffick [sic] in slaves and that before our coming they lived in peace."[36]

The development of large African states along the west coast of Africa and along major interior trade routes was often driven by the desire to exert control over the maritime trade and to take advantage of the European demand for slaves. The kingdom of Segu relied on selling war captives into the Atlantic slave trade and incorporated some of them into its armies. While capturing warriors and selling them was probably not the main motive for the expansion of Segu, it certainly helped enlarge its military force and finance its wars of expansion.

The kingdom of Dahomey captured Whydah in 1727, advancing to the Atlantic Coast. After Dahomey destroyed the port of Jakin in 1732, Whydah became the exclusive outlet for the maritime trade on the Slave Coast. According to Robin Law, "The general view of contemporary European observers, that Agaja (King of Dahomey) sought control of Ouidah [Whydah] principally in order to secure more effective and unrestricted access to the European trade, remains persuasive."[37]

Two of the major polities that developed in West Africa, Asante in the Gold Coast and Dahomey in the Slave Coast, tried to protect their own people from the Atlantic slave trade. But this did not mean they opposed enslavement and sale of other peoples, including their close neighbors.[38] There were substantial numbers of Fon and Arada listed in American notarial documents. But this designation might have been broad. Arada was a commonly used ethnic designation in St. Domingue/Haiti. Very few Mahi or Savaru, neighbors to the north regularly raided for slaves by Dahomey, have been found listed in notarial documents in North America. One Mahi and one Savaru were found in documents in Bahia, Brazil, dating from between 1816 and 1850.[39] Marisa Soares has found that Mahi and Savaru who spoke Gbe languages eagerly differentiated themselves from Dahomeans in religious brotherhoods in Rio de Janeiro during the eighteenth century.[40]

European trade goods made modest contributions to the needs of Africa. The most useful products introduced by Europeans were the food crops domesticated over thousands of years by Native Americans. They included maize/corn, manioc/cassava, pineapples, avocados, tomatoes, peanuts, white potatoes, some sweet potatoes, squash, pumpkins, and some forms of peppers and beans. African goods had been produced to high standards and traded over great distances many centuries before the Atlantic slave trade began. Textiles and medals were often of high quality. The Atlantic slave trade imported massive quantities of cheap substitutes to exchange for slaves and other goods, disrupting to some extent the established, traditional trade networks from the coastal regions of Africa into the interior and creating enclave economies along the coasts to supply the Atlantic slave trade. Europeans brought in and exchanged some useful products: various forms of currency including cowries from the Indian Ocean, cheap cloth—at first mainly from India and later in the form of mass-produced textiles from Britain—iron, copper, brass and other metals also from Britain, and luxury goods from all over the world.

Some of the imported products were destructive and addictive. Europeans introduced large quantities of firearms, including some cannons, and gunpowder. Regardless of their quality, muskets and rifles had a profound military and psychological impact in Africa and certainly helped escalate warfare and slave raiding. Warfare was subsidized by the sale of captured warriors and of villagers kidnapped in warfare as well as in private raids. The role of addiction in promoting the Atlantic slave trade is only beginning to get the attention it deserves. Tobacco domesticated by Native Americans was introduced. Some varieties were cultivated in Africa, but the market for tobacco in Africa was specialized. Powerful, cheap, sweetened tobacco from Bahia, Brazil, was in great demand along the Slave Coast. Virginia tobacco was popular in Upper Guinea. Light alcoholic beverages — palm wine, for example — existed in Africa before the Atlantic slave trade began. European and American slave traders introduced increasingly potent alcohol, first mainly wine and then brandy and rum. Such imports clearly undermined the physical and mental health of many Africans and made them increasingly dependent on the Atlantic slave trade.[41]

In West Central Africa, Portuguese wine was introduced very early. It was overproduced abundantly in Portugal as well as in its Atlantic Islands off the coast of Africa. The sale of wine in Africa was an especially profitable trade for Portugal because export and re-export of goods to Africa from Asia and northern Europe via Portugal raised costs and reduced profits. It played a ceremonial role in the process of trade negotiations. It was sometimes used to intoxicate African rulers and merchants in order to promote trade and obtain the best terms. The sale of wine was widespread in West Central Africa before 1640. But the introduction of rum with much higher alcohol content was particularly devastating. The first references to the sale of distilled rum in West Central Africa date from the beginning of the 1640s. Dutch traders began to sell rum to obtain control of the slave trade in the port of Mpinda on the Atlantic coast on the south bank of the Kongo River. Enslaved Africans from the kingdom of Kongo as well as some from north of the Congo River were shipped through this port.[42]

Although the Dutch captured Luanda, Angola, in 1641, the Portuguese and Afro-Portuguese continued to control the trade routes of its hinterland. After 1648, when the Dutch were chased out of Luanda by a Brazilian fleet led by Salvador da Sá, Brazilian merchants began to replace Portuguese slave traders in Angola, expanding direct trade between Brazil and Luanda. They sold extremely potent Brazilian rum (*cachaça* or *gerebita*) and bought large numbers of enslaved Africans "produced" by escalating warfare.[43]

For over a hundred years, New England rum played a significant role in the Gold Coast and Greater Senegambian slave trade. It was extremely popular in the Gold Coast, where 80.8 percent (n = 198) of the 245 voyages leaving from Rhode Island with identified buying regions in Africa sold their cargoes.[44] In Greater Senegambia, New England rum and Virginia tobacco were in great demand. Neither West Indian rum nor French brandy would do. During the American Revolution, in the absence of New England rum, the slave trade there nearly collapsed.[45] In Sierra Leone during the early 1790s, one observer wrote, "Without rum [exchanged for rice and for slaves], we must already shortly starve."[46] New England rum and gold were the only products that attained the status of currency. Joseph E. Inikori's studies of British exports to West Africa show that between 1750 and 1807, "spirits" were 5 percent or less rising to over 10 percent thereafter and then 20 percent during the 1840s. Evidently, British "spirits" were not popular when New England rum was available.[47]

African slavery in the Americas is usually discussed within the context of the need for brute, unskilled labor on sugar, rice, indigo, coffee, and cotton plantations. But Africans were especially needed in the Americas because of their skills. Spain and Portugal began to colonize the Americas well over a century before Britain and France. The Spanish American colonies focused mainly on the mining of silver, gold, and precious stones and the large-scale construction of harbors, docks, warehouses, roads, bridges, houses, churches, cathedrals, and fortresses. Skilled labor was desperately needed, and African skills were known long before the conquest and colonization of America began. The Native American population was decimated by conquest, warfare, forced labor, and diseases spread from Europe and Africa to which they had no immunity. While protection of Native Americans was couched in religious, humanitarian, and ideological terms, the main reason why these protective policies were adopted was to stop the total destruction of the native labor force in Spain's colonies so they could continue to be exploited through forced labor on heavy construction projects and by paying tribute in the form of food, clothing, craft products, labor, and currency. Although many Africans were relied on for their skills, especially in port cities, some of them were systematically substituted for Native Americans in the most brutal and dangerous occupations in early Spanish America—in mines, on sugar plantations, and in pearl-diving. Spain soon outlawed Indian slavery because it feared the utter annihilation of the Indian population in its American colonies. Slavery of Africans and their descendants remained legal in Spanish America throughout the entire colonial period and well after independence in many Latin American nations.

The colonization of America depended very heavily on skills brought from

Africa. Enslaved Kongo Africans developed and worked in the copper industry at Santiago de Cuba where they remained in high demand for centuries.[48] Africans who were experienced gold miners were in demand very
early in Colombia to develop mining there. Africans designated as "Minas"
were brought to Brazil from gold-producing regions of West Africa, including Greater Senegambia and the Gold Coast, in order to discover and develop panning and digging for gold.[49] Enslaved Africans were blacksmiths,
metallurgists, toolmakers, sculptors and engravers, silversmiths and gold-
smiths, tanners, shoemakers, and saddle-makers. They were designers and
builders of warehouses and docks, barracks and homes, public buildings,
churches, canals, and dams. They were coopers, draymen, and coach drivers;
breeders, groomers and trainers of horses; and cowboys skilled in cattle rear-
ing and herding. They were hunters and fishermen, as well as pearl divers.
They were ship builders, navigators, sounders, caulkers, sailmakers, ship car-
penters, sailors, and rowers. They were indigo-makers, weavers and dyers of
cloth, tailors and seamstresses. They were basket weavers, potters, and salt-
makers. They were cooks, bakers, pastry chefs, candy-makers, street vendors,
innkeepers, personal servants, housekeepers, laundresses, domestics, doctors
or surgeons, and nurses. They cultivated corn, rice, garden crops, tobacco,
poultry, pigs, sheep, and goats.[50]

For four centuries, the political and economic elites of the nations of
Europe and the Americas were enriched by the foreign and domestic slave
trade and the unpaid labor of slaves. The transatlantic slave trade was enor-
mously profitable to the crowned heads of Europe. Licensing and taxing of
the Atlantic slave trade became a major source of wealth for the Iberian kingdoms. The Spanish crown reaped extraordinary revenues by selling licenses
to engage in the Atlantic slave trade and then collecting tax on every slave
landed while passing all risks on to the Atlantic slave traders. The English
crown invested in and profited directly from the Atlantic slave trade. The
French crown subsidized the Atlantic slave trade by paying a gratuity to the
maritime slave traders for each African landed in France's American colonies. This subsidy encouraged the slave trade to French colonies so the crown
could then profit by taxing its wealthy sugar islands in the Caribbean and
the valuable products they produced and exported. French rulers, merchants,
maritime traders, and sugar refiners reaped a windfall.

A vast amount of the wealth accumulated by European nations derived directly or indirectly from the Atlantic slave trade and slavery. Eric R. Williams
argued that Britain's industrial revolution was financed by the wealth derived
from the Atlantic slave trade and slavery in its colonies in the Americas. The
Williams thesis, published in 1944, has held up very well against criticism

leveled against it ever since. It is valid beyond Britain, although perhaps on a more modest scale. Its greatest weakness is that it does not make the necessary global links among European nations involved in the Atlantic slave trade and slavery in the Americas.[51] Joseph Inikori has corrected this. He discusses the role of the English slave trade and slavery in the Americas in the industrial revolution in England in a global context over the *longue durée* (between 1650 and 1850), emphasizing the growing hegemony of Britain in international maritime trade, including the transatlantic slave trade, the production in the Americas of increasing quantities of export commodities produced by cheap African labor, and the rise of the shipbuilding, banking, and insurance industries in England to support this trade. His work is well informed by a comparative approach; but it tends to downplay the wealth accumulated by other European and American powers through the exploitation of Africa and Africans. Inikori's definitive work concerning England should inspire other scholars to focus on these same questions in regard to Spain, Portugal, France, the Netherlands, the United States, Brazil, and Spanish America.[52]

At many times and in many places, African coastal polities exerted considerable power and control over conditions of trade with maritime slave traders. But the Atlantic slave trade and slavery in the Americas formed a system that operated over a span of four centuries. It ripped out Africa's most precious possession, its people, to create the wealth and power of faraway lands at an extremely high cost in suffering and human lives. This simple fact is not debatable.

CHAPTER TWO

Making Invisible Africans Visible:
Coasts, Ports, Regions, and Ethnicities

We are called, we are named just like a child is given a name and who, like a child, do not have a say in the choice of our own name.
—Olabiyi Yai, in *African Ethnonyms and Typonyms*, 1978

Qui se disent leur nation Bambara. [They say their nation is Bambara.]
—From a slave sale document in Louisiana, 1799

Studies of the African diaspora in the Americas began mainly during the early twentieth century among anthropologists: most notably Nina Rodriguez in Brazil and Fernando Ortiz in Cuba, and then a generation later by Frances and Melville Herskovits in the United States. Fieldwork was a primary methodology. They often studied communities of African descent in the Americas, linking them with particular regions or ethnicities in Africa by seeking out shared cultural traits. Their work is very useful, informative, and fascinating, and their methodologies are more sophisticated than some recent critics have been willing to acknowledge. Nevertheless, their approach poses problems for the study of the African diaspora in the Americas. Religion, worldview, and esthetic principles—including the styles and social role of the plastic arts, music, musical instruments, and dance—are among the most enduring and resilient cultural heritages. But they are also the most generalized. There are many common cultural features in Africa. It is not always easy to disaggregate which features are characteristic of any particular ethnicity or region. Very few scholars are familiar with a substantial number of African languages. Some seize on a word or a name they know and extrapolate it broadly to prove the presence and influence of a particular African ethnicity in the Americas. But the same or similar names and words exist in several African languages and can have the same, a similar, or a different meaning. The result is sometimes romanticized and inaccurate views of the influence of particular African ethnicities and languages. Swahili becomes the "African language," but few speakers of Swahili were brought to the

Americas. "Yoruba" becomes the African ethnicity, although "Yoruba" presence in the Americas before the late eighteenth century (recorded as "Nago" or "Lucumí" in American documents) was not very substantial. Except for Louisiana, where Nago were 4 percent of identified ethnicities, the presence of Yoruba in the United States was insignificant. They were important in St. Domingue/Haiti (Nago) after 1780, in Cuba (Lucumí) during the nineteenth century, and, most significantly, in nineteenth-century Bahia, Brazil (Nago).

During the last few decades, anthropologists have taken the lead in denying the significance of African ethnicities in the Americas. Their arguments include questioning both the accuracy and the significance of these designations in American documents as well as the very existence of African ethnicities in Africa. Based on his studies of documents in Cuba, Moreno Fraginals has written:

> The main trend at present (perhaps due to the influence of Roger Bastide) is to attach little importance to ethnic references; the assumption is that they were imposed arbitrarily by the slave-trader so as to trick his clients, or that this must have been affected by the traders' geographical ignorance of the zone in which they were operating or by pseudoscientific prejudices of the time. We maintain the complete opposite. Our basic assumption is that the slave trade was the business that involved the greatest amount of capital investment in the world during the eighteenth and early nineteenth centuries. And a business of this size would never have kept up a classificatory scheme had it not been meaningful (in overall general terms, in keeping with reality) in designating in a *very precise* way the merchandise that was being traded.[1]

We will see that there is strong evidence that Africans often identified their own ethnicities recorded in American documents. The knowledge and perceptions of the slave traders had much less to do with this process than scholars have assumed.

The assumption of timelessness is a basic methodological flaw of anthropology. But it is a problem shared by many historians of the African diaspora. They sometimes project patterns in times and places with which they are familiar to all times and places. In their eagerness to make sense of vast, complex data, scholars sometimes embrace abstract, generalized concepts, which obscure rather than reveal the past. Studies of the African diaspora in the Americas need to be concrete and contextualized. Peoples and their cultures evolved and changed on both sides of the Atlantic. There was no single pattern of creolization either in Africa or in the Americas. Slavery as well as other forms of exploitation of labor varied greatly over time and place.

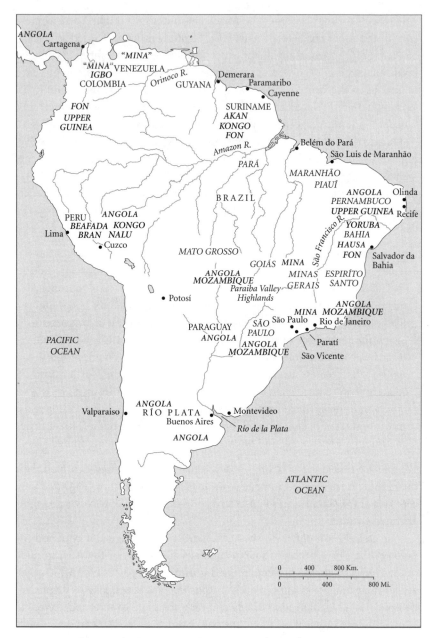

Map 2.1. African Ethnicities Prominent in South America, 1500–1900

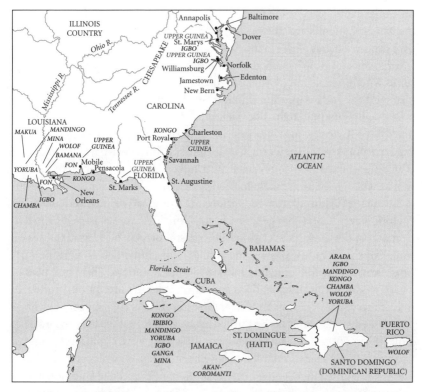

Map 2.2.   African Ethnicities Prominent in North America and the
Caribbean, 1500–1900

Thanks to computer applications to history, it is now possible to organize
huge amounts of data, thereby facilitating comparisons of patterns over time
and place. DNA studies are the newest frontier for exploring the roots of
African-descended peoples in the Americas.

The study of transatlantic slave trade voyages is not enough. These documents do not list and rarely mention African ethnicities. Documents generated by these voyages can at best give us African coasts or ports of origin
and/or ports in the Americas where slaves were first sold. More rarely, the
numbers, genders, or age categories of the slave "cargoes" were listed. The
proportions of African ethnicities exported from African coasts and ports
changed over time. After enslaved Africans arrived in American ports, they
were normally sold and then often transshipped to other places, sometimes
outside the colony or country where they first landed. Studies based entirely

on transatlantic slave trade voyages need to be supplemented by studies of the transshipment slave trade as well as other types of documents generated over time in various places in the Americas. These studies can help us discover which Africans from which regions, ethnicities, and genders found themselves where, when, and in what proportions. Such studies far transcend local history. They have important implications for the study of the African diaspora throughout the Americas as well as for African history. Patterns of introduction of African ethnicities into the Americas are mirror images of their export from Africa. They can help us understand when particular African ethnicities started to become deeply victimized by the Atlantic slave trade as well as where they were finally located.

Ethnicities exported from the various African coasts defined and named by Atlantic slave traders changed. The same ethnicities were exported from two or more of these coasts over time. The coastal origins of transatlantic slave trade voyages can give contrasting results with ethnic descriptions of Africans derived from documents generated in the Americas. This book tries to avoid making artificial separations among Africans exported from more than one of these African coasts. It is often best not to treat African coasts defined and named in various ways by European slave traders as entirely separate regions. Firm boundaries among some of these coasts are an illusion. Some of Curtin's African coastal definitions have been cogently challenged. Boubacar Barry has convincingly argued that it is often awkward and questionable to separate "Senegambia" from "Sierra Leone." Curtin's "Windward Coast" designation presents problems discussed below.

I argue that our best evidence for the distribution of Africans at their final destinations in the Americas is in documents containing "nation" descriptions of enslaved Africans, despite the fact that these ethnic designations are sometimes unclear and equivocal. The Mexican scholar Gonzalo Aguirre Beltrán published a pioneering work about African ethnicities in North America. He made systematic studies of American documents over time and place and linked them to developments in Africa as well as with patterns in the transatlantic slave trade. His work focused on Mexico and the Caribbean through the seventeenth century. James Lockhart studied African ethnic designations in Peru during the mid-sixteenth century, but his data are thin. Gabriel Debien and his colleagues studied African ethnicities listed in documents in the French West Indies dating almost entirely from the eighteenth century. Philip D. Curtin relied heavily on the work of these three scholars.[2] Colin Palmer's book about Mexico discusses African ethnicities there.[3] Subsequent studies have usually been based on larger numbers of African ethnic designations listed in American documents. During the past three decades, some scholars have made major contributions to our knowledge of documents listing African ethnic designations. Their work is studied and cited throughout this book.

The introduction of Africans into the Americas was a complex process. It involved vast regions of the world over nearly four centuries. It must be placed within the context of ever changing patterns over time and place on both sides of the Atlantic as well as at sea. Primary sources exist, and very important books and articles have been published in major European languages: English, French, Spanish, Portuguese, Dutch, German, Danish, and Russian. There are important sources published in Arabic as well as in African languages written in Arabic script.[4] There are invaluable oral histories as well. Many studies have been published about various regions of Africa and the Americas at specific times and places. There are other fine scholarly works about the slave trade of specific European and American nations.

Two important syntheses of the Atlantic slave trade and slavery in the Americas were recently published in English. Both books—one by Robin Blackburn, the other by Hugh Thomas—discuss African slavery and the Atlantic slave trade over the centuries, the *longue durée*. They rely on the literature in major European languages, avoiding the narrow English focus of some historians. Organizing and synthesizing this vast, difficult, and unwieldy body of knowledge is a major achievement. But neither of these books discusses the African ethnicities involved in the Atlantic slave trade, limiting their usefulness for this study.[5]

Many of the most prominent historians of the Atlantic slave trade, especially those writing in English during the past thirty-five years, have been fascinated by quantitative studies. The first major work using quantitative methods was Philip D. Curtin's pioneering book *The Atlantic Slave Trade: a Census*, published in 1969. This bold, imaginative, impressively researched work has inspired more than one generation of historians to search for greater precision in estimating the numbers of Africans loaded aboard slave trade ships in Africa and landed in the Americas. Some of these historians were Curtin's distinguished students. But until recent years, few of them followed Curtin's interest in African ethnicities.

There are conflicting interpretations of the number of Africans removed from Africa and landed in the Americas. Joseph E. Inikori has pointed out that many voyages involving smuggling and piracy were obviously undocumented and that many slave trade voyages went directly from the Americas to Africa and back, bypassing Europe. Many of them have been overlooked or undercounted by historians working mainly in large, centralized archives in Europe. Inikori raised Curtin's estimate of 9.55 million Africans put on land in the Americas to about 15.4 million.[6] Hugh Thomas gives a higher estimate of the numbers of transatlantic slave trade voyages, raising David Eltis's estimate from approximately 40,000 voyages to 50,000. Thomas estimates that about 2 million enslaved Africans left for the Americas from Senegambia and Sierra Leone alone, a much higher figure than most historians allow. This book confirms and explains the substantial undercount of voyages from Greater Senegambia.[7]

African, Spanish, Portuguese, and Latin American scholars have appreciated Curtin's work. But some of the most prestigious among them have remained reasonably skeptical about the limits of quantification, regardless of how sophisticated, when it is based on uneven and inadequate data. They, as well as Curtin, have emphasized the importance of understanding the historical context in which these voyages took place. Some have pointed out that for various reasons these Atlantic slave trade documents reported falsified information. Many documents are still to be found or are missing. Other voyages were never documented. Thus, quantification alone is a limited tool in the absence of a deepening of our knowledge, understanding, and appreciation of studies relying on unquantifiable sources.[8] Many fine historians have assiduously collected, translated, annotated, and prudently used traditional sources despite changing fads and often without the support and recognition they deserve. Their work, some of it cited in this book, is essential in putting flesh on the bare bones of quantitative studies and ensuring that they are used judiciously.

The Trans-Atlantic Slave Trade Database is the best recent synthesis of the work of the quantification school of Atlantic slave trade studies.[9] It is an extremely useful compilation of research carried out mainly during the past thirty years and, especially important, a computerization of much of the known information about transatlantic slave trade voyages. It was published as a relational database on a compact disk with a search engine, which allows for rapid answers to questions about documented and studied transatlantic slave trade voyages as well as comparison of broad patterns over time and place. Some of these results are of transcendent importance. For example, they indicate that individual transatlantic slave trade voyages collected their "cargoes" overwhelmingly from the same African coast, often from only one or two ports. A very important, valid conclusion is that African ethnicities were not nearly as fragmented by the transatlantic slave trade as scholars as well as the wider public have long believed.[10]

Obviously, many important questions about the transatlantic slave trade cannot be answered by studying The Trans-Atlantic Slave Trade Database alone. Missing and uneven data about voyages as well as inaccurate interpretations of geographic terms have led at times to inaccurate and distorted conclusions. Contrasting uses of the geographic term "Angola" by British and other European slave traders and "Angola" as an ethnic designation by slave owners add to the confusion. The documented British slave trade has been extensively studied, overemphasizing this trade compared to that of other countries. Manolo Florentino has pointed out that more than twice as many enslaved Africans were brought to Brazil than to the British colonies. Africans arriving on voyages to the British Caribbean were much more likely to be transshipped to colonies of other powers, especially to Spanish and French colonies, than Africans arriving in Brazil, although a relatively small number were transshipped south from Brazil to Spanish Río de la Plata (now Argentina and Uruguay) and west to Upper Peru (now Paraguay and Bolivia), Lower Peru, and Chile.[11] The deficit in Portuguese and Brazilian voyages in *The Trans-Atlantic Slave Trade Database* is widely recognized, including by its creators. Post-publication revisions have already added about 7,000 voyages, most of them Portuguese and Brazilian.

The truth is, we do not know and probably never will know how many enslaved Africans were loaded onto Atlantic slave trade ships in Africa and how many disembarked in the Americas. How representative are the voyages included in *The Trans-Atlantic Slave Trade Database*? My research into unusually rich documents housed in Louisiana archives reinforces the conclusion that direct voyages between Africa and the Americas have been undercounted. More studies of other American ports should be revealing. This database is a very large sample showing important trends. It should neither be dismissed nor turned into a fetish used uncritically. Its potential for answering pivotal questions has only begun to be explored.

African coasts defined in Philip D. Curtin's influential work have remained largely in vogue and were adopted in full by the creators of the *Trans-Atlantic Slave Trade Database*. Curtin's demarcation of territories along the West African coast clearly proceeded from the outside perspective of European and American slave traders rather than from the indigenous view of the peoples inhabiting various African regions. Distinguished historians have challenged two of these coastal definitions. Boubacar Barry defines the region between the Senegal and the Sierra Leone rivers as Greater Senegambia. Cultural interpenetration among ethnic groups throughout this region was intense over many centuries. Languages of two major language groups, Mande and West Atlantic, are spoken throughout this vast region.[12] Mandingo was the lingua franca. Separating Senegambia and Sierra Leone creates awkward problems when ethnic designations in American documents are used to define coastal origins. Timing is an important factor. Some ethnicities found frequently in

American documents — for example, the Fulbe (listed in documents as Fula, Fulani, Poulard, Peul) — migrated south and east over vast distances. During the 1720s, because of the growing desiccation of their grazing lands, many Fulbe migrated with their herds of cattle from the banks of the Senegal River and established the Fula Alamate in Futa Jallon. By 1780, they were heavily engaged in warfare with the Mandingo in the region defined by Curtin as Sierra Leone. Many Fulbe and Mandingo captives were exported from ports in Sierra Leone.[13]

The same ethnicities were exported from more than one region or coast. The American data can give us ethnicities present at a particular time and place. They may not correspond to African ethnicities sent from any particular port or coast. The study of African ethnicities in the Americas requires mining of data from both sides of the Atlantic over time. For example, after 1750 African ethnicities normally associated with Senegal narrowly defined arrived in the Americas on voyages that had left from Sierra Leone. Atlantic slave trade voyages from Sierra Leone increased more rapidly than voyages from Senegal narrowly defined. More Temne, Kisi, and Kanga appear in American documents during the last half of the eighteenth century. But the percentage of ethnicities associated with Senegambia narrowly defined does not in fact decline in documents recorded in the Americas. Fulbe and Hausa were exported from African coasts located further south and east over time: from the Slave Coast during the eighteenth century; from the Bight of Biafra as well during the nineteenth century.

The term "Windward Coast" as used by Atlantic slave traders designated an imprecise location in Africa. It could refer to anywhere from the Gold Coast to Greater Senegambia as well as to what it is widely understood to mean: Liberia and the Ivory Coast. In 1980, Armah, Jones, and Johnson published the first challenge to Curtin's definition of the "Windward Coast," the coast of present-day Liberia and the Ivory Coast. They concluded that the term was vague, that it did not always conform to Curtin's geographical definition, and that the numbers of enslaved Africans exported from Curtin's "Windward Coast" were substantially exaggerated. Michael A. Gomez included voyages listed as coming from the Windward Coast among voyages coming from Sierra Leone. The region defined by Curtin as the "Windward Coast" posed many difficulties for maritime slave traders because of severe surf and by effective, ongoing resistance to the slave trade by the Kru people, who were highly skilled mariners living there. From the earliest years of the Atlantic slave trade, they refused to supply enslaved Africans to the maritime slave traders. They were highly skilled navigators, boatmen, and swimmers and provoked and assisted revolts among Africans imprisoned aboard Atlantic slave trade ships anchored along their shores. The Kru described as *mala gente* (bad people) were considered very dangerous by the slave trade captains. In order to obtain slaves, the captains had to send crews in small boats to surprise, assault, and kidnap their victims. These raids were dangerous to the raiders and unproductive in collecting slaves.[14] When European slave traders had to raid directly for slaves it usually meant there was no existing export market for slaves. They surely would have preferred to purchase enslaved Africans rather than run the risks involved in raiding directly for them. Over time, a few enslaved Africans were exported from the Windward Coast. But the Atlantic slave trade from this coast has been significantly exaggerated. After the Gold Coast began to export large numbers of slaves, starting in the 1650s, the Ivory Coast continued to export ivory rather than slaves.

In *The Trans-Atlantic Slave Trade Database*, 252 voyages (41.6 percent of 606 voyages) were recorded as coming simply from the "Windward Coast." This could mean anywhere from Greater Senegambia/Upper Guinea to the Bight of Benin. The number of slaves bought at the first port of purchase along this "Windward Coast" is missing in the case of 98.5 percent of the recorded voyages. Only 62 of the voyages (10.2 percent) are known to have resulted in the sale of slaves in the Americas. Many of them could have been stop-offs for wood, water, and food and for the purchase of other products. Our most knowledgeable experts advise that we exclude the Kanga from the Windward Coast and include them in Sierra Leone. If we exclude the Kanga, African ethnic designations from Curtin's "Windward Coast" are extremely rare in American documents. Armah, Jones, and Johnson pointed out that there were very few in the lists of African ethnicities of slaves studied by Gabriel Debien and his colleagues. The only possible exception is Cape Lahou — actually a port, not an ethnic designation — which Debien included in the Gold Coast. Debien found 26 Kanga and 25 Cape Lahou among 6,188 slaves in British-occupied St. Domingue in 1796–97.[15] David Geggus counted 253 ethnicities from the Windward Coast in his more recent study of 13,344 slaves in St. Domingue. Among them 124 were listed as Mesurade/Kanga. No other ethnicities were listed for this coast. Only one Caplao was found in Louisiana documents: a 25-year-old cook named Joseph who was first sold in 1815. Some of the smaller Caribbean islands listed more "Cape Lahou." Guadeloupe probate inventories listed 49 "Caplaous" (7 percent of Africans of identified ethnicities) between 1770 and 1789.[16] Barry Higman found 231 Cape Lahou among 2,638 Africans of identified ethnicities and no Kanga in the St. Lucia registration lists of 1815; no Cape Lahou and 140 Kanga were among 2,986 Africans of identified ethnicities in the St. Kitts lists of 1817; 473 KwaKwa (Kwa language group speakers whom we include with Lower Guinea), 160

Cape Lahou, and 270 Kanga in the 13,398 Trinidad entries of 1813; 62 Kanga and no Cape Lahou in the 1,136 slaves listed for Berbice in 1819. No Africans from the Windward Coast by any possible definition were listed among slaves in Anguilla in 1827.[17] The data published after 1980 confirm that Curtin's "Windward Coast" was hardly involved in the Atlantic slave trade unless we include Cape Lahou as part of the Windward Coast; in any case, Cape Lahou became involved late and in small numbers. Well into the nineteenth century, the British relied mainly on Kru mariners along the inhospitable shores of the Ivory Coast for help in suppressing the illegal slave trade. But by then some Krumen had become involved in the illegal maritime slave trade as well, and they might have been instrumental in sending a few Africans to the Americas from Liberia and the Ivory Coast.[18]

In order to grasp the changing patterns of export of Africans of various ethnicities, we need to transcend the concept of African coasts as defined by European slave traders and look at the changing internal patterns in Africa. Ethnicities living near the Atlantic Coast were very likely to have been shipped from ports on the coasts where they lived. But there is disagreement among scholars about how quickly and profoundly the Atlantic slave trade involved peoples living considerable distances inland from these coasts. Peoples in Africa were often mobile to escape from slave raiding, expanding desiccation, famine, warfare, and state formation. By the eighteenth century, some of the same African ethnicities from the West African Middle Belt located to the north of the coasts of Lower Guinea began to be shipped to the Americas from all three of the Lower Guinea coasts named by Atlantic slave traders. For example, Chamba were shipped from the Gold Coast and the Slave Coast. By the nineteenth century, Hausa were being shipped from the Slave Coast and from the Bight of Biafra.

Documents listing and describing enslaved Africans throughout the Americas are uniquely valuable. But like all forms of historic evidence, they have their strengths and their weaknesses. One of their greatest strengths is that they are voluminous. Slaves were legally defined as property, and as a result there is often more information listed in documents about them than about free people. Many documents contain detailed descriptions of slaves: their names and the names of their masters, their genders, ages, skills, illnesses, family members, personalities as perceived by their masters, origins (including sometimes African ethnic designations), and their prices. When slaves were interrogated, they often identified their own ethnicities (described as nations or *castas* in documents) or the ethnicities of other Africans. There is a whole world of known, unknown, and still to be studied documents describing slaves and sometimes recording their testimony when they were in-

Table 2.1.   Origin Information for Slaves in Louisiana Documents

Origin Identified			Percentage
African-born			
	"Nation" given	8,994	55.9
	Guinea or Coast of Guinea	1,043	6.5
	Other coastal or port origin	148	.9
	"African," no further details	831	05.2
	"Brut" only, new Africans	3,046	19.0
	Born before slave trade began	2,037	12.7
	Total	16,099	54.1
American-born			
	Louisiana Creole	9,814	72.1
	British America	2,183	16.0
	Non-British Caribbean	1,414	10.4
	Native American	207	0.2
	Total	13,618	45.9
Grand total		29,769	

Source: Calculated from Hall, *Louisiana Slave Database, 1719–1820.*
Note: Atlantic slave trade voyages excluded. Category "other" (n = 52) not included.

terrogated for various reasons: mainly for running away or for involvement in conspiracies and revolts against slavery. The information about slaves in documents throughout the Americas is so massive that it is only now possible to begin to make sense of it thanks to advances in information technology. This new frontier of historical scholarship can begin to restore the severed links among Africans in Africa and their descendants in the Americas.

Documents generated in the Western Hemisphere are clearly the richest source of information about the origins and ethnicities of enslaved Africans. But they vary greatly in quality and quantity of information, mainly in accordance with the languages in which they were written. In Latin America, all transactions involving slaves were public records maintained in chronological order by notaries working in specific places and can be studied systematically over time and place. Documents written in French are by far the most informative. French documents normally list hundreds of distinct African ethnicities. These listings are rarely port or other geographic designations.

French-language documents are abundant, well organized, and generally well preserved, often in bound volumes. For St. Domingue/Haiti, they are housed in the French Colonial Archives in Aix-en-Provence, France. They have not yet been systematically studied. In Louisiana, the notarial documents are housed in parish courthouses. Almost all of these documents dating between 1723 and 1820 have been studied and databased. The richness of information about African ethnicities in French-language documents in the Americas explains why historians who have used them—for example, Gabriel Debien and his team of researchers, David Geggus, and I—are convinced of the significance of ethnic identifications in American documents.

English-language documents contain the least information about African ethnicities. British colonies did not have notaries to keep transactions involving slaves as public records. Therefore many sales of slaves, inventories of slaves after the death of masters, wills, marriage contracts, and other types of documents were private papers of individuals. Many of these documents have not been preserved. Others are scattered and difficult to obtain and study over time and place. The richest, most reliable information about African ethnicities in English-language documents have been found in the registration lists of slaves in preparation for general emancipation in the British West Indies. African ethnic information about them was recorded in formerly French islands as well as in Trinidad, which was settled largely by French Creole-speaking masters and slaves from Martinique. Barry W. Higman used these registration lists for his sophisticated studies of slavery in the British West Indies. Aside from these lists, newspaper advertisements for runaway slaves are the major source of information about African ethnicities in English-language documents. Daniel Littlefield pioneered their study for South Carolina. His detailed, sophisticated analysis remains unsurpassed. Michael A. Gomez effectively used advertisements for runaway slaves in his study of African ethnicities in the United States. Douglas B. Chambers has collected ethnicity information from newspaper advertisements for runaway slaves in Jamaica.[19]

In documents recorded in Brazil and in Spanish America, broad African coastal or regional designations predominated, and we find fewer specific African ethnicities recorded than in French documents. While Spanish and Portuguese colonists and officials grouped Africans under large regional or coastal denominations, Africans in these Iberian colonies in the Americas made finer distinctions among themselves, which sometimes emerge in the documents, especially records of court testimony in which Africans identified their specific ethnicities. Although some Africans exposed to others of closely related ethnicity in the Americas tended to overcome their more narrow, localized identities and identified themselves more broadly, they often resisted the extremely broad designations projected on them by Iberian slave traders and colonial officials.[20] Except in Santiago de Cuba, where French refugees from St. Domingue/Haiti were a significant portion of the population, slaves recorded in sales documents in Cuba were listed under broad

Table 2.2.   Africans with "Nation" Designations Sold in Cuba, 1790–1880

Ethnicity	Number Sold	Percentage
Karabalí (Calabar)	1,873	27
Kongo	1,901	28
Ganga (Kanga)	1,118	16
Lucumí (Nago/Yoruba)	640	9
Mandingo	663	9
Other	712	10
Total	6,917	100

Source: Adapted from Bergad, Iglesias García, and Barcia, *The Cuban Slave Market, 1790–1880*, 72, table 4.7.

regional categories regardless of their ethnicities: For example, "Karabalí" for slaves from the Bight of Biafra; "Mandinga" for slaves from Senegambia; "Ganga" (probably derived from Kanga) for slaves from Sierra Leone; "Ashanti" for slaves from the Gold Coast; "Lucumí" for slaves from the Slave Coast; "Congo" for slaves from West Central Africa.

Moreno Fraginals has found some specific ethnic designations listed among slaves inventoried after the death of masters. We do not know where in Cuba these inventories came from, but if they follow the patterns of sales documents, a very high percentage of specific ethnicity information came from French-language documents in Santiago de Cuba.

In Cuba as well as in Brazil, official mutual aid societies were organized and named in accordance with the broad African coastal or regional designations most familiar to masters and colonial authorities. But they were often reorganized internally in accordance with ethnicities recognized by their African members. In Cuba, for example, the name of an African coast or the largest and best-known ethnicity arriving from that coast was used as the designation for a particular Cabildo de Nacion, even though it likely encompassed quite distinct peoples. The Cabildo de Karabalí included the Igbo, speakers of a Kwa language, and the Ibibio, speakers of a Northwest Bantu language. Some of these Cabildos de Naciones disintegrated along ethnic lines.[21]

In Latin American countries where the conversion of Africans to the Catholic faith was a priority and the Catholic Church maintained records of vital statistics as sacramental documents (births, marriages, and deaths), some information about African ethnicities was put on paper. For the reasons discussed below, even the best of those records need to be used with caution.[22] Although the documents concerning adult baptisms reflected the

Table 2.3. Africans with Ethnic Designations Recorded on Cuban Sugar and Coffee Estates

Ethnic Designation	1760–69		1800–20		1850–70		Total	%
	Number	%	Number	%	Number	%		
Kongo	1,305	30.3	1,201	22.21	1,532	16.71	4,038	21.6
Karabalí	1,090	25.31	1,380	25.53	1,589	17.37	4,059	21.7
Lucumí*	354	8.22	453	8.38	3,161	34.52	3,968	21.2
Mandingo	560	13.0	1,037	19.18			1,597	9.0
Mina	248	5.8	365	7.0	363	4.0	976	5.2
Arara**	168	3.9					168	0.9
Ganga***	151	3.5	409	7.57	1,053	11.45	1,613	8.6
Macuba	134	3.11					134	0.7
Mozambique	117	2.72					117	0.6
Mondongo			201	3.72			203	1.1
Bricamo			199	3.68			199	1.1
Marabi					269	2.95	269	1.4
Bibi****					268	2.94	268	1.4
Others	180	4.18			942	10.13	1,122	6.0
Total	4,307		5,245		9,177		18,731	

Source: Adapted from Moreno Fraginals, "Africa in Cuba," 190–91, tables 2–4.

*Yoruba

**Arada/Aja/ Fon

***Also written "Canca" or "Canga"

****Ibibio

African population better than other sacramental records, in Brazil they did not list specific ethnicities, and the broad coastal designations that were recorded did not reflect their proportions among African slaves. In baptismal documents in eighteenth-century Rio de Janeiro, denominations for African origins were few and very broad: Mina, Guinea, West Coast, Cape Verde, and "Contracosta" (meaning East Africa). Slaves from West Central Africa— Kongo and Angolans—were most likely to have been baptized before they left Africa. They would be underrepresented in baptismal records and over-represented in church membership lists because of their exposure to Christianity in Africa. Islamized Africans from Upper Guinea were probably most likely to resist baptism and would therefore be underrepresented in sacramental records. Africans from the Slave Coast, listed in Brazilian documents under the broad denomination "Mina," were rarely baptized in Africa and were therefore baptized in Brazil in higher proportions. In Brazil as well as in Louisiana, and possibly elsewhere, adult women accepted baptism more readily than adult men. Therefore, Africans from the Slave Coast, listed as

Mina in Brazil, would have been overrepresented partially because of a higher proportion of women among them.[23]

Some designations that appear to be ethnicities actually refer to regions. Early Spanish-language documents lumped all Africans from the same region under the name of the most widely known ethnicity from that region. During the fifteenth century, for example, slaves in Valencia, Spain, were designated by the names of the major ethnicities living in large regions of Greater Senegambia. "Jalof" meant all of northern Upper Guinea, "Mandega" meant central Upper Guinea (from the Gambia to the Rio Geba), and "Sape" meant southern Upper Guinea. According to George E. Brooks, "Sape" meant the Bullom or Temne ethnicity.[24]

Marisa Soares has discovered and studied remarkable documents about the Mahi (Maki) groups organized within the Irmandade da Mina (Brotherhood of Mina) in Rio de Janeiro, Brazil, during the eighteenth century. The Mahi lived north of the kingdom of Dahomey. They were heavily raided after Dahomey captured Whydah and established itself on the Atlantic Coast during the late 1720s, when the Mahi began to arrive in Brazil in significant numbers. The Mina Irmandade divided itself into two major groups: the Dahomeans (Fon) and other lesser-known groups who had been raided by Dahomeans for slaves. These ethnicities identified themselves as Mahi (Maki), Agolin, Savaru, and Sanno. They all spoke the general Mina language of Brazil, "lingua geral da Mina," demonstrating a seemingly contradictory process of integration and disintegration along ethnic lines. Each ethnicity within this brotherhood elected its own kings, queens, and regents. The first Mahi king, Capitão Ignacio Gonçales Monte, was elected in 1764. He claimed descent from the kings of Mahi. These Mahi rejected the Dahomeans as pagans.[25]

Portuguese and Brazilian documents commonly identify Africans by the port from which they left[26] or, in the case of Mozambique, from the region from which they were exported.[27] Thus West Central African ports of origin were often used for names of Africans in Brazil: for example, Fortunato Cabinda, José Benguela. Broad regional designations were often included in slaves' names: for example, Domingos Mina, Vitorino Moçambique.

The meanings of these "nations" recorded in American documents are not obvious. There is no detailed, existing body of knowledge about historical African ethnicities either in Africa or in the Americas. Ethnic designations and identities changed on both sides of the Atlantic during the 400 years of the Atlantic slave trade. It is easy to get lost in the maze of hundreds of nominal designations of a great variety of peoples over four centuries. Scholars often focus on how Europeans in Africa identified African ethnici-

Mozambique Africans in Brazil. (Johann Moritz Rugendas, *Voyage pittoresque dans le Brésil*, 1835.)

ties. But the relevance of observations of Europeans in Africa about Africans brought to the Americas is often questionable. There is strong evidence that specific ethnic designations recorded in American documents were often self-identifications. For example, masters could not possibly have been familiar with the hundreds of ethnic designations listed in French documents.

While many scholars look to Africa to understand how Europeans desig-

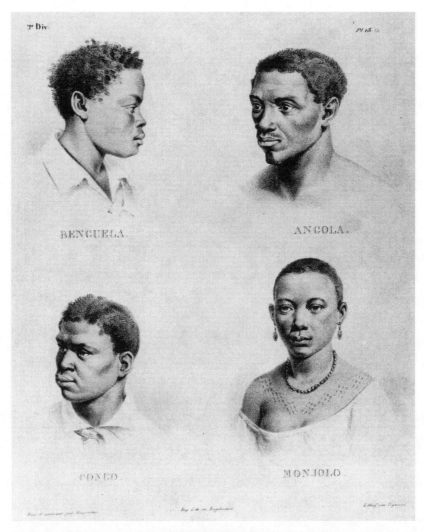

West Central Africans in Brazil. (Johann Moritz Rugendas, *Voyage pittoresque dans le Brésil*, 1835.)

nated Africans of various ethnicities over time and place, our most reliable information is how Africans identified themselves in the Americas. Except in the case of the recaptives from illegal slave trade voyages brought to Sierra Leone during the first half of the nineteenth century, self-identified African ethnicities are rare in historical documents in Africa.[28] But they are frequent in the Americas. Some of our best, most detailed information comes from

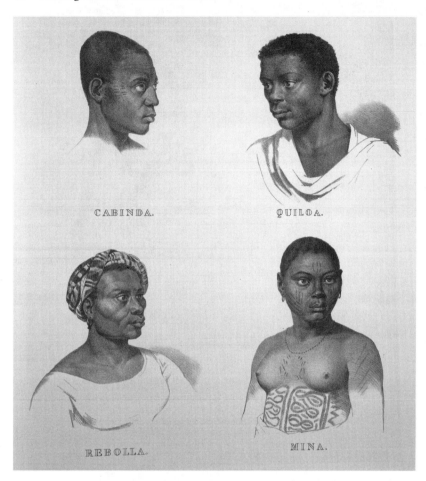

CABINDA.

QUILOA.

REBOLLA.

MINA.

Each of these four images represents a different African "nation" in Brazil. (Johann Moritz Rugendas, *Voyage pittoresque dans le Brésil*, 1835. From the website "The Atlantic Slave Trade and Slave Life in the Americas: A Visual Record,"<http://hitchcock.itc.virginia.edu/Slavery>.)

Louisiana. The total slave population of early Louisiana was small compared to that of many other places in the Americas. But the richness of the information, especially about African ethnicities, is certainly unique for documents about slaves who became part of the population of the United States and quite possibly for documents generated in any other place in the Americas.

The *Louisiana Slave Database, 1719–1820*, systematically sheds light on the circumstances under which African ethnicities were identified. All extant

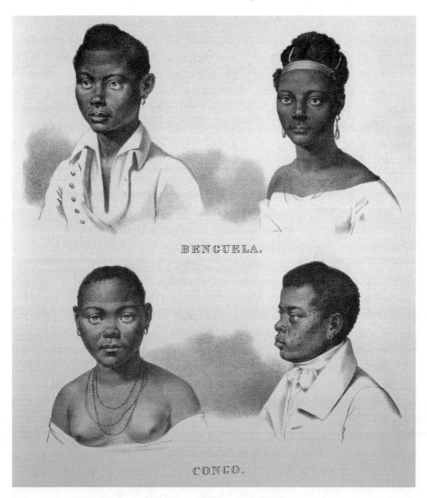

Men and women from Benguela and Kongo living in Brazil.
(Johann Moritz Rugendas, *Voyage pittoresque dans le Brésil*, 1835.
From the website "The Atlantic Slave Trade and Slave Life in the Americas:
A Visual Record," <http://hitchcock.itc.virginia.edu/Slavery>.)

documentation indicates self-identification or, on occasion, identification by
other Africans. The clearest cases of self-identification involved slaves testify-
ing in court proceedings. These interrogations almost always involved recaptured runaways and slaves accused of involvement in conspiracies or revolts
against slavery. When they were sworn in, they were normally asked, among
other standard questions, "What is your nation?"

When asked to identify other slaves, they often identified their African "nation" as part of the description. Since there were substantial numbers of Africans of the same ethnicity and region throughout Louisiana, deliberate misrepresentation of African ethnicities would pose problems. Although Africans were often multilingual, language use among new Africans might make misrepresentation difficult. Some Africans no doubt identified with larger, better-known ethnicities found in the Americas that were closely related to them. But the great variety of ethnic designations found in Louisiana documents would minimize, but not exclude, this possibility.

The 8,994 records in the *Louisiana Slave Database* containing specific African ethnicity information involve 217 different ethnicities, many of them spelled in a variety of ways. Among them 96 have been identified, although identifications remain to be further refined by input from other scholars. There are 121 ethnic designations (consisting of only 152 individuals) whose "nation" was recorded but cannot as yet be identified. Most of the identified ethnicities and all of the unidentified ones were represented by very few individuals, often only one. Among the 8,842 Africans of identified ethnicities (excluding "Guinea" and ethnicities listed but unidentified), 96.2 percent (n = 8,508) were clustered among 18 ethnicities ranging between a low of 66 records for the Edo of the Bight of Benin to a high of 3,035 for the Kongo of West Central Africa.[29] Although the nominal designations of the most frequent ethnicities varied over time and place, all of them can be found in substantial numbers in documents throughout the Americas. African ethnicities described in very few documents are of particular interest to specialists in African history, but they are too few in number for use in studies of the distribution of African ethnicities in the Americas.

Table 2.4 shows the changing patterns of introduction of the most frequent African ethnicities in Louisiana over time and by gender. By selecting smaller time periods and particular locations, we can study the pattern of the appearance of African ethnicities in Louisiana documents in great detail. These studies, including age studies, can throw light on the patterns of export from Africa.

The *Louisiana Slave Database*, our most detailed, sophisticated tool about African ethnic designations in the Americas, indicates that when new Africans were first sold, their ethnicities were rarely identified. The longer Africans remained in Louisiana, the more likely were their ethnicities identified. If these patterns in Louisiana can be generalized, it appears that Africans in the Americas, not slave traders or masters, identified African ethnicities recorded in American documents. Sales documents, especially of newly arrived Africans (described as "new Africans" in English, *brut* in French, *bozal* in Span-

Table 2.4. Eighteen Most Frequent Ethnicities by Gender in Louisiana,
1719–1820

Ethnicity		Male	Female	Total
Bamana	Number	413	53	466
	Percentage	88.6%	11.4%	100.0%
	% of Total	4.9%	.6%	5.5%
Mandingo	Number	617	305	922
	Percentage	66.9%	33.1%	100.0%
	% of Total	7.3%	3.6%	10.9%
Nar/Moor	Number	101	35	136
	Percentage	74.3%	25.7%	100.0%
	% of Total	1.2%	.4%	1.6%
Poulard/Fulbe	Number	160	50	210
	Percentage	76.2%	23.8%	100.0%
	% of Total	1.9%	.6%	2.5%
Senegal/Wolof	Number	363	234	597
	Percentage	60.8%	39.2%	100.0%
	% of Total	4.3%	2.8%	7.1%
Kisi	Number	51	35	86
	Percentage	59.3%	40.7%	100.0%
	% of Total	.6%	.4%	1.0%
Kanga	Number	210	129	339
	Percentage	61.9%	38.1%	100.0%
	% of Total	2.5%	1.5%	4.0%
Aja/Fon/Arada	Number	126	117	243
	Percentage	51.9%	48.1%	100.0%
	% of Total	1.5%	1.4%	2.9%
Chamba	Number	276	139	415
	Percentage	66.5%	33.5%	100.0%
	% of Total	3.3%	1.6%	4.9%
Hausa	Number	122	11	133
	Percentage	91.7%	8.3%	100.0%
	% of Total	1.4%	.1%	1.6%
Mina	Number	430	198	628
	Percentage	68.5%	31.5%	100.0%
	% of Total	5.1%	2.3%	7.4%
Nago/Yoruba	Number	247	111	358
	Percentage	69.0%	31.0%	100.0%
	% of Total	2.9%	1.3%	4.2%
Edo	Number	38	28	66
	Percentage	57.6%	42.4%	100.0%
	% of Total	.5%	.3%	.8%

Table 2.4.   Continued

Ethnicity		Male	Female	Total
Igbo	Number	287	237	524
	Percentage	54.8%	45.2%	100.0%
	% of Total	3.4%	2.8%	6.2%
Ibibio/Moko	Number	61	21	82
	Percentage	74.4%	25.6%	100.0%
	% of Total	.7%	.2%	1.0%
Calabar	Number	88	59	147
	Percentage	59.9%	40.1%	100.0%
	% of Total	1.0%	.7%	1.7%
Kongo	Number	2,064	924	2,988
	Percentage	69.1%	30.9%	100.0%
	% of Total	24.4%	10.9%	35.4%
Makwa	Number	67	35	102
	Percentage	65.7%	34.3%	100.0%
	% of Total	.8%	.4%	1.2%
Total	Number	5,721	2,721	8,442
	Percentage within Gender	67.8%	32.2%	100.0%

Source: Calculated from Hall, Louisiana Slave Database, 1719–1820.

ish), tend to lump Africans into only the few best-known ethnicities or coastal origins when they give such descriptions at all. Enslaved Africans who had been in the Americas for several years and were then resold had their specific ethnicities recorded more often than newly arrived Africans. The inventories of Africans on estates after their masters died offer much more numerous and detailed ethnic designations than any other type of document. In probate inventory documents generated after the deaths of masters as well as in sales documents listing and describing slaves in Louisiana, several notaries explained that they could not list the African "nation" of particular slaves because these slaves did not know their nation: for example, Quebra, "does not know his nation;" Marie, "does not know her nation;" Francine, age twenty-three, a woman from Guinea, "does not know the name of her nation."[30]

Aside from this impressive, but still largely anecdotal evidence, overall patterns revealed by calculations drawn from the *Louisiana Slave Database* make an even more convincing case that enslaved Africans themselves — rather than masters or appraisers — normally identified their ethnicities. The longer Africans remained in Louisiana, the more likely it was that their specific African ethnicities would be identified. Of new Africans sold in Louisiana, 81.7

percent (n = 2,860; t = 3,499) were listed simply as *brut* or *bozal*, and 3.0 percent (n = 106) gave their African coastal origins only. Only 15.3 percent (n = 553) listed specific ethnic designations. The mean age of new Africans listing numeric ages was 19.2 (n = 2,867). When Africans with recorded ethnicities and not listed as *brut* or *bozal* were sold, their mean age was 26.4 (n = 3,946). They were mainly resold slaves who had been in Louisiana for an average of seven years. When Africans with recorded ethnicities were inventoried and appraised in probate documents after the deaths of masters, their mean age was 34.5 (n = 4,489). They had been in Louisiana for an average of 15 years. The mean age of all Africans with numeric age and specific African ethnicity information recorded was 31.2 (n = 8,226). Slaves with recorded African ethnicities were 68.3 percent (n = 4,750; t = 6,955) of all African slaves listed in probate documents; 46.4 percent (n = 3,448; t = 7,435) listed in sale documents; and 46.6 percent (n = 796; t = 1,709) listed in all other types of documents. These figures exclude towns, villages, coasts, ports, or other geographic designations. The largest number of coastal designations by far were listed as Guinea or the Coast of Guinea: a total of 1,052 records, which have been excluded from the calculations given above.

To recapitulate, new Africans were the least likely to have their ethnicities recorded in documents. Africans who had been in Louisiana for several years and were resold were much likely to have their ethnicities recorded. Africans who had been in Louisiana for many years and were inventoried and sold after the master's death were most likely to have their ethnicities recorded. A credible explanation is that new Africans had the greatest difficulty communicating and therefore could not identify their ethnicities. But after they had been in Louisiana for a number of years, they could communicate better. The longer they had been in Louisiana, the more likely they could communicate and identify their ethnicities. It is reasonable to conclude that the African ethnic designations listed in Louisiana documents overwhelmingly involved self-identification by Africans. The role of maritime slave traders in this process was apparently quite limited. Neither masters nor appraisers could possibly have been familiar with the hundreds of ethnic designations listed in these documents. We can safely minimize their role in identifying the African ethnicities of slaves brought into Louisiana and probably into other places in the Americas as well. This surprising pattern of when, where, and how African ethnicities were identified calls into question the assumption of very rapid loss of particular African ethnic self-identifications during the process of creolization. The extent to which these patterns can be confidently generalized throughout the Americas will have to await databased studies from other colonies, nations, and regions.

It is obvious that names for places, regions, and peoples in Africa need to be examined carefully. Few historians who study African ethnicities in the Americas view them as "tribes."[31] "Tribe" is a static term with heavy overtones implying primitiveness. It assumes that all Africans identified themselves according to kinship when in fact the basis for group identification among Africans varied greatly and changed over time and place. In the process of state building, strong matrilineal traditions were a seriously destabilizing force, especially in polygamous societies. For example, in Angola, in order to destroy the power of matrilineal descendants, the Imbangala (Jaga) prevented their wives from having children, sometimes killing their wives and their biological children, or excluding them from their communities. They adopted captured children who were not related to them by blood. Elite men sometimes married slave women to thwart the ambitions, demands, and conflicts among their co-wives and children. In the Upper Niger region during the eighteenth century, the expanding Segu "Bambara" state was constructed and consolidated by substituting age-group affiliation and personal loyalty for descent.[32] Thus traditional hierarchies based on kinship and descent were destroyed as new polities were created demanding new loyalties.

Many Africans had a broad, politically based identification with ancient and more recent empires, kingdoms, and smaller polities. Some groups of Africans were assigned nominal designations by other African groups but of course maintained their own names and identifications among themselves. Some Atlantic slave traders referred to peoples by using port, regional, coastal, and other geographic designations. For example, the Portuguese named the Bissago Islands after the Bissago people who lived there.[33] Common, mutually intelligible, and closely related languages were important but not necessarily decisive factors in identity. For example, the Bamana ("Bambara") and the Mandingo spoke mutually intelligible Mande dialects but they had historic and religious conflicts resulting in the maintenance of separate identities in the Americas as well as in Africa. Africans from the Slave Coast in Brazil spoke the common lingua geral da Mina created in Brazil, but those raided and enslaved in Africa by the kingdom of Dahomey distinguished themselves from and remained hostile to the Dahomeans.

Designations for African regions as well as for ethnicities varied among European slave traders. British traders in Africa referred to all of West Central Africa as Angola and English-language documents in the Americas tended to list all West Central Africans as Angolans. English slave trade documents indicating port of origin in West Central Africa are vague, further obscuring the origins of English voyages to West Central Africa. Among the 933 English voyages to West Central Africa recorded in *The Trans-Atlantic Slave*

Trade Database, 68.7 percent (t = 641) list the principal port of slave purchase simply as Angola.[34] French- and Spanish-language documents tend to list all West Central Africans as Kongo: for example, 93 percent (n = 4,561) in the lists from eighteenth-century St. Domingue studied by David Geggus.[35] Michael Gomez's calculations from Gabriel Debien's collection of ethnic designations in St. Domingue during 1796 and 1797 indicate that all West Central Africans were listed as Kongo (n = 1,651).[36] In the *Louisiana Slave Database*, 97 percent (n = 3,152) of Africans from West Central Africa were listed as Kongo. Only 25 were listed as Angolans, 18 of whom had been brought in from South Carolina in 1783 by Dr. Benjamin Farar. Although all West Central Africans were normally recorded as Angolans in British colonies, runaway slave ads in Jamaican newspapers after 1775 (1776–95 and 1810–17) described 499 of them as Kongo while only 27 were described as Angolans. Five were described as Angolans and none as Kongo before 1776, indicating perhaps increasing precision as more West Central Africans entered Jamaica over time.[37] Several ethnicities from West Central Africa recorded in significant numbers were not listed simply as Kongo or Angolan; they were, instead, listed as Mungola in Jamaica, Monjolo in Brazil, Mandongo in Louisiana and Cuba, and Mondongue in St. Domingue. But relatively few documents created in the Americas list a significant number or variety of distinctive West Central African ethnicities. The partial explanation for this is perhaps the specific pattern in which fishing communities along the Kongo River were populated, which resulted in close linguistic and kinship relationships among peoples living over wide geographic areas.[38] Mary Karasch has found an array of specific ethnicities from West Central Africa described in travelers' accounts in Rio de Janeiro during the nineteenth century.[39]

Some designations that scholars have taken to mean a port or a coastal designation had other meanings. In Louisiana and no doubt elsewhere in the Americas as well, "Senegal," a coastal designation, meant Wolof. During the first years of the African presence in Louisiana, Le Page du Pratz, director of the Company of the Indies, noted that the Wolof were called Senegal by the French colonists but they continued to be called Wolof ("Djolaufs") among themselves.[40] "Mina" normally did not mean slaves coming through the fortress/port of São Jorge da Mina (Elmina) on the Gold Coast. It was a designation referring to different ethnicities over time and place, but it certainly sometimes meant people from Little Popo, originally Akan speakers who had migrated from west of the Volta River. They were often designated Mina-Popo in Brazil and Cuba. Popo was usually written "Pau Pau" in English. The designations "Mina-Nago" and even "Mina-Congo" were sometimes found in Brazil.[41]

Some Africans in the Americas, when asked to identify their "nation," replied with the name of their village or district. But this did not necessarily mean that they lacked a broader self-identity or that they were so isolated as to have no concept of other peoples. Isolation was far from universal among Africans involved in the Atlantic slave trade. Ancient, extensive trade networks involving the sale of products made throughout Africa linked coastal with interior regions and across the Sahara and the Indian Ocean. This active trade predated the Atlantic slave trade by many centuries. Except for bringing in slaves for sale in the ports, the Atlantic trade weakened commercial links with the interior. Warfare, conquest, kidnapping, and slave raiding escalated at the expense of production and internal trade. As the price of slaves rose over the centuries and cheap East Indian and then British textiles conquered the African market, African production tended to lose its economic incentives.[42] The maritime slave trade created enclave economies along the coasts geared toward supplying the ships, especially with food for the voyages. Although the Atlantic slave trade introduced new products from all over the world to exchange for a variety of African products—including gold, copper, and other currencies, ivory, gum, pepper and other spices, textiles, kola nuts, rice, millet, sorghum, yams and other foods as well as slaves[43]—a blanket rejection of Walter Rodney's argument that Europe underdeveloped Africa is not warranted.[44]

Patterns of self-identity among Africans differed from region to region in Africa and the Americas. For example, in Greater Senegambia, the Wolof and the Mandingo came from stratified societies with a long tradition of state formation and self-identity. Fulbe herdsmen and warriors, heavily Islamized and quite mobile, relocated great distances south and east of their original home along the middle reaches of the Senegal River to protect their herds from drought and desiccation. In their migrations through West Africa, the Fulbe were also active in warfare and the capture and sale of slaves. These ethnicities identified themselves clearly as distinct peoples living in extended geographic areas. Africans from small, local communities in parts of Upper Guinea, along the Bight of Biafra, or in parts of West Central Africa where bureaucratic, stratified state systems were less common generally identified themselves in terms of their immediate vicinity. To cite an example from a document from Opelousas, Louisiana, dating from 1802: Celeste, the thirteen-year-old Creole daughter of an African slave couple, was accused of assaulting her master with an axe and nearly killing him. When her parents were called on to testify, they both explained that they did not know their ages and professed no religion. There is little doubt about the father's ethnicity; he was a self-identified Mandingo, a heavily Islamized ethnicity. Celeste's mother testified that her "country" was called "Yarrow" (Jarrow?), which was the name she used for herself.[45] A slave in Maryland, Yarrow Mahmout, lived to be very old while openly practicing the Muslim faith. The personal or place name Yarrow might have had a religious significance.[46]

It is obvious that over four centuries the meanings of these nominal designations changed. Some peoples were assigned names by their neighbors, or by other Africans. But when one group of people was named by another, they nevertheless had various bases for self-identification and their own names for themselves. Africans had group identities in Africa as well as in the Americas. To deny that ethnicities existed in Africa and assume that the many and varied African ethnic designations recorded in documents in the Americas did not originate in Africa but were created in the Americas is worse than being named by others. It denies the roots of peoples in Africa, including their names, homogenizes them, and renders them invisible. Africans are the only peoples who have been subjected by scholars to this level of denial.[47]

It is understandable that some scholars throw up their hands in the face of the bewildering number of African ethnic designations with changing spellings, pronunciations, and meanings recorded in several languages over many centuries in vast regions on both sides of the Atlantic. Nevertheless, we can go far by concentrating on the relatively few African ethnicities most frequently listed in documents throughout the Americas, despite the fact that they were often recorded under various names. We have seen that the best evidence we now have indicates that these ethnic designations were normally self-identifications by Africans in the Americas rather than identifications by slave traders on either side of the Atlantic or at sea.

The study of African ethnicities in the Americas has been widely neglected during the past three decades. The influential Mintz-Price thesis was first published in 1976.[48] It claimed extreme diversity among and random distribution of Africans brought to the Western Hemisphere. This work has several virtues, including its partial emphasis on changes over time. It emphasizes the importance of the early, formative period of creolization in the Americas, although no pattern of creolization can be confidently generalized. Unfortunately, the most influential conclusion of the Mintz-Price thesis is flawed by its static approach to the Atlantic slave trade as well as its projection of patterns supposedly found in one, small place in the Americas to all of the Western Hemisphere. It collapses time and then calculates the percentage of Atlantic slave trade voyages arriving in Suriname from various African coasts. In generalizing this flawed finding, the thesis concludes that the impact of particular African regions and ethnicities on the formation of Afro-Creole cultures in the Americas was nonexistent or insignificant. But Africans from the same regions and ethnicities arrived in various places in the Americas in waves and were often clustered over time and place. Dynamic perception and comparative analysis reveal clustered patterns while static perception gives the false impression of random, dispersed patterns. The Mintz-Price thesis had a chilling effect on studies of African ethnicities in the Americas. Such studies became almost a heresy among influential scholars in the United States. The influence of the thesis spread abroad as well, although it was greeted with less enthusiasm in Latin America than elsewhere.[49] The work of historians—especially minorities and/or women working in the United States—who even mentioned African ethnicities has yet to get the recognition it deserves. Much of that work is discussed and cited in this book.

A growing number of historians of Africa, the transatlantic slave trade, and the African diaspora in the Western Hemisphere are focusing on the patterns of introduction of Africans of various coastal origins and ethnicities throughout the Americas over time and place. These studies have shown that Africans were often clustered in the Americas rather than randomized or deliberately fragmented. This conclusion has been reinforced by the publication of computerized relational databases created from massive collections of documents generated by transatlantic slave trade voyages as well as by the publication of other databases created from more varied types of documents generated in the Americas.[50] These innovative tools help us refine studies of the pattern of introduction of Africans over time and place as well as other key questions about the slave trade and slavery in the Western Hemisphere. They allow us to avoid the mistake of distorting this complex history by collapsing time, and they enable us to begin to better evaluate and transcend the limitations of previously available evidence.

Much historical interpretation has, up to now, relied heavily on anecdotal evidence collected from travelers' accounts, which were sometimes plagiarized, falsified, or sensationalized to appeal to a public hungry for information about "exotic" peoples and places; administrative reports, which were often self-serving distortions by more or less well informed and observant bureaucrats; and reports of missionaries, which were often better informed because the authors had closer and more sustained contact with the peoples they were writing about, but such reports need to be carefully studied and used judiciously because they are often marked by prejudice and stereotypes. Thus the secondary literature has been constructed to a great extent from sources of uneven quality. Many questionable conclusions have been accepted as truth and repeated by historians from one generation to the next. This writer believes that the creation of databases constructed from large numbers of generally less self-serving documents organized in time series can help save history from nihilistic tendencies within the postmodernist school, which subjectivize history and reduce it to literary criticism. (To the postmodernist, one person's myth is often as good as another's.)

Some scholars advance and defend the concept that ethnicity has nothing to do with Africans but is a mere construct dating from the end of the nineteenth century, when the colonial period began in Africa. According to this argument, European missionaries, anthropologists, and administrators invented African ethnicities in order to create conflicts among the peoples they ruled. Joseph C. Miller, grounded in the history of West Central Africa, where distinctive ethnicities were less developed than in some other West African regions and the terms "Kongo" and "Angola" were widely used by Europeans for a great variety of peoples, properly calls for more contextualized studies by historians who posit ethnic continuities among Africans brought to the Americas.

There is only an element of truth to the argument that European colonizers of Africa constructed African ethnicities. During much of the era of the Atlantic slave trade, and in most locales where it was conducted, maritime slave traders and their hierarchies of administrators and missionaries lacked access to the interior regions of Africa. They were often confined to the coast, and sometimes to ships docked offshore. Within Africa, creolization developed as a normal process of contact among peoples incorporating new cultural and linguistic groups into other groups and polities. During the Atlantic slave trade, increasing warfare and raids among ethnicities for captives to sell into the Atlantic slave trade aggravated ethnic conflicts. The creation and promotion of rigid, mutually exclusive antagonisms among ethnicities in Africa were a product of policies of social control as European colonizers advanced into the interior of the African continent.

Indeed, the political motivations for the denial of the existence of African ethnicities in Africa are laudable. The Cold War was a hot war in Africa as the dominant world powers sought to use African clients in proxy wars against each other. Ethnic conflicts continue to be aggravated and manipulated to exploit the natural resources of Africa, tear and mutilate her social fabric, and destroy her peoples. Ethnic conflicts are often promoted by outsiders, including arms merchants and multinational corporations allied with some of the elite or would-be elite within various African states to facilitate the exploitation of gold, diamonds and other precious gems, copper, uranium, oil, and other natural resources.[51]

Scholars who deny the historical existence of African ethnicities prior to the late nineteenth century sometimes acknowledge that their conclusions are based on studies of conditions in Southern Africa, often in places where the

Atlantic slave trade was of minor significance. Nevertheless, some of them confidently project these conclusions backward in time over four centuries to regions from which the vast majority of Africans were brought to the Americas. They then conclude that African ethnicity in all times and places was a European construction imposed on Africans. The Atlantic slave trade obviously took place during precolonial times when, except in West Central Africa, the European administrative presence was often confined to Atlantic and Indian Ocean ports and fortresses and sometimes merely to ships docked offshore. Ethnicities existed in Africa and interacted widely not only before the colonial period but also long before the Atlantic slave trade began. The great Senegalese scholar Cheikh Anta Diop emphasized the fundamental unity among all Africans and their common descent. But he never denied the existence of African ethnicities.[52] Boubacar Barry described an ongoing process of creolization in Africa among ethnicities with ancient identities. He wrote that in Greater Senegambia, long before the Atlantic trade began,

> people switched ethnic groups and languages. There were Toures, originally Manding, who became Tukulor or Wolof; Jallos, originally Peul [listed as Poulard in Louisiana documents], became Khaasonke; Moors [listed as Nar(d) in Louisiana documents] turned into Naari Kajor; Mane and Sane, originally Joola surnames, were taken by the Manding royalty of Kaabu. There was, in short, a constant mixture of peoples in Senegambia, destined for centuries to share a common space. Senegambia, in some respects, functioned like a vast reserve into which populations in the Sudan and the Sahel habitually poured surplus members. In their new home the immigrants created a civilization of constant flux. . . . Nowhere in this Senegambia . . . did any Wolof, Manding, Peul, Tukolor, Sereer, Joola, or other ethnic group feel they were strangers.[53]

The denial of the history and even the existence of many African peoples on both sides of the Atlantic reinforces the concept of the generic African, distancing and dehumanizing Africans in the minds of peoples throughout Europe and the Americas. It severs the ties between Africans who remained in Africa and those who were shipped to the Americas, as well as the ties between their descendants.

Finally, let us look at the great abundance and variety of African names of slaves recorded in the *Louisiana Slave Database*. These 5,647 distinctive African names remain to be fully studied and explained. The possibilities are open ended. The vast majority of slaves with African names—5,980 (57.7 percent)—fell into the category of slaves of unidentified ethnicities or birthplaces. We do not know if they were Africans or Creoles. In order to respect

Table 2.5.   Distribution of African Names among Louisiana Slaves by Origin

Where Born	Total Number	With African Names	Percentage with African Names
Africa	16,089	3,228	20.1
British colonies	2,183	238	10.9
Non-British Caribbean	1,414	163	8.7
Louisiana (Creoles)	9,814	731	7.4
Louisiana (Native American)	207	23	11.1
Unidentified	62,262	5,980	9.6
Total	91,969	10,368	11.3

Source: Calculated from Hall, *Louisiana Slave Database, 1719–1820.*

what was literally contained in the documents, these individuals were not coded as Africans. If they had been, the proportion of identified birthplaces as well as the proportion of Africans in the *Louisiana Slave Database* would have been much higher. This decision is buttressed by Philip D. Morgan's findings that in the British mainland colonies, which became part of the United States, African-born slaves usually had Anglo names but they passed on African names to large numbers of their American-born children.[54]

Unless the names included a clear ethnic designation, such as Louis Congo or Samba Bambara, "nation" designations, rather than personal names, were relied on to identify African ethnicities. Naming patterns were fluid on both sides of the Atlantic, and Africans often changed their names. Some Africans adopted the names of others in order to honor them. Enslaved Africans sometimes took the name of a friend or a shipmate or someone they met shortly after landing as a means of identification with this person or out of respect. African names spread among a variety of African ethnicities and regions. Africans of various ethnicities used the same personal names.[55] Names with particular meanings among certain ethnicities can be found among other ethnicities: for example, Samba, Comba, Kofi, and other Akan names representing the day of the week on which the person was born. A few Creole slaves took an African ethnic designation as their name, or part of their name, as a way of identifying with the ethnicity. There is the case of a Creole slave, Joseph Mina, who took the ethnic name of the Mina slaves who reared him.[56] A few other names of Creole slaves included African ethnic designations: for example, Edouard dit Kanga, Felipe alias Bambara, Louis Kiamba, Senegal, and Maniga. The most startling case was François dit Congo, a four-year-old quadroon slave who was sold in 1817 with his mulatto mother under the condition that both of them be immediately freed, although it was illegal to free anyone under the age of thirty by that date. Here was a second-generation Creole who was three-quarters white with an African ethnic designation as part of his name. But these cases are rare enough to ignore in calculations.

The widespread survival of African names among Louisiana slaves and those in British colonies is unusual in the Americas. In Brazil and in Spanish America we find fewer African names in lists of slaves because enslaved Africans had normally been baptized and given Christian names either in Africa or shortly after they arrived in the Americas. But in Rio de Janeiro during the nineteenth century, an African port designation was often added to the slave's Christian name. African names were more likely to be found in British colonies where the Christianization and baptism of slaves were less common. In Louisiana 10.9 percent of slaves coming from English-speaking colonies or countries had African names. The African names among slaves in St. Domingue were found in highest proportion among Africans from Senegambia.[57] In Louisiana as well, Africans shipped from Senegambia retained African names out of proportion to their numbers in the slave population. For example, the Bamana were 5.5 percent of the most frequent African ethnicities but had 10.3 percent of the African names. The Mandingo were 10.9 percent but had 12.7 percent of the African names. The Wolof were 7 percent of the most frequent ethnicities and had 9 percent of the African names. The proportion of African names was higher than could be expected by their numbers among the Nar/Moor and the Fulbe as well. Many of these names were Africanized Islamic names. Africans from the Bight of Benin did not have a higher than proportional retention of African names although they often resisted Christianization. One reason could be that few of them were Islamized. At the other end of the scale, the Kongo were 35.7 percent of the most frequent ethnicities but had only 29.6 percent of the African names. This difference could reflect the fact that many more Kongo than other ethnicities had been baptized and Christianized in Africa and their names were passed down through the generations.

It is a humbling thought that Africans continued to identify with their particular African ethnic and regional origins long after they arrived in the Americas. Many of them retained their African names decades after they arrived, and some of them passed them on to their children born in the Americas. This evidence would indicate that African ethnic and regional identities survived for a longer period of time than most historians and anthropologists believe. In order to understand the process of creolization in various regions in the Americas, we indeed need to ask, "Which Africans?"

CHAPTER THREE

The Clustering of African Ethnicities in the Americas

[Falupos and Arriatas are] the mortal enemies of all kinds of white men. If our ships touch their shores they plunder the goods and make the white crew their prisoners, and they sell them in those places where they normally trade for cows, goats, dogs, iron-bars and various cloths. The only thing these braves will have nothing to do with is wine from Portugal, which they believe is the blood of their own people and hence will not drink.
— Manuel Alvarez, *Ethiopia Minor and a Geographical Account of the Province of Sierra Leone* (c. 1615)

Despite the staggering number of Africans introduced into the Americas during the Atlantic slave trade and their crucial role in creating its wealth and forming its cultures, their origins in Africa remain obscure. There is still a widespread belief among scholars as well as the general public that Africans dragged to various places in the Americas were fractionalized and diverse, culturally and linguistically. Therefore, few of the newly arrived Africans could communicate with each other, and there was little or no basis for transmission of elements of the cultures of specific African regions and ethnicities to specific places in the Americas. This conclusion is based on anecdotal evidence as well as more complex errors in methodology. Over several generations, historians have cited statements by European and American observers at various times and places in Africa and the Americas that in order to discourage revolts, communication among new Africans was suppressed by separating and fractionalizing the various African ethnicities during their transport on Atlantic slave trade voyages as well as after they arrived in the Americas. Studies of the coastal origins of Atlantic slave trade voyages to particular places in the Americas have collapsed time, ignoring wave patterns clustering voyages originating from particular African regions, and then presented this flawed conclusion as evidence to demonstrate great diversity in the origins of enslaved Africans. Monolingual Anglophone historians have relied excessively on English-language documents and publications containing much less information about African ethnicities than documents and publications in Portuguese, Spanish, and especially French.

We now know for certain that Atlantic slave trade ships did not meander along several African coasts collecting enslaved Africans and bringing them to many different places in the Americas. Individual Atlantic slave trade ships collected Africans overwhelmingly from the same coast, usually from only one or two ports on each coast, and brought them largely to the same American port. Why? Because the longer enslaved Africans remained aboard slave trade ships, the more likely they would die before they could be sold. It is hard to believe that humanitarian concerns were a significant influence on decisions made in the Atlantic slave trade business. But spoilage of the "cargo" seriously compromised the profitability of the voyage.

If we count all the peoples of the huge African continent and the many languages they speak, we might conclude that Africans brought to the Americas were extraordinarily diverse. If we limit ourselves to the African regions from which slaves were brought in significant numbers, this diversity is substantially reduced. If we total the African coastal origins of slave trade voyages to particular regions in the Americas over several decades or centuries and collapse the span of time, we conceal the fact that Africans from the same regions and ethnicities arrived at various places in the Americas in waves.[1] If we look at the changing ethnic composition of slaves exported from various African coasts over time, what we know about the patterns of the transshipment trade of Africans within the Americas, and the distribution of new Africans after their final sale, we can see further evidence of clustering of ethnicities and speakers of mutually intelligible languages on Atlantic slave trade voyages as well as after they arrived at their final destinations. We can discern the clustering of Africans from the same regions and ethnicities in local districts and on estates. This trend was almost universal: in Peru and Mexico during the sixteenth century and the first half of the seventeenth; in Brazil throughout its history; in St. Domingue/Haiti during the eighteenth century; and in mainland North American colonies and the subsequent states of the United States as well as the British West Indies during the eighteenth and nineteenth centuries. Gabriel Debien studied patterns of acquisition of new slaves on two large sugar estates over time, concluding that additional slaves were purchased from Atlantic slave trade ships in groups of ten, twenty, or thirty. "Once they were Nagos, another time Aradas, another time Ibos or Sosos, each voyage debarking one nation at a time, or else the manager preferred to take the same ethnicity from each arriving ship."[2] B. W. Higman wrote that in the British West Indies during the nineteenth century "particular source regions were more likely to predominate and a single ethnic group often accounted for a large proportion of the slaves from a particular region."[3] Aside from being clustered on estates, they were clustered in local districts. Enslaved Africans were often quite mobile and sought out their fellow countrymen living nearby.[4]

If we look at the bewildering variety of African ethnic designations recorded in documents in the Americas, we might come down, again, on the side of great diversity. Although a large variety of particular African ethnic designations can be identified in documents, few of them can be found with significant frequency. Thus, although Africa is a huge continent with many different peoples, only some of them were involved in the Atlantic slave trade, and relatively few African ethnicities were brought to the Americas in significant numbers.

There are multiple reasons for this clustering. Various African coasts were drawn into substantial involvement in the transatlantic slave trade in sequence over several centuries. During its early stages, European maritime trade with Africa often did not focus heavily on buying slaves to ship to the Americas. European traders named many African coasts after the major trade goods they purchased there: for example, the Gold Coast, the Pepper Coast, the Grain Coast, the Ivory Coast, the Slave Coast. During the first 150 years of the Atlantic slave trade, enslaved Africans were at first shipped mainly to Portugal, the Cape Verde Islands, the island of São Tomé, or to the Gold Coast in West Africa. The Portuguese demand for slaves for labor in Africa and these Atlantic islands off the African coast impinged sharply on the number of slaves available for the transatlantic slave trade. Neither the Cape Verde Islands nor the island of São Tomé was populated when the Portuguese first colonized them. In 1493, Portugal sent about 2,000 Jewish children under the age of eight, both male and female, to São Tomé. They had been taken away from their families in Portugal and baptized before they were deported. Most of them died shortly after they arrived. Only about 600 survived. Some of them married among themselves in the Catholic Church and had children. Most of them mated with or married Africans. Their African mates were described as very rich and intelligent. Their descendants became some of the Afro-Portuguese of Lower Guinea and West Central Africa.[5]

These Portuguese-colonized Atlantic islands off the African coast were launching pads for trade and colonization on the African mainland. Enslaved Africans were imported from the continent to produce very valuable trade goods. Salt, cotton, and luxurious textiles were produced in the Cape Verde Islands. They were the main products exchanged for slaves and other goods in Greater Senegambia. Throughout the centuries luxurious *panos* (lengths of cloth) produced in the Cape Verde Islands continued to be in very high demand on the adjoining African continent. As late as 1805, ships en route to Greater Senegambia stopped in Santiago, Cape Verde Islands, to purchase *panos* "greatly valued as an article of trade."[6] These Atlantic islands became the major place for exchange of domesticated plants and animals; techniques of cultivation; construction of buildings, ships, and docks; and manufacture of a variety of goods familiar in Europe, Africa, and the Americas. During the sixteenth century, the island of São Tomé was the world's leading sugar producer. By the 1560s, the sugar industry of São Tomé began to be undermined by slave runaways and revolts and later by Dutch raids, invasions, and occupations.

There was relatively little demand for Africans in the Americas during the sixteenth century. Shipping technologies to the Americas were underdeveloped. Before the full impact of the demographic disasters unleashed by Spanish and Portuguese exploration, conquest, and occupation of the Americas, Native American labor was more available and certainly cheaper.[7] This situation changed after about 1590, when the sugar industry of São Tomé collapsed and the Brazilian sugar industry became predominant. Between 1595 and 1640, Portugal held the *asiento* (contract) to supply African slaves to Spanish colonies. Cheap slaves could be obtained in Angola because of severe, extended drought and escalating warfare involving Portuguese and Dutch occupations and battles among Portuguese and Dutch allies and clients.

Once Brazil became the world's leading sugar producer, São Tomé and the Cape Verde Islands evolved into major entrepôts for the transatlantic slave trade. Africans enslaved on the continent were disembarked and refreshed with food and water, and then they worked to produce valuable trade goods while awaiting ships to take them to Portugal, to the Gold Coast, or to the Americas. Portuguese settlers of these Atlantic islands moved on to the African coast and established trading posts and settlements. They were called *lançados*.[8] Some of them were New Christians or *conversos*: Jews fleeing religious persecution in Portugal. Many of them moved to African communities on the mainland where religious differences were better tolerated, and they reconverted to Judaism. By 1629, there were Jewish synagogues in Recife (now Rufisque) and Cayor in Senegambia.[9] With the exception of the Jewish female children sent to settle the island of São Tomé in 1493, the *lançados* were almost entirely males. They mated with and married African women, often elite women. Their mixed-blood descendants were skilled traders, mariners, and linguists who enjoyed the great advantage of being resistant to African diseases. They played a major role in extending Portuguese trade and influence to the African continent. São Tomé developed an important shipbuilding industry. The Portuguese relied heavily on the skilled mariners of

São Tomé and the ships built there to penetrate and conquer West Central Africa.

The *lançados* and their descendants developed the earliest Creole languages. These Portuguese-based Creoles were no doubt the seed for subsequent Creole languages based on French, Spanish, and English vocabularies. Cape Verdean Creole was the first Portuguese-based Creole language in Greater Senegambia. São Tomé Creole was introduced into and developed in West Central Africa. The Portuguese *lançados*, their dependents (called *grumetes*), and their descendants became part of the influential Afro-Portuguese communities located along the coasts of West Africa and the riverine trade routes into the interior. They were established in enclaves, gradually influencing the surrounding areas. The Afro-Portuguese lived in places close enough to the Atlantic coast to allow for links with maritime traders. It is probably an exaggeration to describe the early generation of African slaves introduced into the Americas as a Creole generation, especially if this implies heavy European cultural influence among a significant number of Africans brought in as slaves. In coastal regions, African cultural influences based on the interpenetration of various African ethnic groups dominated the process of creolization. For example, in the coastal trading community of Luanda, Angola, 200 years after its founding by Portugal, African languages and traditional African religions continued to predominate.[10] Many enslaved Africans were brought from the interior, especially after 1650, when the Dutch, English, and French transatlantic slave traders became well established.

Before 1650, the Gold Coast and the Slave Coast were an insignificant source of slaves for the Americas. The Gold Coast was a primary market for the sale of enslaved Africans within Africa. Some Africans from the Slave Coast arrived in Cartagena de Indias during the first half of the seventeenth century, but the voyages from this region were very few in number. Greater Senegambia and West Central Africa were the only significant regions of origin for the transatlantic slave trade before 1650.

Another reason that the early Atlantic slave trade focused on relatively few coasts is because it was effectively resisted in some places. During the first two centuries of the Atlantic slave trade, few enslaved Africans were collected east of Greater Senegambia/Guinea all the way to the Slave Coast. There was no significant export of slaves from Liberia, the Ivory Coast, the Gold Coast, or the Volta River basin. European ships trading along the coast between Greater Senegambia/Guinea and the Slave Coast bought gold, ivory, grain, and pepper and supplied themselves with wood, food, and water to continue their voyages. The Loango Coast between Cape Lopez Gonzalez and the mouth of the Congo/Zaire River was not involved in the early maritime

Vue de Ben dans le pays de Cayor près Gorée.

Africans taken as slaves in eighteenth-century Senegal. (René Claude Geoffroy de Villeneuve, *L'Afrique, ou histoire, moeurs, usages et coutumes des africains: Le Sénégal*, 1814. Courtesy of Special Collections, University of Virginia.)

slave trade. Before 1650, the Atlantic slave trade remained very sparse along these many coasts. Ivory and red-wood dyes were exported from Mayombe. The slave trade at Gabon was limited because of the defiance of its inhabitants. They had a bad reputation among the crews of the Atlantic slave trade ships. They were advised to trade from their boats and avoid going ashore unless they were well armed. Resistance to the slave trade along the Gabon Coast continued over the centuries, forcing the Atlantic slave traders to concentrate on other coasts.[11] Throughout the centuries of the Atlantic slave trade, ships trading in Senegambia and at Gabon/Cape Lopez were up to eight times more likely to experience revolts among their "cargo" than ships trading from the Slave Coast and fourteen to thirty times more likely to experience revolts than those trading at the Bight of Biafra or in West Central Africa.[12]

Peoples living along other shores were difficult for the maritime slave traders to deal with. Shortly after they first arrived in Greater Senegambia, the Portuguese discovered that the Bissagos, living on islands at the mouth of

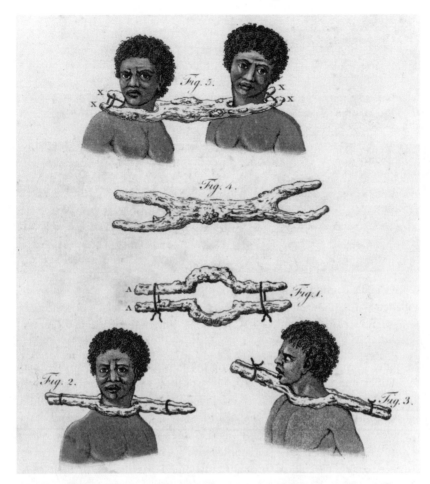

Wooden collars used in the slave trade. (Thomas Clarkson, *Letters on the slave-trade, and the state of the natives in those parts of Africa, . . . contiguous to Fort St. Louis and Gorée,* 1791. Courtesy of The Library Company of Philadelphia.)

the Geba River in Upper Guinea made very effective use of arrows poisoned with the spines of a fish called Bagre, which killed instantly. The Bissagos were skilled boatmen and pirates who became active kidnappers of other ethnicities to sell into the Atlantic slave trade. Near the end of the sixteenth century, the Balantas or Bagos as well as the Kru of Liberia refused to sell slaves to the Europeans. The Felupos or Diola living along the lower Casamance River in Greater Senegambia/Guinea refused to trade with the Portuguese at all.

A slave coffle coming from the interior in Senegal. (René Claude Geoffroy de Villeneuve, *L'Afrique, ou histoire, moeurs, usages et coutumes des africains: Le Sénégal*, 1814. Courtesy of Special Collections, University of Virginia Library.)

At night, they cut the ropes anchoring the Portuguese ships, causing them to founder, and then they attacked. Many of them would not accept ransom for the Portuguese they captured and killed them instead. Resistance to the slavers continued throughout the Atlantic slave trade. At the very end of the nineteenth century, two Felupos living in Guinea-Bissau said, "We never were slaves. We never enslaved or sold our fellows."[13] There was ongoing, armed resistance to the slave traders throughout Igboland over the centuries. John N. Oriji denies "that the slave trade was a normal commercial transaction which was conducted largely in the hinterland through peaceful means. The Igbo example clearly shows that slavery and the slave trade were the primary cause of violence in the West African sub-region for over three centuries. It is also clear that without the stiff resistance mounted by many individuals and communities, slavery would have had a more devastating impact in the hinterland."[14]

As late as the 1820s, after three and a half centuries of Portuguese presence in Mozambique, the Portuguese were confined to the coast and were not allowed to enter the Makua or Yao territories. In 1857, when the slave trade involved so-called contract workers, the Makua beat off Portuguese traders trying to enter their territory and threatened to attack Portuguese coastal

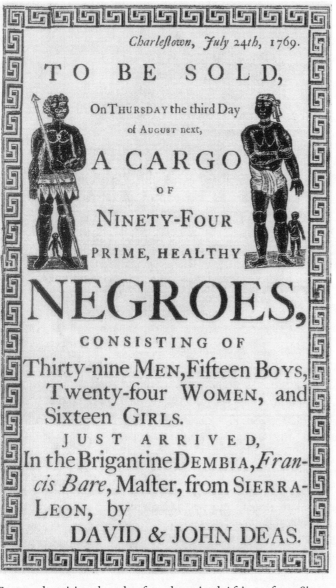

Poster advertising the sale of newly arrived Africans from Sierra Leone in Charleston, South Carolina, July 24, 1769. (From the website "The Atlantic Slave Trade and Slave Life in the Americas: A Visual Record," <http://hitchcock.itc.virginia.edu/Slavery>.)

Revolt aboard a slave ship, 1787. (William Fox, *A Brief History of the Wesleyan Missions on the West Coast of Africa*, 1851.)

settlements. The Portuguese governor-general agreed not to seek "contract laborers" from their country and thereby avoided war.[15]

Throughout West Africa, armed resistance to enslavement continued along the coasts, in the interior, along the rivers, in runaway communities, in slave pens, and aboard slave trade ships docked along the West African coasts as well as at sea.[16] But the Atlantic slave traders calculated African resistance on land and sea as an inevitable cost of their lucrative trade. African resistance could at best limit it.

Until about 1650, when the Portuguese monopoly of the Atlantic slave trade was destroyed, there were only two African regions sending large numbers of enslaved Africans across the Atlantic: Greater Senegambia and West Central Africa. Africans from these two regions were clustered in the Americas. During the first half of the seventeenth century, West Central Africans were brought to Spanish North America in increasing numbers, especially to Mexico and eastern Cuba. Greater Senegambians were brought to northeastern Brazil during the sixteenth century and to far northeastern Brazil (Maranhão and Pará) after 1750. But Greater Senegambians were most heavily clustered in the circum-Caribbean and Peru, and West Central Africans in Brazil.

During the seventeenth century, the English and the French began to establish trading companies operating in West Africa. After 1650, more African regions, especially the Gold Coast and the Slave Coast, became deeply involved in the Atlantic slave trade. But piracy at sea remained pivotal because of nearly unabated warfare among the European powers. Even in peacetime, large numbers of armed, unemployed seamen and former privateers were widespread throughout the Atlantic world. Estimates of the Atlantic slave trade to the Americas remain uncertain. Surviving researched documents alone tell only part of the story and give us only some of the numbers.

By the late seventeenth century, the Dutch, then the English, and then the French managed to open up the slave trade along the Loango Coast of West Central Africa north of the Congo River. This was a slow process and began mainly with the purchase of ivory. There was evidently no pool of slaves available to sell. Raids to produce slaves were eventually extended inland both north and south of the tumultuous Congo River. The Vili were the major slave raiders and sellers. During the eighteenth century, the Loango Coast became the primary source of West Central Africans in the British, French, and Dutch colonies. Substantial numbers of Kimbundu speakers from the hinterlands of Luanda, Angola, were shipped to the Loango Coast via the Malebo (Stanley) Pool. While there was significant overlap between Kikongo language group speakers shipped mainly from the Loango Coast and Kimbundu language group speakers shipped mainly from Luanda, "Angolans" in the British colonies as well as "Congo" in the French and Spanish colonies in North America were likely to be Kikongo language group speakers.

West Central Africa poses particular problems for our discussion of African ethnicities. There were conflicting usages of the terms "Congo" (Kongo) and "Angola" as coastal terms for Atlantic slave trade voyages as well as for individuals recorded in documents in the Americas. Compared to the other regions discussed, West Central Africa was the source of relatively few specific ethnicities recorded in American notarial documents in any significant numbers. A few more specific ethnic designations from West Central Africa appear in American documents as the slave trade from this region escalated during the late eighteenth and the first half of the nineteenth century. But the history, language, and culture of these peoples were so close that referring to most of them as "Kongo" is reasonable. Especially in Brazil, "Mozambique" was commonly used as a generic term for various ethnicities from that Southeast African region. More specific ethnic designations of peoples from Mozambique, mainly Makua, appear with greater frequency in French-language notarial documents.

Aside from timing, there were other factors clustering Africans from the same regions and ethnicities in the Americas. Particular African and American regions were linked by propinquity and by winds and currents affecting the length of voyages from various African coasts to various places in the Americas, as well as by the market for products sold by Atlantic slave traders along particular African coasts. Trading networks involving various types of credit arrangements, including pawnship, were established among African, Afro-European, European, and American traders.[17] The North Atlantic system linked Greater Senegambia/Upper Guinea with the United States, the Caribbean, and far northeastern Brazil (Maranhão and Pará). The South Atlantic system linked Central Africa, especially Angola and Mozambique, with southeastern Brazil and the Río de la Plata (now Argentina and Uruguay). Ships leaving Portugal for Angola had to pass near northeastern Brazil. Proximity and winds minimized travel time between Angola and southeastern Brazil.[18] African slavery thrived in all regions of Brazil during four centuries. Brazil was by far the greatest consumer of slaves in the Western Hemisphere.

African demand for goods sold by the Atlantic slave traders linked African and American regions. We have seen that New England rum and Virginia tobacco were very popular in the Gold Coast and Sierra Leone. The taste for tobacco was specialized. Cheap, strong, sweetened tobacco produced in Bahia, Brazil, was in great demand at Whydah and the Slave Coast.[19] Neither tobacco nor gold were important imports in West Central Africa. The Loango Coast of West Central Africa was not a significant market for rum. But Brazilian rum was an essential import in Angola.

African ethnicities were clustered in the Americas because of the preference of slave owners of various regions for particular African ethnicities. There were several important reasons for these preferences. Slave owners were motivated to purchase Africans with the knowledge and skills they needed the most. The cultivation and processing of indigo, the blue dye used for cotton cloth, was a technology long known by Africans from Upper Guinea. During the late sixteenth century, indigo was the major item sold to the Portuguese along the Nuñez River. Small quantities of indigo were used as currency.[20] In Louisiana, indigo production did not begin until Africans began to arrive from Senegal.[21] During the eighteenth century, indigo became a major export crop from St. Domingue/Haiti, Louisiana, Carolina, and Central America.

The clearest example of African technology transfer to the Americas is the production of rice. Several prominent historians have argued that early slave trade voyages from Madagascar first introduced to the Americas rice and the complex technology for its cultivation. A substantial number of voyages from Madagascar to Barbados and Virginia between 1675 and 1724 have been documented. Although the British never managed to establish a permanent colony in Madagascar, they were active exporters of enslaved Africans from there, especially to Jamaica and Barbados. A census in Barbados at the end of the seventeenth century counted 32,473 slaves, half of them from Madagascar. Some of these Madagascans were surely transshipped from Barbados to Carolina, accompanied masters who were relocating there, or arrived directly on voyages of the many English and American pirates actively trading for slaves in Madagascar between 1688 and 1724. *The Trans-Atlantic Slave Trade Database* gives the impression that the slave trade from Madagascar was largely a British operation. Among forty-seven voyages of ships with national registry recorded in this database, forty-two (89.4 percent) were of British registry. But many early Dutch voyages as well as voyages of ships of other national registry, including Portuguese and Brazilian, were not recorded in this database, to say nothing of the many voyages of European and American pirates operating in Madagascar.[22]

Greater Senegambia/Upper Guinea was a major cradle of domestication and cultivation of rice as well as of many other food crops. Rice was domesticated there independently of the Asian variety.[23] Generations of rice growers experimented with mini-environments, developing and adapting their techniques to varied and changing climatic conditions. Wet rice was widely cultivated using complex irrigation techniques.[24] Africans from Upper Guinea were prized in Carolina and Georgia because of their skills in rice cultivation. They were less feared in the United States than in the demographically imbalanced Caribbean sugar islands, where black slaves vastly outnumbered whites. Voyages recorded in *The Trans-Atlantic Slave Trade Database* allow us to generalize findings to other rice-cultivating regions in the Americas as well. Although only 12.9 percent of the voyages entered in this database brought Africans from Senegambia and Sierra Leone, they were 46 percent of voyages to rice-growing regions.[25] The high proportion of missing voyages from Greater Senegambia in this database allows us to tilt toward an even higher number.

Mining was another important technology transferred from Africa to the Americas. By the middle of the sixteenth century, Africans who were experienced gold miners were in demand in Colombia. Runaway slaves in Colombia were listed as "Minas" (miners). Although the meaning of the term is unclear, it changed over time and differed in various places. These "Minas" were probably experienced miners from the goldfields of Bambuk or Buré in Greater Senegambia. Africans designated as "Minas" were brought to Brazil from gold-producing regions of West Africa, including Greater Senegambia and the Gold Coast, to develop the gold-mining industry of Brazil. They were used to discover gold and develop panning and digging for it.[26] Kongo were

Table 3.1.   Transatlantic Slave Trade Voyages Bringing
Enslaved Africans to Rice-Growing Regions

Destination	Number of all Voyages	Voyages from Senegambia/ Upper Guinea
South Carolina	556	230 (44%)
Georgia	60	37 (62%)
Mississippi Delta	31	21 (68%)
Florida	7	6 (86%)
Northeast Brazil	87	47 (54%)
Total	741	341 (46%)

Source: Calculated from 13,072 voyages recorded in *The Trans-Atlantic Slave Trade Database* indicating both major buying and selling regions.
Note: Three voyages to the Mississippi Delta missing from *The Trans-Atlantic Slave Trade Database* were added. The numbers of voyages do not reflect the number of slaves. Voyages from Senegambia, narrowly defined, carried a significantly smaller number of slaves than voyages from other regions. Voyages from the "Windward Coast" are excluded here.

clustered in Santiago on the eastern end of Cuba to develop and work in the copper mines.[27]

While Africans with especially needed skills were favored in various parts of the Americas, specific African ethnicities were preferred for other reasons. It has become a false truism that masters were always inclined to fractionalize new Africans so they could not communicate with each other, thereby minimizing revolts among them. While this was certainly true in some cases, some masters preferred new Africans with whom they were familiar and who spoke languages understood and spoken by the slaves they already owned. There was a certain logic to bringing in Africans from "nations" who were already present in substantial numbers. The upside of creating a Tower of Babel on estates was often outweighed by the ability of partially resocialized Africans who had arrived earlier to communicate with and help resocialize newcomers. For example, in Louisiana in 1730, a master sent "un nègre de son pays" (a black from his country) to talk to a newly arrived slave whom he suspected of malingering.[28] Le Page du Pratz, director of the Company of the Indies in Louisiana, who returned to France in 1732, advised Louisiana slave owners that new Africans from Guinea all believed that the French intended to kill them and drink their blood and they would kill themselves or run away shortly after they arrived unless they were reassured by the presence of older slaves from their nations.[29] Moreau de St.-Méry wrote that while some St. Domingue planters hesitated to buy Igbo slaves because of their suicidal tendencies, others preferred them because they were very attached to each other and "the newly arrived find help, care, and example from those who have come before them."[30] A chain migration pattern has been identified for free immigrants. Those who arrived early attracted more immigrants from the same places of origin in the Old World. A modified pattern of chain migration applied to African slaves as well. Some masters preferred Africans of ethnicities who arrived early and purchased slaves from these same African "nations" when they could.

As they arrived on Atlantic slave trade voyages, new Africans were often transshipped to other regions and colonies. Patterns of this transshipment trade must be better known and understood before we can draw firm conclusions about the distribution of Africans from particular coasts and ethnicities in many places in the Americas. This is especially true for major transshipment points. With a few outstanding exceptions, very little research on this trade has been done, and little is known about it. Although at first blush the transshipment slave trade from the Caribbean seems likely to have fragmented Africans of the same regions and ethnicities because of the large numbers of ships arriving from a variety of African coasts, there was a countervailing trend indicating that preferences among both sellers and buyers tended to cluster rather than fragment arriving Africans. Some masters sent their own ships to purchase enslaved Africans from preferred coasts on Atlantic slave trade voyages as they arrived in Caribbean ports. Some of them sent their ships directly to preferred African coasts, cutting out the very expensive Caribbean middlemen. Daniel Littlefield has made very convincing links between the British Atlantic slave trade and the transshipment trade from the Caribbean. His work has revealed careful patterns in marketing that tended to cluster Africans transshipped from the British Caribbean to places where they were preferred.[31] Colin Palmer has discussed preferences for African ethnicities in the transshipment trade from the British West Indies to the United States and to Spanish America between 1700 and 1740. Between 1702 and 1714, before the British *asiento* (contract) to supply new Africans to the Spanish colonies began, at least 18,180 new Africans were transshipped from Jamaica. Fully 59.2 percent (n = 231) of British voyages bringing new Africans to Spanish American colonies between 1714 and 1740 were transshipments from Jamaica.[32] More recently, David Eltis has discussed the impact of preferences for Gold Coast/Slave Coast Africans in Jamaica. His conclusion is that "on Jamaican plantations at least, the estimate of two-thirds of all slaves coming from the Gold Coast–Slave Coast regions is very much a lower bound figure, with the true figure perhaps in excess of eighty percent."[33]

The preference for Gold Coast and Slave Coast Africans in Jamaica probably explains why the stated preferences of British mainland masters for Africans from the Gold Coast was not reflected in the transatlantic slave trade voyages to the United States. Ships of United States registry brought Africans they collected on the Gold Coast mainly to Jamaica and Barbados. The sharp preference for Gold Coast/Slave Coast Africans in Jamaica probably limited the transatlantic slave trade voyages from these regions to the United States and diminished their transshipment from the British Caribbean to the British mainland colonies as well. Documented Atlantic slave trade voyages from the Slave Coast to the Anglo–United States during both the colonial and the national periods are minimal.

We have little direct evidence concerning place of birth or of socialization among Africans transshipped from the Caribbean to the Anglo–United States; our knowledge about their African coastal or ethnic origins is similarly limited. But we know that they were not likely to be either born or socialized in the Caribbean. Masters were reluctant to buy Caribbean-born or socialized slaves, and for good reasons. They often had hidden illnesses, or their masters and the colonial authorities were trying to get rid of them because they were uncontrollable. Lorena S. Walsh has discerned this pattern for the Chesapeake. She argues that prestigious historians have exaggerated the number of Caribbean-born slaves brought into the British mainland colonies and states. This is certainly true for Louisiana, where the evidence is absolutely clear.[34]

Our newest and most systematic data about the trade in slaves shipped from Caribbean ports is from Spanish Louisiana. This colony relied very heavily on the transshipment trade rather than on the transatlantic slave trade. It is certain that almost all slaves shipped to Louisiana from the Caribbean were new Africans purchased from transatlantic slave trade voyages as they arrived in various Caribbean ports. There were both push and pull factors clustering rather than fragmenting transshipped Africans. As these voyages arrived in the Caribbean from Africa, selections among Africans from various coasts were made at the transshipment point. Africans arriving on ships coming from preferred coasts were chosen, and Africans coming from forbidden coasts were rejected. For example, a document dating from 1765 indicates that the Bight of Biafra was a forbidden coast for maritime slave traders bringing new Africans from Caribbean islands to Louisiana.[35] This document explains why Peter Hill, captain of the sloop *Little David*, which left New York for Barbados, failed to carry out instructions to purchase between 80 and 100 newly arrived enslaved Africans to bring to the Iberville coast on the west bank of the Mississippi River opposite Baton Rouge. Captain Hill explained, "On my arrival at Barbados after doing everything in my power to fulfill the directions given me . . . and finding no probability of succeeding . . . I proceeded (in accordance with previous instructions) for the Island of Jamaica. . . . But after waiting there till the 16th of August and to that day there having but three ships arrived from Africa, two of which were of the countries excepted against and the other cargo in so bad condition that I could not Pick out the number wanted in Tolerable Order." He could not fulfill the contract, which proved costly to his sponsors, who were successfully sued by the potential buyers of these slaves.[36] Evidence from transatlantic slave trade voyages arriving in Jamaica during this time period indicates that the two ships bringing in Africans from "the countries excepted against" came from Bonny, a port on the Bight of Biafra. During this time period, such "cargoes" were probably mainly Igbos. Enslaved Africans from the Bight of Biafra were underrepresented in Spanish Louisiana, although a high proportion of voyages from the Bight of Biafra arrived in Jamaica and Cuba, both major Caribbean transshipment points for Africans brought to Louisiana.

Going beyond this one very informative, but still anecdotal document, there is significant information in the *Louisiana Slave Database* about slaves arriving on transshipment voyages. During the entire Spanish period we have records for 2,920 individual slaves shipped to Louisiana from the Caribbean. These figures cannot be extrapolated over time. The transatlantic slave trade as well as the transshipment trade in slaves waxed and waned with prosperity, conditions in Africa, warfare among the European powers, levels of privateering and piracy, and considerations of social control, especially after the Haitian Revolution began in 1791. The import of slaves to Louisiana was restricted or outlawed throughout the 1790s. Nevertheless, much smuggling no doubt took place.[37]

Among the 2,920 records describing individual slaves who arrived on ships from the Caribbean during the Spanish period (1770–1803), the origins of 967 of them were identified. Among them, 97.3 percent (n = 941) were Africans. Among these Africans, 97 percent (n = 913) were listed as *brut* or *bozal* (the French and Spanish designations for new arrivals from Africa); no other information about the origins of 87.2 percent (n = 796) of these new Africans was recorded. More specific origin information was given for 136 of them: 115 were identified by specific African ethnicities and 21 by coastal origins only. Evidence at the point of sale of these new Africans arriving on transshipment voyages from the Caribbean indicates a clustering rather than a fragmenting or randomizing of Africans of the same ethnicity. Among the slaves transshipped to Louisiana from the Caribbean, there were Africans listed as Mandingo, Kongo, and Makua. Each ethnic group was probably purchased from the same Atlantic slave trade voyage and brought over in groups on the same transshipment voyage. Many of the slaves listed under the same ethnicity were sold to the same buyer in Louisiana. Only one of the buyers, Hilario Boutte, can be identified as a jobber or reseller. In 1785, thirteen Mandingo arrived from Jamaica on the *Cathalina*. They were sold to four different buyers in lots of six, five, one, and one. In 1787, ten Mandingo were brought in from Martinique on the ship *Nueva Orleans*. They were all sold to the same buyer. Nine Kongo slaves brought in from St. Domingue in 1786 on the *Rosaria* were all sold to the same buyer. Ten Kongo slaves who arrived from Martinique on the *Nueva Orleans* in 1787 were sold to the same buyer as well. The thirty-nine Kongo slaves arriving on the *Abentura* from Havana in 1796 were sold to various buyers in lots ranging between eight and one. The seventeen Makua arriving from St. Domingue on the *Maria Magdalena* in 1785 were sold as follows: three lots of four; one lot of three, and two lots of one. The Makua ended up mainly in Pointe Coupée Parish: 54.8 percent of them (n = 23) were recorded on estates probated there.

Information about the transshipment of Africans can also be found in voyages listed in Spanish customs documents, but they are very far from complete. By 1782, slaves entered Louisiana duty-free, and the Spanish authorities were therefore not motivated to keep track of them. Except for the year 1786, information in Spanish customs documents about slaves imported into Louisiana is very sparse. The Spanish Custom House List for 1786 (see table 3.2) claimed to provide complete information, but it did not. Some voyages arriving from the Caribbean in 1786 sold slaves in Louisiana but were not listed in this document. There were 1,204 transshipped slaves sold in Louisiana in 1786 as opposed to 957 listed in the Spanish customs documents for that year.[38] Nevertheless, the 1786 customs document is quite revealing about patterns of the transshipment slave trade to Louisiana from the Caribbean and has implications for other places in the Americas as well. It reveals a whole world of voyages, some of them bringing in substantial numbers of new Africans as they arrived in the Caribbean on transatlantic slave trade voyages. These transshipment voyages were not part of a large, reasonably well-documented, international network of slave trade voyages. Nor were they small, insignificant voyages either in number of voyages or numbers of slaves brought in by each shipment. For each voyage, the document includes the number of slaves brought ashore, the name of the ship, its captain and/or owner, the island of embarkation, and the date of arrival in Louisiana. It reveals that these voyages were initiated and carried out entirely by Louisiana merchants, ship captains, and slave masters, usually overlapping categories. In a large majority of instances, the captain was the owner of the ship and the sponsor of the voyage.

Table 3.2.   Spanish Custom House List of Slaves Arriving
in Louisiana from Caribbean Islands during 1786

Origin of Voyage	Slaves Landed	Captain/ Owner	Total from Each Island
Guadeloupe	40	Yes	40 (4%)
Jamaica	93	Yes	
	9	Yes	
	59	Yes	
	100	Yes	
	52	Yes	
	56	No	
	52	No	
	60	No	481 (50%)
Martinique	102	Yes	
	60	Yes	162 (17%)
St. Domingue	10	Yes	
	105	Yes	
	135	Yes	
	24	No	274 (29%)
Grand total			957

Source: Calculated from Papeles Procedentes de Cuba, Correspondencia de
la Intendencia con la Aduana Estados mensuales de derechos de entrada y
salida, 1786–87, Relacion que manifiestan el numero de Negros llagados a
esta Ciudad, Legajo 575, folio 89.
Note: 765 slaves (80 percent) were landed by ships in which the captain
was also the owner of the ship and of the slaves purchased.

Thus there was another world of slave trade voyages organized by slave
owners who sent their own ships to the Caribbean or to Africa to collect slaves
for their own use. These newly arrived Africans do not normally appear in
sales documents in the Americas. If the captain was not the shipowner, he
was given a few slaves from the "cargo" to sell as partial compensation for his
services. Nevertheless, we find significant traces of these imported slaves in
Spanish documents in Louisiana after Spain required that sellers of slaves indicate, under penalty of confiscation, how they had acquired any slave they
sold.[39] The master would often explain that he had brought the slaves he was
selling over in his own ship, usually giving its name. The slaves almost always
had been purchased in a Caribbean port.[40] But sometimes the customs documents indicate an African port, such as Guinea La Cayana (a location that
remains unidentified). Table 3.2 reveals that 80 percent of these enslaved Africans arrived on voyages in which the captain was also the owner.

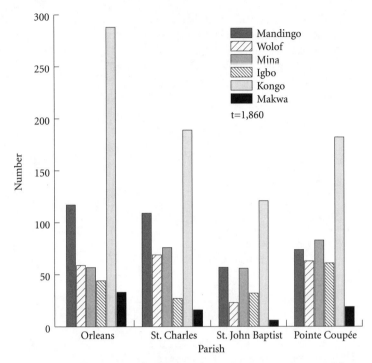

Figure 3.1.   Clustering of African Ethnicities in Louisiana Parishes, Spanish Period (1770–1803). Calculated from Hall, *Louisiana Slave Database, 1719–1820*.

The main Caribbean transshipment points for Spanish Louisiana were Jamaica, St. Dominigue, Martinique, and, after 1790, Cuba. In Louisiana documents, Africans do not at all reflect the African coastal regions of transatlantic slave trade voyages arriving in these islands during the relevant time periods. The clustering of African ethnicities during the transshipment trade from the Caribbean is evident from the heavy concentration of Africans from the Bight of Benin in Spanish Louisiana (1770–1803), especially along the Mississippi upriver from New Orleans.

The last documented transatlantic slave trade voyage from the Bight of Benin arrived in Louisiana in 1728. During the Spanish period in Louisiana (1770–1803) the transatlantic slave trade to Martinique had evidently greatly diminished. There were only twenty-three transatlantic slave trade voyages to Martinique recorded in *The Trans-Atlantic Slave Trade Database* between 1750 and 1795, the year the foreign slave trade to Louisiana was outlawed.[41] Only three of these voyages (11.5 percent) arrived in Martinique from the Bight of Benin, and only one of them during the 1780s when the transshipment

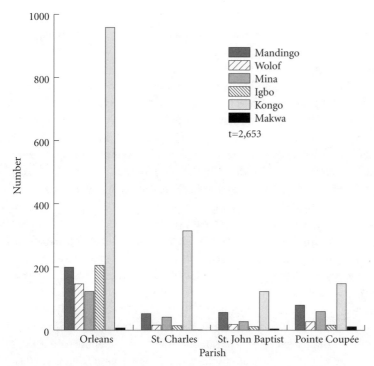

Figure 3.2.   Clustering of African Ethnicities in Louisiana Parishes,
Early U.S. Period (1804–1820). Calculated from Hall, *Louisiana
Slave Database, 1719–1820.*

trade from the Caribbean to Louisiana was most active. St. Domingue/Haiti
was still importing Africans from the Bight of Benin, but the most common
African coast of origin had shifted heavily to West Central Africa. Jamaican imports were predominantly from the Gold Coast, but Gold Coast slaves
were extremely rare in Louisiana. The Bight of Biafra was important in the
Atlantic slave trade to Cuba as well as to Jamaica during the 1780s and 1790s,
but relatively few Africans from this coast were found in Spanish Louisiana
documents. Linking the dates of arrival of transatlantic slave trade voyages in
these islands with transshipment voyages to Louisiana reveals that the Bight
of Benin did not figure at all prominently as the major buying region during these years.[42] We can only account for the clustering of Africans from the
Bight of Benin in Louisiana through vigorous choice during the course of
the transshipment trade from the Caribbean. They were heavily selected from
among the voluminous voyages arriving in St. Domingue and Jamaica during the 1780s when the transshipment trade to Louisiana escalated or from
voyages arriving in Cuba after 1790 as the transshipment trade shifted toward

that island. Africans from the Bight of Benin were present in Louisiana since the earliest years of colonization, demonstrating a significant continuity over many decades. Clustering of Africans from the Bight of Benin in upriver parishes continued through 1820.

During 1800, the foreign slave trade to Louisiana was reopened. Three transatlantic slave trade voyages were licensed by Spain and arrived in Louisiana during 1803. After Louisiana was taken over by the United States in late 1803, the foreign slave trade was immediately outlawed, but the transshipment trade from east coast ports of the United States remained legal. Once the Louisiana Territory came under United States control, the Kongo of West Central Africa became heavily clustered in Orleans and St. Charles Parishes, where the sugar industry was rapidly growing. The two documented Atlantic slave trade voyages arriving in Louisiana after the Louisiana Purchase were British ships bringing Kongo from West Central Africa. During the early U.S. period (1804–20), slaves transshipped to and sold in Louisiana arrived mainly on maritime voyages from east coast ports of the United States: Baltimore, Charleston, and Norfolk. They were overwhelmingly newly arrived Africans. Between 1804 and 1809, 63.5 percent (n = 172) of slaves arriving by sea and sold in Louisiana with recorded birthplaces were new Africans listed as *brut*. In 1808, thirty Kongo arrived on the transshipment voyage of the ship *Ana*. A surprisingly small number of slaves sold from ships arriving from east coast ports were born or were socialized in the United States. Sales documents dating from between 1810 and 1820 list 325 slaves brought from east coast ports of the United States. Very few birthplaces of slaves arriving by sea were recorded after 1810.

Many American-born slaves were no doubt brought by their masters by land, downriver, or by sea and were therefore not sold in Louisiana. Some documents record slaves who were probably sold down the Mississippi River by slave traders from Kentucky and Tennessee. We know where the slave traders lived, but not where the slaves they sold came from.

After the Louisiana Purchase in 1803, there was substantial smuggling of new Africans into the territory. The documentation for illegal voyages is, of course, thin. But young Africans of various ethnicities listed in Louisiana documents between 1804 and 1820 shed considerable light on the African ethnicities of smuggled slaves.

A comparison of the mean age of various African ethnicities recorded in Louisiana documents between 1800 and 1820 makes it abundantly clear that massive smuggling of new Africans was taking place. Very few ethnicities reflected a significant rise in mean age, which would have indicated that these Africans were elderly survivors of the legal slave trade. Young Africans were

Table 3.3.   Birthplace or Ethnicity of Slaves Arriving
in Louisiana by Ship from East Coast Ports of the
United States, 1804–1809

Birthplace or Ethnicity	Number	Percentage
British Mainland Creole	9	3.3
Maryland	2	.7
Virginia	1	.4
Carolinas	2	.7
Native American	1	.4
St. Domingue	3	1.1
Martinique	1	.4
Mandingo	5	1.8
Fulbe/Pular	1	.4
Wolof	6	2.2
Gola	1	.4
Chamba	1	.4
Hausa	1	.4
Mina	11	4.0
Birom	1	.4
Kongo	45	16.5
Africa	9	3.3
New Africans	174	63.5
Total	274	100.0

Source: Calculated from Hall, *Louisiana Slave Database, 1719–1820.*

renewing the slave population. Table 3.4, calculated from the *Louisiana Slave Database*, is a selection of Africans of the most numerous ethnicities. This table reveals certain trends. The most significant is that there was massive smuggling of Africans into the Lower Mississippi Valley after the foreign slave trade was outlawed. It shows which ethnicities were most heavily victimized by this illegal slave trade and which were not. Judging by the substantial rise in their mean age over time, the Pular (Fulbe) and the Nard (Moor) seemed to have been the least affected. The ethnicities with dropping or nearly stable mean ages — Wolof, Kisi, Chamba, Nago, Hausa, and Mandongo as well as those categorized simply as African or of unrecognized African nation — were probably the most victimized since they were being rapidly renewed by young people. The majority of the most numerous African ethnicities show a slight increase in mean age, about two years, which would indicate that they, too, were being substantially renewed from Africa.

Historians have missed these numerous voyages, and no doubt similar ones initiated in other colonies, because they have emphasized centralized,

Table 3.4. Mean Age of Africans in Louisiana, 1800–1820

| | 1800–1809 | | 1810–1820 | | |
Ethnicity	Number	Mean Age	Number	Mean Age	Total Number
Bamana	83	38.68	98	40.46	181
Mandingo	239	33.12	257	35.26	496
Nard (Moor)	18	39.89	18	47.28	36
Pular (Fulbe)	49	36.07	52	44.39	101
Wolof	104	29.14	176	29.90	280
Guinea or Coast of Guinea	290	35.91	136	37.12	426
Kisi	21	43.14	18	37.28	39
Kanga	90	30.67	90	32.64	180
Aja/Fon/Arada	44	36.48	37	38.64	81
Mina	140	31.61	181	33.52	321
Chamba	98	38.46	92	38.83	190
Hausa	22	34.55	73	32.12	95
Nago (Yoruba)	67	40.49	58	38.41	125
Igbo	120	31.69	171	33.58	291
Ibibio/Moko	29	27.03	24	31.67	53
Calabar	44	31.87	29	35.55	73
Kongo	759	26.53	1,237	28.51	1,996
Mandongo	10	30.60	11	29.27	21
Makua	21	35.24	13	39.39	34
Africa	75	37.77	384	32.41	459
Unidentified	25	34.12	23	33.96	48
New Africans	337	18.66	20	23.06	357
Total	2,840	30.05	3,280	32.33	6,120

Source: Calculated from Hall, *Louisiana Slave Database, 1719–1820.*
Note: "Africa" means identified only as "African." "Unidentified" means nation given but unidentified. "New African" means identified as a newly arrived African but no nation information given.

mainly European archives containing records for large, commercial voyages. Most of these informal voyages were probably never documented at all. More studies of private papers and maritime documents housed in ports throughout the Americas might find traces of other such voyages. A significant number of them no doubt went directly to Africa, cutting out the expensive Caribbean middlemen and going to preferred coasts, especially to Greater Senegambia, a comparatively near destination where the slave trade was sometimes firmly in the hands of Afro-Europeans.

This chapter has argued that, although at some times and places newly arrived Africans were deliberately or randomly fragmented by the Atlantic slave trade, there were predominant countervailing patterns that tended to cluster new Africans from the same ethnicities and regions. These patterns resulted from the following factors: the tendency to load and ship enslaved Africans as quickly as possible from one coast; the gradual introduction of new regions of Africa into significant participation in the transatlantic slave trade over several centuries; geographic patterns involving distance, winds, and currents facilitating contact between specific African and American regions; traditional trading networks involving preferences for specific American products as well as long-established credit relationships on both sides of the Atlantic, including pawnship relationships in Africa;[43] resistance to the Atlantic slave trade along various coasts of Africa, forcing the maritime slave traders to rely on fewer African coasts and regions; preferences for Africans from specific coasts and ethnicities, greatly influenced by African skills and technology transfer from Africa to the Americas; and preferences for Africans who were first brought into specific American regions. All of these factors established historical trade networks linking regions of Africa with regions of the Americas. Patterns in the maritime transshipment slave trade tended to cluster new Africans in places of their final destination.

The concluding four chapters of this book will link African regions and ethnicities with regions in the Americas over time.

CHAPTER FOUR

Greater Senegambia/Upper Guinea

The blacks of the rivers and ports of Guinea . . . we refer to, because of their excellence, as of law [having a written religion with ethical-legal traditions]. They are much more faithful than all the others, of great reason and capacity, more handsome and attractive in appearance; strong, healthy, and capable of hard work; and for these reasons it is well known that all of them are more valuable and esteemed than any of the other nations. These peoples and coasts are numerous, and referring to all of them would be an exhausting and infinite task. But giving some information about them would be pleasant, advantageous, and even very necessary to our task. Among them are Wolof, Berbese, Mandinga, and Fula: others Fulupo, others Banun; or Fulupo called Boote; others Cazanga and pure Banun; others Bran; Balanta; Biafara; and Biofo; others Nalu; others Zape; Cocolis and Zozo.

—Alonso de Sandoval, *Un tratado sobre la esclavitud*, 1627.

This chapter challenges some of the prevailing wisdom among historians who minimize the demographic and cultural contribution of peoples from Greater Senegambia to many important regions in the Americas. During the first 200 years of the Atlantic slave trade, Guinea meant what Boubacar Barry defines as Greater Senegambia: the region between the Senegal and the Sierra Leone rivers. In Arabic, "Guinea" meant "Land of the Blacks." It referred to the Senegal/Sierra Leone regions alone. In early Portuguese and Spanish writings, "Guinea" meant Upper Guinea. Early Portuguese documents and chronicles called the Gold Coast, the Slave Coast, and the Bights of Benin and Biafra the Mina Coast.[1] In the writings of Alonso de Sandoval, "Guineans" meant Greater Senegambians. As late as the nineteenth century, "Guinea" continued to mean Upper Guinea to other Atlantic slave traders as well. When King James I chartered the first English company to trade with Africa in the early seventeenth century, the Portuguese and Spanish usage of the term "Guinea" was initially adopted. The English company was named the Company of Adventurers, and it was to trade specifically with " 'Gynny and Bynny' (Guinea and Benin)."[2] After the northern European powers began to enter the Atlantic slave trade legally and systematically in the 1650s, "Guinea" was gradually extended to mean the entire West African coast from Senegal

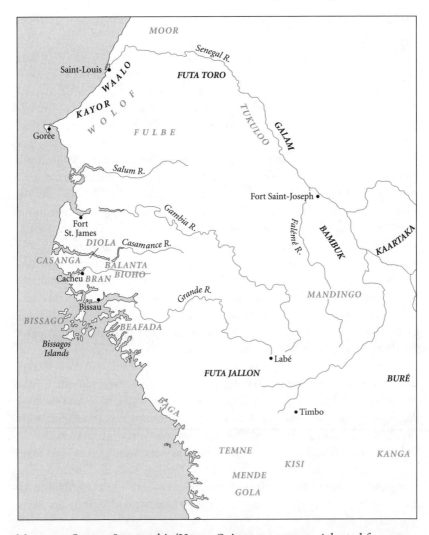

Map 4.1.   Greater Senegambia/Upper Guinea, 1500–1700. Adapted from a
map by Boubacar Barry, in *UNESCO General History of Africa*, vol. 5, ed.
B. A. Ogot (Berkeley: University of California Press, 1992); copyright © 1992
UNESCO.

down through Angola. But the meaning of "Guinea" continued to depend
on time and place and was far from precise or universal. It often continued
to mean Greater Senegambia among Iberians and at times among Atlantic
slave traders of other nations as well. A French document dating from 1737
ordered a ship to go to Africa and get slaves from "the Coast of Guinea or else-

where."[3] There is credible evidence that as late as 1811 "Guinea" or the "Coast of Guinea" still referred to Africans from Sierra Leone.

Greater Senegambia is much closer to Europe and North America than any other region of Africa. Voyages were much shorter. The earliest Atlantic slave trade began in this region. Half a century before the "discovery," conquest, and colonization of the Americas began, African slaves, mainly Senegambians, were brought to Portugal by ship, sold in the active slave market in Lisbon, and then resold throughout the Iberian Peninsula. The earliest information we have about them comes from Valencia, Spain. Their "nation" designations have been interpreted as regional rather than ethnic, cultural, or linguistic. They include "Guine," "Jalof" (Wolof), and, by the 1490s, "Mandega" (Mandingo). The Mandingo were Mande language group speakers, descendants of the peoples of the Mali Empire who were prominent conquerors, traders, and interpreters of languages throughout Greater Senegambia. Many speakers of West Atlantic languages had been conquered, displaced, and/or acculturated by Mande language speakers.[4] African ethnicity and regional names overlapped. According to Stephan Buhnen, in these documents "Jalof" meant all of northern Upper Guinea, "Mandega" meant central Upper Guinea (from the Gambia to the Rio Geba), and "Sape" meant southern Upper Guinea (to the Sierra Leone River).[5]

Many enslaved Africans brought to the Iberian Peninsula and their descendants were converted to Christianity and spoke Portuguese and/or dialects of Spanish. The Wolof were prominent among them.[6] They were referred to as "Ladinos," meaning Latinized Africans. After the conquest and colonization of the Americas began, enslaved Africans continued to be introduced into the Iberian Peninsula. They and their descendants were among the first Africans and peoples of African descent brought to the Americas as "Ladinos." The comparatively rapid voyages from Greater Senegambia to the Caribbean encouraged populating early Spanish America with Africans from Greater Senegambia.

The earliest importation of enslaved Africans to Spanish America was to the island of Santo Domingo in 1502. After the conquest of Mexico in 1519, Mexico (New Spain) became an important destination as well. In keeping with Spain's laws and policies enforcing religious conformity throughout its empire, the first African slaves brought to Spanish America were Ladinos. But the Ladino slaves encouraged and helped the surviving Arawak Indians of Santo Domingo to rebel against the Spanish colonists. Hoping to bring in slaves who were more ignorant of Spain and Spanish ways and therefore less dangerous, the Spanish began bringing in enslaved Wolof from Africa instead of Ladinos, despite the fact that the Wolof were Islamized. But they turned

Table 4.1. Length of Slave Trade Voyages Arriving in Cartagena de Indias,
1595–1640

Place of Purchase	<1 year	1–2 years	2–4 years	>4 years
Senegambia	16	6	5	—
Angola	—	29	13	3
São Tomé	—	—	6	5
Arda (Allada)/Slave Coast	—	—	1	—

Source: Calculated from Vila Vilar, *Hispanoamérica y el comercio de esclavos*, 148–52.
Note: The length of slave trade voyages begins with their departure from Europe and includes the voyage to West Africa, time on the West African coast, the voyage across the Atlantic to the Americas, and the return to Europe.

out to be as rebellious as the Ladinos. They, too, encouraged and helped the Arawak to revolt against the Spanish and became repeatedly and universally prohibited in Spanish America. Nevertheless, Wolof continued to arrive in substantial numbers.[7]

During the closing decades of the sixteenth century, the Portuguese *lançados* gradually established a fortified slave-trading post on the Cacheu River in Greater Senegambia.[8] The catchment area of this post was referred to in Portuguese documents as the Rivers of Guinea. In Spanish and Portuguese documents, "Ríos de Guinea" meant the region between the Casamance and the Sierra Leone rivers.

Although Brazil is widely associated with West Central Africa and the Slave Coast, Greater Senegambia was an important source of Africans brought to Brazil. Costa e Silva has called the last half of the sixteenth century the Guinea phase of the slave trade to Brazil.[9] Dutch and then French and British slave traders largely displaced the Portuguese in Greater Senegambia during the seventeenth century, but Portugal maintained a relatively minor presence at its trading posts of Cacheu and Bissau. During the last half of the eighteenth century, far northeastern Brazil was colonized and developed with Africans from Greater Senegambia. The Maranhão Company was chartered in 1755 and held a monopoly of the Portuguese and Brazilian slave trade from Upper Guinea for twenty years. Its slave trade brought Africans mainly to Maranhão and Pará in northeastern Brazil, a rice- and cotton-producing region located in the North Atlantic system of winds and currents. It was a hard sail from Greater Senegambia to southeastern Brazil but an easy sail to the far northeast. Portuguese officials were afraid that newly arrived Africans would be transshipped to the Caribbean from Maranhão because it was an easy sail and prices of slaves in the Caribbean were higher.[10]

In much of Spanish America during the first two centuries of colonization, Greater Senegambians remained predominant. Geographic proximity, preferences for "Guineans" (meaning Greater Senegambians), favorable winds and currents, and shorter voyages allowing for smaller ships and crews and fewer supplies were important reasons for this early pattern. Between 1532 and 1580, Greater Senegambians were 78 percent of recorded African ethnicities in Peru and 88 percent in Mexico, with 20.4 percent recorded as Wolof, 18.7 percent as Biafara, and 15.9 percent as Bran.[11]

Between 1580 and 1640, the crowns of Spain and Portugal were merged but their colonies were administered separately. The papacy had given Portugal a monopoly over the maritime trade along the West African Coast. But the Spanish crown managed to profit handsomely from the slave trade. The *asiento* licenses sold by the Spanish crown allowed Portuguese merchants to supply African slaves to Spain's colonies in the Americas. These licenses were sold at high prices and sometimes resold by their purchasers. They represented a significant part of the revenue of the crown of Spain. They were paid in advance, placing all financial risks on the slave traders. The Spanish crown managed to recoup most of the profits made by the transatlantic slave traders to whom they sold these licenses. These *asentistas* were mainly *conversos* or New Christians: Jews who had converted to Christianity to avoid expulsion from their Iberian homelands. Many of them had fled from Spain to Portugal, where they were somewhat better tolerated. After most of the New Christian Atlantic slave traders had made their fortunes, they were hauled before the Inquisition in Spanish America; their property was confiscated; and they were tortured and executed: an excellent way for the crown to recoup their profits.[12] The Spanish crown also collected a head tax on every slave arriving from Africa and sold in the Americas. This tax was high: between one-third and one-fourth of the sale price of each slave. All of the goods produced in the Americas and exported to Spain were heavily taxed again: the royal fifth, 20 percent of the price of precious metals; another special tax to cover the costs of protecting the fleets that carried American-produced goods to Spain; the tithe (10 percent) collected by the Roman Catholic Church (whose finances the Spanish crown controlled in the Americas); and sales taxes on all products bought or sold in or exported from Spanish America.

The Portuguese *asiento* documents are voluminous and well preserved. Enriqueta Vila Vilar established that there was a serious undercount of Africans who were actually brought ashore to avoid paying the head tax on them. Based on her work, Philip D. Curtin acknowledged his serious undercount of the Atlantic slave trade to Spanish America during the first half of the seventeenth century.[13] But the implications of Vila Vilar's work concerning the numbers of enslaved Africans brought to the Americas as well as the significance of Greater Senegambians among African slaves in the Americas have still not been widely recognized by historians. Greater Senegambia was a major formative African regional culture in the Caribbean and the Gulf of Mexico and surrounding coastal areas as well as along the west coast of South America. This includes the early Spanish Caribbean, especially the island of Santo Domingo and what is now Mexico, Venezuela, Colombia, Ecuador, and Peru. From the earliest years of colonization in the Caribbean, enslaved Africans helped Native Americans revolt against the Spanish colonists. Runaway slaves and runaway slave communities cooperated with pirates and assisted invasions by rival European powers. By the seventeenth century, Spanish American colonial authorities began to lose their taste for Greater Senegambians, especially for the Wolof. They were considered too dangerous and rebellious. Although the import of Wolof into Spanish colonies was repeatedly forbidden, they continued to be brought in in substantial numbers.[14]

An interesting early example of the prohibition of Wolof by Spanish colonial authorities is a promulgation relating to Puerto Rico (called San Juan Island) issued in 1532 by the Council of the Indies in Spain:

> All the destruction caused on San Juan Island and the other islands by the revolt of the blacks and the killing of Christians there were done by the Gelofes living there who by all accounts are arrogant, uncooperative, troublesome and incorrigible. Few receive any punishment and it is invariably they who attempt to rebel and commit every sort of crime, during this revolt and at other times. Those who conduct themselves peacefully, who come from other regions and behave well, they mislead into evil ways, which is displeasing to God, our Lord, and prejudicial to our revenues. This matter having been examined by the members of our Indies Council, and considering the importance for the proper peopling and pacification of these islands that no Gelofe should be moved there, I hereby command you for the future to ensure that no one, absolutely no one, transfers to India, islands and terra firma of the ocean any slave from the Island [sic] of Gelofe without our express permission to that end: any failure in this regard will result in confiscation.[15]

The Trans-Atlantic Slave Trade Database distorts this period because of misinformation about the meanings of geographic terms defined therein. The voyages listed in the appendix of the Vila Vilar book were entered. But errors involving the meaning of Guinea, the Rivers of Guinea, and the coastal origin of Africans shipped via the Cape Verde Islands, plus the omission of a

Table 4.2. Voyages to Cartagena de Indias with
Known African Provenance, 1595–1640

Place of Departure	Number	Percentage
Upper Guinea	55	48.2
Angola	46	40.4
São Tomé	11	10.0
Arda (Allada)/Slave Coast	2	1.4
Total	114	100

Source: Calculated from Vila Vilar, *Hispanoamérica y el comercio de
esclavos*, appendix, cuadros 3–5.

significant number of voyages coming from these islands, resulted in a serious undercount of Africans brought from Greater Senegambia/Upper Guinea
to Spanish America between 1595 and 1640. The database put slaves on voyages coming from Ríos de Guinea and Guinea among Africans of unknown
coastal origin. Ríos de Guinea was not listed as a buying region. Both of these
coastal origins with clear meanings during the Portuguese *asiento* to Spanish America (1595–1640) cannot be disaggregated because there is only one
numeric code in the database for voyages of unknown African coastal origin.

Before enslaved Senegambians were shipped to the Americas, they were
often first landed at the Cape Verde Islands. When transatlantic slave trade
ships loaded their slave "cargoes" there, they almost invariably originated in
Greater Senegambia. *The Trans-Atlantic Slave Trade Database* records only
three voyages' loading their slave "cargo" in the Cape Verde Islands during
the Portuguese *asiento* period (1595–1640). There was then a brisk traffic in
slaves to Spanish America from these islands. All seventeen of the other voyages coming from the Cape Verde Islands recorded in this database took place
after 1818, when the Atlantic slave trade above the equator was being suppressed by British patrol ships.

Alonso de Sandoval wrote that Portuguese *asiento* slave trade voyages were
coming from only four places in Africa: the Cape Verde Islands, the Rivers of
Guinea, the island of São Tomé, and Luanda, Angola. Sandoval's information
about the African coastal origins of the Portuguese *asiento* voyages is con-
firmed by Enriqueta Vila Vilar's study of the Portuguese *asiento* documents.
The numbers of slaves successfully transported is impossible to calculate. If
numbers were recorded, they were substantially underestimated to avoid paying the head tax to the Portuguese crown.[16]

Trading networks radiated from the Cape Verde Islands to Greater Senegambia. A variety of goods were sold, including salt, which was obtained free

Table 4.3.   African Region of Origin of Peruvian Slaves Calculated from Ethnic Descriptions, 1560–1650

Region	All Afro-Peruvians	Bozales
Guinea-Bissau and Senegal	2,898 (55.1%)	1,281 (55.9%)
Other West Africa	635 (12.0%)	248 (10.8%)
West Central Africa	1,735 (32.9%)	766 (33.4%)
Total	5,278	2,295

Source: Calculated from Bowser, *The African Slave in Colonial Peru, 1524–1650*, 40–43, tables 1–2.

in Cape Verde and sold at a high price and/or exchanged for slaves in Greater Senegambia. Cotton, very expensive textiles (*panos*), and rum were shipped to several places in the Ríos de Guinea region. The result was a substantial sale of enslaved Africans to the Cape Verde Islands, many of whom ended up in the Americas. These complex trading links were extremely profitable and therefore concealed by Portuguese chroniclers, but they were revealed by Dutch reports collecting intelligence about the Portuguese trade in the region.[17]

Many Greater Senegambians arrived in the Caribbean, Mexico, and Cartagena de Indias in Colombia. They were the majority in Peruvian documents between 1560 and 1650 (about 55 percent). West Central Africans were about 33 percent, and many of them were shipped from the Río de la Plata on the southeast coast of South America via Upper Peru. African ethnicities transshipped from Cartagena de Indias to Peru were mainly from Greater Senegambia. Their origin is very clearly reflected in ethnic descriptions in notarial documents from early Peru.

Africans from the Bights of Benin and Biafra (referred to by Frederick Bowser as "Other West Africa") did not appear in Peruvian slave lists in significant numbers before 1620. Africans from Lower Guinea were never more than 12 percent among Africans in Peru through 1650. They were fewer among *bozales* (newly arrived Africans) than among those who had been in Peru longer (12 percent versus 10.8 percent), indicating that clustering of Africans from the two major African regions was increasing rather than diminishing. Greater Senegambians were a substantial majority in Peru despite West Central Africans' entering Upper Peru from the east coast of Spanish America via the Río de la Plata (now Argentina and Uruguay); about 1,500 to 3,000 enslaved Africans from Angola were brought in each year during the first half of the seventeenth century. Some of them were transshipped to and remained in Paraguay, Upper Peru (Bolivia), and Chile, but some of them no doubt arrived in Lower Peru as well.[18]

Although the substantially shorter time required for voyages between Greater Senegambia and the circum-Caribbean was a major factor linking this region with early Spanish America, preference for Greater Senegambians (called Guineans) loomed large. That preference was very clear and significant and continued strong throughout the Portuguese *asiento* slave trade to Spanish America (1595–1640). Records show that in Cartagena 48.2 percent of voyages came from Upper Guinea and 40.2 percent from Angola — and the ships from Angola normally carried many more enslaved Africans. Thus Greater Senegambians were further clustered during transshipment. Although the numbers game is fruitless because of misrepresentations in these *asiento* documents, there is no doubt that a substantially higher percentage of Greater Senegambians first taken to Cartagena ended up in Peru. Guineans were highly esteemed, and Peruvians had the silver with which to pay for them. They were so highly valued that their importation to the Americas as slaves was partially subsidized by the Spanish crown. Contracts signed with suppliers of African slaves during the 1580s provided that only one-fourth of the sale price of Guinea slaves was to be paid to the crown as a tax, as opposed to one-third of the price of slaves from other regions of Africa. Contracts signed with African slave traders after 1595 required that the greatest possible number of Guinea Africans be supplied. In 1635, an attempt was made to route all Guinean slaves to Spanish America.[19] Africans arriving from Greater Senegambia brought substantially higher prices than Africans arriving from Angola, although this price differential could partially reflect the fact that Angolans arrived in worse condition because of the longer voyages they endured. In 1601, a Portuguese *asentista* wrote that Guineans (Greater Senegambians) sold for 250 pesos in Spanish American ports, while Angolans sold for 200 pesos. In 1620, Guineans sold for between 270 and 315 pesos, while Angolans sold for 200 pesos.[20]

Based on his knowledgeable and sophisticated analysis of the African ethnic descriptions collected by Aguirre Beltrán, Frederick Bowser, James Lockhardt, and Colin Palmer, Stephan Buhnen was astounded by the extent of the clustering of African ethnicities in early Spanish America:

> For the period 1560–91, we observe the amazing fact that more than half of all African slaves (54.2 per cent) and two-thirds of all Upper Guinean slaves (67.2 per cent) in Peru came from a tiny area of about twenty square kilometers stretching from the lower Casamance (River) to the River Kogon. This was the settlement area of the southern Banol, the Casanga, Folup, Bran, Balanta, Biafara, Bioho, and Nalu. It covers the Western half of Guinea Bissau and a narrow strip of southernmost Senegal. . . . And within this small area, two ethnic groups supplied

staggering numbers: 21.3 per cent of all African slaves in our sample were Bran (n = 282) and 21.4 per cent were Biafara (n = 283).

This region was near the Portuguese slave-trading post of Cacheu. The Bran were cultivators of wet rice produced in reclaimed mangrove swamps. Their population density allowed them to withstand the impact of the Atlantic slave trade to a greater extent than could many other African peoples.[21]

Sandoval explained in great detail why Spanish officials and colonists in the Americas prized Senegambians (whom he referred to as Guineans) above Africans from any other region. He praised their intelligence, strength, resiliency, temperament, and musicality:

> These Guineans are the blacks who are most esteemed by the Spanish; those who work the hardest, who are the most expensive, and whom we commonly call of law. They are good natured, of sharp intelligence, handsome, and well disposed; happy by temperament, and very joyous, without losing any occasion to play musical instruments, sing, and dance, even while they perform the hardest work in the world . . . without fatigue, by night or by day with great exaltation, shouting in an extraordinary way and playing such sonorous instruments that their voices are sometimes drowned out. One admires how they have the heart to shout so much and the strength to jump. Some of them use guitars similar to ours in their style. There are many good musicians among them.

Catholic missionaries took due note of the mechanical and metallurgy skills of Senegambians. But they mistakenly assumed they had learned these skills from Spanish Gypsies: "From the communication they have had in the ports with the Spanish, they have learned many mechanical skills. Mainly, there are a large number of blacksmiths using the techniques of the Gypsies of Spain. They make all the arms which we ask them for and whatever curiosities we desire."

Sandoval described a process of transculturation among Guineans and Iberians: "It is these Guineans who are closest to the Spanish in law and who serve them best. The ways of the Spanish please them, even though they are gentiles. It is important to them to learn our language. They delight in dressing themselves festively in the Spanish way with our clothing which we have given them or which they have bought. They praise and extol our holy Law and feel that their own is bad. Virtue is such a beautiful thing that even these people love it to the extent that they have many Spaniards in their lands and much clothing and other things from Europe in their houses."

But the acculturation process went both ways. "Many Spaniards and other

Christians of various nations live with them voluntarily in the interior of their land and do not wish to leave them because of the broad freedom of conscience they enjoy there. They die not only without God, but without worldly goods for which they have worked so hard because the king of the land inherits all of it when they die." [22]

Sandoval was no doubt referring to the *lançados*, many of whom were New Christians (*conversos*). The Portuguese chronicler Alvares de Almada described one of the most remarkable of them: a man named João Ferreira, a Jewish native of Crato, Portugal, who was called Ganagoga by the blacks. In the Biafara language, "Ganagoga" means "one who speaks all languages." Ganagoga made a living by selling ivory down the Senegal River. He was reported to be actively trading in ivory in 1591. Ganagoga married a daughter of the Grand Fulo (Fulani), had a daughter by her, and became a powerful political figure.[23]

After Portugal separated from Spain in 1640, Spanish slave traders dominated at Cacheu in Greater Senegambia. Their undocumented voyages paid no taxes to Portugal. We only know about them because they appear in documents in the form of unsuccessful Portuguese efforts to repress them.[24]

By the mid-seventeenth century, Africans and their descendants in the Caribbean began to outnumber whites very substantially. This demographic imbalance escalated during the eighteenth century. Because of their reputation as rebels, Greater Senegambians became less welcome. Although Greater Senegambians were feared in Spanish colonies, they were readily accepted — if not preferred — in the colonies eventually incorporated into the United States, where black/white ratios were much more manageable and therefore security problems did not loom as large. The Greater Senegambians' skills were especially needed in rice and indigo production and in the cattle industries of Carolina, Georgia, the Florida panhandle, and Louisiana. During the eighteenth century, Greater Senegambians were more clustered in colonies that became part of the United States than anywhere else in the Americas. These colonial regions include the Carolinas, Georgia, Louisiana, the lower Mississippi Valley, and the north coast of the Gulf of Mexico extending across Texas, Louisiana, Mississippi, Alabama, the Florida panhandle, and, to a lesser extent, Maryland and Virginia. The Stono Rebellion of 1739 has focused attention on West Central Africa as a source for enslaved Africans brought to South Carolina. But a majority of Atlantic slave trade voyages arrived in South Carolina from West Central Africa during only one decade: between 1730 and 1739. The Stono Rebellion of 1739, well described as a Kongo revolt, evidently discouraged South Carolina planters from bringing in more West Central Africans. Thereafter, Greater Senegambia became

Phillis Wheatley, circa 1773, around age twenty. She was from Gambia and most likely a Mandingo. (Phillis Wheatley, *Poems on Various Subjects, Religious and Moral*, 1773.)

the major source of Atlantic slave trade voyages for the rest of the eighteenth century. But the number of slaves on voyages arriving from Greater Senegambia was substantially smaller than on voyages arriving from other African regions. West Central Africa did not become a significant source of Africans for South Carolina again until 1801: only six years before the foreign slave trade to the United States was outlawed on January 1, 1808. From the study of transatlantic slave trade voyages, it appears that during the eighteenth century the United States was the most important place where Greater Senegambians were clustered after the northern European powers legally entered the Atlantic slave trade. Studies of transatlantic slave trade voyages to the United States are reasonably revealing about trends in ethnic composition because there was no large-scale, maritime transshipment trade to colonies of other nations. This conclusion must be qualified because of the unknown, and probably unknowable, extent and ethnic composition of new Africans transshipped from the Caribbean to the east coast ports of the United States. But it is likely that Greater Senegambians were quite significant in this traffic because of selectivity in the transshipment trade from the Caribbean. From the point of view of African ethnicities arriving in South Carolina, the artificial separation between Senegambia and Sierra Leone obscures the picture. Thus the role of Greater Senegambians was very important in South Carolina. There is evidence that Senegambians were clustered regionally in the

Job Ben Solomon, an
educated Fulbe Muslim who
was sold into slavery around
the age of twenty-nine.
(Rare Books and Special
Collections, Library of
Congress. From the website
"The Atlantic Slave Trade
and Slave Life in the
Americas: A Visual Record,"
<http://hitchcock.itc.virginia
.edu/Slavery>.)

Chesapeake and probably elsewhere as well, especially on the Sea Islands
off the coast of South Carolina and other rice-growing areas of South Carolina, Georgia, and Florida.[25] The patterns for Louisiana are clear and not at
all speculative. Greater Senegambians loomed large among Africans there.
In the French slave trade to Louisiana, 64.3 percent of the Africans arriving on clearly documented French Atlantic slave trade voyages came from
Senegambia narrowly defined. Based on *The Trans-Atlantic Slave Trade Database* for British voyages to the entire northern coast of the Gulf of Mexico as
well as additional Atlantic slave trade voyages found in Louisiana documents
that were included in the *Louisiana Slave Database* but not in *The Trans-
Atlantic Slave Trade Database*, this writer's studies show that slave trade voyages coming from Senegambia were 59.7 percent of all documented voyages
coming directly from Africa to Louisiana and the northern coast of the Gulf
of Mexico between 1770 and 1803. Nevertheless, the African coastal origin of
Louisiana slaves during the Spanish period was much more varied than Atlantic slave trade voyages indicate. The vast majority of new Africans arriving
in Spanish Louisiana were transshipped from the Caribbean, especially from
Jamaica, where Gold Coast Africans were preferred and retained.

   In Louisiana, if we exclude Atlantic slave trade voyages and study only descriptions of slaves in internal documents, Africans from "Senegambia" were
30.3 percent and those from "Sierra Leone" were 20.8 percent, or a total of

Abdul Rahaman, born in Timbuktu around 1762, an educated Fulbe Muslim who was sold into slavery at about the age of twenty-six. Engraving of a crayon drawing by Henry Inman, 1828. (*The Colonizationist and Journal of Freedom*, 1834. From the website "The Atlantic Slave Trade and Slave Life in the Americas: A Visual Record," <http://hitchcock.itc.virginia.edu/Slavery>.)

51.1 percent from Greater Senegambia. If we exclude slaves described as being from "Guinea" or the "Coast of Guinea" from the Sierra Leone category, Africans from Sierra Leone drop to 6.7 percent. The result is a minimum of 37 percent of Africans of identified ethnicities from Greater Senegambia in Spanish Louisiana. As we have seen in our discussion of the meanings of "Guinea," there are cogent reasons for tilting toward the higher figure.

In the two major rice-growing states of the Anglo–United States, 44.4 percent of Atlantic slave trade voyages arriving in South Carolina and 62.0 percent arriving in Georgia listed in *The Trans-Atlantic Slave Trade Database* brought Africans from Greater Senegambia. These gross, static figures are impressive enough. But when we break down calculations for Anglo–United States colonies and states over time and place, we see a wave pattern clustering Africans from Greater Senegambia. In South Carolina, 50.4 percent of all Atlantic slave trade voyages to that colony entered into *The Trans-Atlantic Slave Trade Database* arrived between 1751 and 1775, with 100 (35.2 percent) coming from Senegambia and 58 (20.4 percent) coming from Sierra Leone: a total of 55.6 percent coming from Greater Senegambia. As we have seen, both Mandingo and Fulbe were being exported from both of these regions. During this time period, Britain had occupied the French slave-trading posts along the coast of Senegambia. Close to half (44.7 percent) of the British Atlantic slave trade voyages from Senegambia (narrowly defined: excluding Sierra Leone) went to Britain's North American mainland colonies. Five out of six

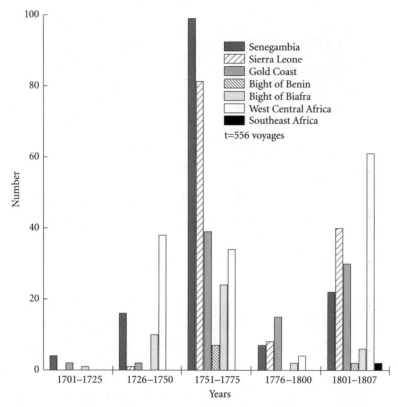

Figure 4.1.   Atlantic Slave Trade Voyages to South Carolina (1701–1807).
Calculated from Eltis et al., *The Trans-Atlantic Slave Trade Database*.
Voyages from "Windward Coast" added to Sierra Leone.

Atlantic slave trade voyages to British West Florida ports along the north
coast of the Gulf of Mexico came from Senegambia narrowly defined. It is safe
to say that between 1751 and 1775, the majority of slaves loaded aboard British
ships leaving from Senegambia were sent to regions that would become part
of the United States. As Yankee traders and Euro-African suppliers took over
the Atlantic slave trade on these coasts during the Age of Revolutions, voyages
bringing Africans to the United States from Greater Senegambia originated
mainly in various ports on the American side, were heavily involved in smuggling and piracy, were never documented in European archives, and were
unlikely to be included in *The Trans-Atlantic Slave Trade Database*. There is
little doubt that most of these voyages brought Greater Senegambians to the
United States and to the British Caribbean.

Although the Igbo from the Bight of Biafra loomed large in the Chesapeake, Greater Senegambia was a formative culture in some regions of the Chesapeake as well. Lorena Walsh has noted that nearly half of the voyages bringing about 5,000 Africans to Virginia between 1683 and 1721 came from Senegambia narrowly defined. There was a clustering of Atlantic slave trade voyages from the same African coasts to regional ports in the Chesapeake.[26]

In sum, *The Trans-Atlantic Slave Trade Database* is probably less useful for Greater Senegambia than for any other African region except perhaps for West Central Africa. While it undercounts the massive Portuguese and Brazilian slave trade voyages coming mainly from Angola, it undercounts voyages coming from Greater Senegambia as well. (The creators of the database, David Eltis, David Richardson, and their associates, are supporting research to correct its deficit in Portuguese and Brazilian voyages. This very difficult task is in the good hands of Manolo Garcia Florentino.) Thus there are a comparatively small number of transatlantic slave trade voyages from Greater Senegambia because in many instances the point of origin was improperly entered. As we have noted before, the database defines the African coast recorded in documents as "Guinea" or the "Rivers of Guinea" as an unknown African coastal origin, writing the mistake into cybernetic stone. These voyages are lumped indistinguishably with unidentified African coasts and cannot be disaggregated for calculations. Propinquity and favorable winds and currents in the North Atlantic system linked Greater Senegambia and the North American continent and continued to dominate maritime trade until the invention and wide adoption of steam engines in ships at sea at the end of the nineteenth century. Shorter voyages allowed for the use of smaller ships requiring fewer supplies and crew members. Rebellions aboard slave trade ships, an extremely serious problem for voyages coming from Greater Senegambia, were less frequent on small ships.

Many of the two-way voyages between North America and Africa were undocumented. Documents for other voyages are probably scattered among surviving documents in ports throughout the Americas. We have seen that there is evidence for ongoing, direct trade involving American slave owners/traders/ship owners, often-overlapping categories, and Euro-African merchants in Greater Senegambia. These small voyages were probably numerous and undocumented. Enslaved Africans were purchased directly by slave owners for their own use rather than for resale in the Americas. These slaves therefore do not show up in European or American sources, either in lists of incoming ships, advertisements for the sale of newly arriving slaves, or documents involving sale of slaves. The large, centralized European archives documenting large, commercial voyages are very unlikely to contain documents involving privately organized voyages initiated in the Americas. Before the outbreak of the French Revolution in 1789, Afro-Portuguese and Yankee traders and smugglers had taken over the slave trade along the coast south of the Gambia River. Jean Gabriel Pelletan, director of the French Company of Senegal in 1787–88, wrote that French slave trade ships rarely stopped between the Gambia and the Sierra Leone rivers because Afro-Portuguese drove their rivals away by force.[27] After the French Revolution began in 1789, these invisible voyages from Greater Senegambia increased sharply. By 1794, Yankee traders had seized control of the maritime slave trade from the French and set up trading stations, although a few voyages were organized by French slave traders under neutral flags.[28] After 1808, when Britain outlawed the Atlantic slave trade, British anti–slave trade patrols began operating along the West Coast of Africa above the equator. Warfare among the major European powers brought the open, large-scale, commercial Atlantic slave trade in Greater Senegambia to a halt. Nevertheless, we find large numbers of young Greater Senegambians listed in American documents during the first few decades of the nineteenth century.

B. W. Higman's detailed, sophisticated study of the slave population of the British West Indies established the importance of Senegambia as a source of slaves during the nineteenth century. From Higman's point of view, the slave trade from Senegambia alone, not including Sierra Leone, "remains grossly underestimated." Writing in 1984, he noted that Roger Ansty recorded a mere 0.7 percent of British slave voyages from Senegambia during the 1800s. *The Trans-Atlantic Slave Trade Database* reveals 1.9 percent. But data concerning the five British West Indies colonies where African ethnicities of slaves were listed in pre-emancipation documents show that between 1817 and 1827 Africans from Senegambia narrowly defined ranged between 10.1 percent and 43.4 percent. Higman's coastal designations were derived from African ethnicity descriptions in American documents, not from documented Atlantic slave trade voyages. These largely complete lists are convincing evidence that there were many more Greater Senegambians brought to the Americas than studies that confine themselves to documented Atlantic slave trade voyages reveal.[29]

THIS CHAPTER WILL CONCLUDE with a discussion of the Bamana, a designation incorrectly spelled and pronounced "Bambara." They were a self-conscious ethnic group exported from Greater Senegambian ports, mainly Gorée and along the Gambia River. Europeans in Africa had broad and sometimes vague definitions of the "Bambara." For example, they designated all slave soldiers as "Bambara." Names, including ethnic names, are a sensitive matter in Africa. During my lecture tour of Francophone Africa in 1987, I was told emphatically and indignantly that I should use the ethnic designation

"Bamana," not "Bambara." David Hackett Fischer had a similar experience during his trip to Mali. I continued to use the spelling "Bambara" because it is universal in European languages. But I now use "Bamana" because "Bambara" is more than inaccurate. It is a sarcastic insult created by Muslim Africans: a neologism that twists this ethnic name to mean "barbarian" (*barbar* in Arabic).[30]

The meaning and identity of "Bambara" must be discussed within the context of changes taking place on both sides of the Atlantic. The French transatlantic slave trade to Louisiana took place almost entirely during the early stages of the formation of the Segu Bamana Kingdom, when small Bamana polities were raiding each other to produce slaves who were then shipped down the Senegal River and sold into the Atlantic slave trade by the Mandingo. According to Philip D. Curtin,

> The "Bambara" slaves shipped west as a result of eighteenth-century warfare or political consolidation could be dissident people who were ethnically Bambara, or they could just as well be non-Bambara victims of Bambara raiders. In any event, the first flow of "Bambara" appears to have come from the northern part of the Bambara region, being transshipped by way of Jara on the Sahel. *Then, from the 1720s, the flow was more clearly from the Bambara core area, and Jahaanke were the principal carriers. This new source of Bambara slaves after about 1715 seems to be associated with the rise of Mamari Kulibali (r. 1712–55) and his foundation of the kingdom of Segu* [emphasis added].[31]

The documented French Atlantic slave trade to Louisiana took place entirely between 1718 and 1731 except for one voyage arriving from Senegambia in 1743. Two-thirds of the Africans arriving on French-period Atlantic slave voyages arrived from Senegal narrowly defined. These are unusually well documented voyages. Because of ignorance of the geographic location of ports of arrival, incorrect information about the French Atlantic slave trade to Louisiana was published in a widely cited article based on calculations from a prepublication version of *The Trans-Atlantic Slave Trade Database* that undercounted voyages from Senegambia to French Louisiana.[32] The published version of the database corrected these omissions from the French period but omitted three clearly documented Atlantic slave trade voyages arriving during the Spanish period in 1803 because of limitations in its search engine or because they could not be found in the Lloyd's List of Atlantic Slave Trade Voyages. Two of these voyages also came from Senegambia narrowly defined.[33]

In my book *Africans in Colonial Louisiana*, based on the number of "Bambara" reportedly involved in the Samba Bambara conspiracy in 1731 and the total number of slaves reported in the 1731–32 censuses, I estimated that about 15 percent of the slaves in Louisiana were Bamana ("Bambara") at the time of the conspiracy. They were far from a majority during the French period, and much less during the Spanish period, although they were clearly overrepresented among those accused of "crimes," including running away, conspiring, and revolting against the French regime.[34] In my discussion of whether the "Bambara" in Louisiana were truly "Bambara" or not, I made a clear distinction between the French period (1719–69) and the Spanish period (1770–1803). Discussing the Spanish period, I concluded with "The Bambara, if such they were . . ."

By the last half of the eighteenth century, the meaning of "Bambara" to Europeans in Africa had broadened substantially. Warriors were at various stages of incorporation into the Bamana language and culture as they were captured in warfare expanding beyond the Bamana core areas. In 1789, Lamiral wrote:

> Of 50 slaves who arrived [in St. Louis from the interior of the continent], there are 20 nations of different customs and language who do not understand each other. Their faces and bodies are scarred differently. These blacks are designated in Senegal by the generic name of Bambara. I have questioned many of them about their country, but they are so stupid that it is almost impossible to obtain a clear notion. One can be tempted to believe that they are taken there in flocks and that they are brought without their knowing where they come from or where they are going. Nothing bothers them, and as long as they are allowed to eat their fill, they will follow their masters to the Antipodes. Their only fear when they are embarked is that they will be eaten by the whites.[35]

Regardless of what "Bambara" meant to Europeans in Africa, it had a clear meaning among slaves in Louisiana. The Bamana in Louisiana knew who they were. In 1764, a group of slaves and runaway slaves were arrested in New Orleans and interrogated. Their leader was Louis dit Foy, one of the uncontrollable slaves who were bounced around the British mainland colonies, the Caribbean, the Illinois country, and South Louisiana. When he was sworn in, he testified that though he was named Louis by the French, his real name was Foy in the language of his country, which he identified as the Bambara nation. The witnesses who testified about Foy, whites as well as blacks, referred to him as Foy, his Bamara (Bambara) name. Andiguy, commandeur of Madame de Mandeville, identified himself as a Bambara and testified that he knew Foy because he was his fellow countryman.

Foy had organized a cooperative network among slaves, runaways, thieves, seamstresses, and street vendors who manufactured and sold clothing, food, and other goods. They held regular social gatherings, including feasts in New Orleans in a cabin in the garden of one of their masters.

Testimony was taken from the accused as well as from other persons, white and black, slave and free. As recorded by the notary, these African slaves expressed themselves fully and eloquently in French, with a few creolisms thrown in. No interpreters were used. Their testimony reveals a network of mainly Mande language group speakers belonging to several different masters in and around New Orleans. When the Africans were asked how they knew each other, they often replied that they were from the same country, which was considered enough of an explanation by their interrogators. They stole a considerable quantity of food, some of which they cooked and ate at their feasts and then sold the rest. Foy, Cesar, a Creole runaway slave, and another slave killed a pig they found on the deserted Jesuit plantation. The pig was so fat that they had to cut it in half to get it over the city wall. Foy sold some of his share of the pig to the slaves of Brazilier living along Bayou St. Jean. He complained that they never paid him, which is why he finally informed on them. He and Cesar gave the rest of the pig to his companions in Cantrell's garden, keeping them in meat for some time.

Comba and Louison, both Mandingo women in their fifties, were vendors selling cakes and other goods along the streets of New Orleans. They maintained an active social life, organized feasts where they ate and drank very well, cooked gumbo filé and rice, roasted turkeys and chickens, barbecued pigs and fish, smoked tobacco, and drank rum. Comba testified from prison. She said her name was Julie dit Comba, her Mandingo name. Other slaves who testified referred to her as Mama Comba. Cantrell's slave Louison also identified herself as a Mandingo. She lived in a cabin in her master Cantrell's garden where they held their feasts. She testified that her close friend Comba, known by the French as Julie, was also a Mandingo. Comba described Louison as *sa paize* (fellow countrywoman). The group included several other male "Bambara" slaves. According to Mama Comba, these "Bambara" men amused themselves very much.

Foy was clearly the brains of the group. A true entrepreneur, he organized and masterminded their economy. It involved the manufacture of garments and the distribution and sale of various stolen items including clothes, jewelry, wood, and food, especially chickens and turkeys because they were hard to trace. He employed slave seamstresses to make the garments, mainly shirts and pants, from cloth he bought or stole. And in fact, according to Mama Comba, Foy boldly used cloth he had stolen to sew garments while sitting at the entrance to the poorhouse where she worked. He employed other slaves to sell his wares, women as well as men, including fellow Bamana belonging to several different masters. Foy was too careful a thief to steal cattle because it could be traced and identified by the hides. He dealt in small objects that were hard to trace and could be easily concealed. He and his salespeople avoided barter, operating with cash, sometimes large amounts of cash, to minimize the risk of being caught with stolen goods.

In this Mande language–group community, the women were mainly Mandingo and the men Bamana, reflecting the very high proportion of males among enslaved Bamana. They maintained their ethnic distinctions although they spoke mutually intelligible dialects of the Mande language as well as French with traces of Louisiana Creole or possibly Louisiana Creole recorded in the documents as French. They identified their own and each others' ethnicities. They shared a long history and closely related culture in Senegambia, their place of origin in Africa. Their gender composition is understandable. The Bamana were mainly war captives brought some distance from the interior, and there were very few women among them. The Mandingo were Muslim, while the Bamana maintained their traditional religion. Mandingo traders were active buying Bamana captives and transporting them to the Atlantic coast for sale into the Atlantic slave trade, but the Mandingo eventually got caught up in the slave trade and were shipped in growing numbers to the Americas as the eighteenth century advanced. Ethnic conflicts in Africa were no doubt forgotten among these kidnapped and enslaved folks in a foreign land where they were happy to find and be able to communicate in their native language with other Africans from their homeland.[36]

In 1799, two adult male slaves were sold into Avoyelles Parish by the slave trader Peytavin Duriblond. It was noted in the sale document: "Qui se disent leur nation Bambara [They say their nation is Bambara]."[37] These Africans identified themselves as Bamana at this particular time and place. I can only accept their self-identification. It is quite possible that some of them arrived during the last half of the eighteenth century and had not always been Bamana. Some of them may have been captives incorporated into the expanding armies of Segu and at least partially socialized into the Bamana language and culture. But if we do not take their word for it that they were indeed Bamana, we will have to assume that ethnicity is genetically based and therefore unchangeable.

CHAPTER FIVE

Lower Guinea : Ivory Coast, Gold Coast, Slave Coast/Bight of Benin

It is marvelous to see the nimbleness and dexterity with which the blacks who live in the Isla de la Palma and on the coast go out to sea to fish in canoes, or better said launches to trade ivory, clothing, and other things they need. . . . [Between Cape Palmas and Mina] the blacks come with canoes which are like a large ship, containing much ivory, clothing, and other things found abundantly in their land to trade for currency, iron, and other things they lack.
— Alonso de Sandoval, *Un tratado sobre la esclavitud*, 1627

In Lower Guinea, the European maritime traders named African coasts for the major products they purchased there. Liberia was called the Pepper Coast and later the Grain Coast. Coasts farther east were named the Ivory Coast, the Gold Coast, and the Slave Coast. They should be looked at internally and should not be treated as entirely separate regions based on what Europeans purchased there. A. A. Boahen includes the Ivory Coast with Lower Guinea.[1]

In dealing with African ethnicities, it is probably best to link the Mande and West Atlantic language group speakers with Greater Senegambia/Upper Guinea and the Kwa language group speakers with Lower Guinea. The Kwa languages spoken by the vast majority of the peoples living near the coasts of Lower Guinea was named after the KwaKwa living in the interior of Liberia and the Ivory Coast. While in Upper Guinea many peoples had been absorbed by the Mane invaders and became speakers of Mande languages, the Kru maintained their linguistic differentiation and spoke Akan, the major language on the Gold Coast.[2] The Kru lived along the Grain Coast (Liberia) and the Ivory Coast and traded along the coasts to the east.

There are important continuities between the Gold Coast and the Slave Coast. The Volta River, an easily permeable barrier, separates these comparatively small regions. It was only after 1500 that the Akan, Ga, and Ewe peoples had migrated from their nearby cradle regions and were differentiated into the ethnolinguistic groups into which they are now divided. The peoples of Lower Guinea were linked through trade along the Atlantic and along coastal

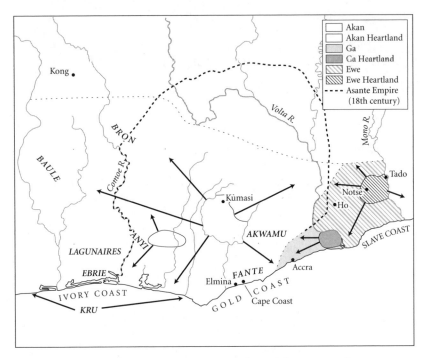

Map 5.1.   Lower Guinea West, 1500–1800. Adapted from a map by A. A.
Boahen, in *UNESCO General History of Africa*, vol. 5, ed. B. A. Ogot
(Berkeley: University of California Press, 1992); copyright © 1992 UNESCO.

lagoons and river systems as well as by trade routes stretching inland all the
way to the Sudan and across the Sahara Desert to the Mediterranean world.
The peoples shipped to the Americas from these coasts interacted through
immigration, absorption, creolization, conquest, enslavement, and common-
alities of language, religion, and worldview. Some slave trade ships loaded
their "cargoes" at both of these coasts. After 1650, Atlantic slave traders from
many European and American nations became very active there. Portugal,
the Netherlands, England, France, Denmark, Sweden, Brandenburg, the British North American colonies, and Brazil eagerly bought slaves. Thirty-two
European fortresses were built along the Gold Coast alone.[3]

    The kingdom of Benin was located to the east of the Slave Coast. Although
Portugal began buying slaves there before the first Columbus voyage to the
Americas, it was a minor source of slaves for the Americas. As early as 1486,
the import of African slaves into Elmina from the Slave Rivers and the kingdom of Benin was important enough for the Portuguese to establish a factor

Akan Peoples, Baule Group, "Spirit Spouse (waka snan)," wood, glass.
(New Orleans Museum of Art: Bequest of Victor K. Kiam, 77.238.)

Edo Peoples, Benin Kingdom, "Hip Ornament in Form of Mask (uhunmwunekhue)," bronze, iron, eighteenth century. (New Orleans Museum of Art: Bequest of Victor K. Kiam, 77.184.)

in that kingdom to regularly supply slaves to be shipped to Portugal as well as to Elmina on the Gold Coast to work in the mines, transport gold and supplies, and load ships. The king of Benin ended the Atlantic slave trade in 1516, mainly because the Portuguese refused to sell him firearms. Thereafter, the Portuguese were only allowed to purchase cloth, pepper, and ivory, but no slaves. Some Edo, the major ethnicity of the kingdom of Benin, continued to be enslaved and sold into the Atlantic slave trade, mainly by the neighboring kingdom of Warri. The kingdom of Benin did not include all the Edo peoples, and its people were not exclusively Edo. It included Yoruba regions to the north and west and Igbo regions east of the Niger River.[4] During the 1690s, protracted civil war resulted in the resumption of the Atlantic slave trade from Benin.[5] But very few Edo appeared in American documents. They were less than 1 percent (n = 66) of the 8,442 eighteen most frequently identified African ethnicities found in Louisiana documents. Only one Edo — in Trinidad — was found in all the other lists of slaves studied in this book; there were none in the French West Indies.

We have seen that most Africans shipped to the Americas during the sixteenth century were Ladinos from the Iberian Peninsula or were brought directly from Greater Senegambia. Before 1650, few Gold Coast or Slave Coast peoples were shipped to the Americas because of the demand for slaves in the Gold Coast. But Africans who were experienced gold miners were in demand early in Colombia and some Akan might have been shipped to Cartagena on the north coast of South America. Runaway slaves in Colombia were listed as Mina, but they could have been experienced miners from the gold fields of Bambuk or Buré in Greater Senegambia rather than Akan miners from the Gold Coast.

The Dutch began trading actively on the Gold Coast and the Slave Coast during the 1630s, the English during the 1660s, and the French during the 1670s.[6] After 1650, Lower Guinea became a very important source of enslaved Africans for the Americas. Africans were exported from the Slave Coast in large and growing numbers during the eighteenth and well into the nineteenth century long after the transatlantic slave trade above the equator had been outlawed by Britain. African polities along the Slave Coast and the Bight of Biafra jealously guarded their shores from European maritime traders, who were confined largely to the coast and whose trade was restricted to relatively few places. Enslaved Africans normally were not baptized before they were shipped to the Americas.[7]

The extent of linguistic continuities in Lower Guinea is debated.[8] Languages of the broad Kwa language group were widely spoken among most of its peoples. But this language group is very broad indeed. Several impor-

Edo Peoples, Benin Kingdom, "Head of Oba (uhumwelao)," brass, iron, late eighteenth century. (Collection of the New Orleans Museum of Art: Gift of anonymous donor, 53.12.)

tant language subgroups. Akan languages, mainly Twi, predominated in the Gold Coast and spilled over into the Ivory Coast to the west and into the Slave Coast to the east. But Gbe languages and Yoruba were most widely spoken in the Slave Coast. The Igbo of the Bight of Biafra spoke still other languages belonging to the broad Kwa language group. Many Igbo could understand each other. If we discuss Lower Guinea as one region, there was greater linguistic diversity among Africans exported to the Americas from there than from elsewhere in Africa. It increased as the slave trade moved inland and large numbers of these and other enslaved Africans were shipped down to all of the coasts of Lower Guinea from the middle Niger River and the Central Sudan. Growing numbers of Africans from the Middle Belt exported from these coasts spoke languages entirely unrelated to the broad Kwa language group. The Chamba spoke a Gur language. Hausa became an important trade language in Lower Guinea, but it is an Afro-Asiatic language unrelated to the broad Kwa language group. The Hausa began to be shipped to the Americas in large numbers quite late: almost entirely after 1790. The Ijo, Ibibio, and Moko exported from the Bight of Biafra spoke Northwest Bantu languages unrelated to Igbo, a Kwa language. The proportion and numbers of Northwest Bantu language group speakers exported from the Bight of Biafra increased sharply during the nineteenth century.

Thus the diversity of languages spoken by enslaved Africans from Lower Guinea was more profound than in other regions deeply involved in the transatlantic slave trade. For example, in Greater Senegambia, which was permeated by the Mande language group, Mandingo was the lingua franca for centuries before the Atlantic slave trade began, widely understood by speakers of West Atlantic languages and normally mutually intelligible among the many speakers of Mande dialects. Throughout the centuries of the Atlantic slave trade, it continued to be the dominant lingua franca in Upper Guinea, with Portuguese Creole as a secondary language.[9] The Bantu languages spoken in West Central Africa were closely related.

Nevertheless, the wave pattern in exporting enslaved Africans from particular regions of Lower Guinea to particular places in the Americas compensated to a great extent for this growing linguistic diversity. Large numbers of Africans speaking very similar or mutually intelligible languages were heavily clustered over time and place in the Americas. Speakers of the Gbe sublanguage group were exported from the Slave Coast in substantial numbers.[10] Other neighboring Gbe language group speakers—for example, the Mahi—were raided for slaves by the kingdom of Dahomey, and conflicts between the Fon/Dahomeans ("JeJe" in Brazil) and the smaller peoples and polities of Gbe speakers raided by them for slaves continued in Brazil, leading to the

AN INTERESTING NARRATIVE.

BIOGRAPHY

OF

MAHOMMAH G. BAQUAQUA,

A NATIVE OF ZOOGOO, IN THE INTERIOR OF AFRICA.
(A Convert to Christianity,)

WITH A DESCRIPTION OF THAT PART OF THE WORLD:

INCLUDING THE

Manners and Customs of the Inhabitants,

Their Religious Notions, Form of Government, Laws, Appearance of the Country, Buildings,
Agriculture, Manufactures, Shepherds and Herdsmen, Animals, Marriage and Funeral Cere-
monies, Dress, Trade and Commerce, Warfare, Slavery, with an Account of Mahommah's early
life, Education, Capture and Slavery in Africa and Brazil, Escape, Reception by Rev. W. L.
Judd, Baptist Missionary at Port au Prince, Conversion to Christianity, Baptism, his Views,
Objects and Aim, &c.

WRITTEN AND REVISED FROM HIS OWN WORDS,

BY SAMUEL MOORE, ESQ.,

*Late publisher of the "North of England Shipping Gazette," author of
several popular works, and editor of sundry reform papers.*

C234
169

MAHOMMAH G. BAQUAQUA,
Engraved by J. G. Darby, from a Daguerreotype by Sutton.

DETROIT:
Printed for the Author, Mahommah Gardo Baquaqua,
BY GEO. E. POMEROY & CO., TRIBUNE OFFICE.
1854.

Mahommah Gardo Baquaqua, whose mother was a Hausa and whose father was a Dendi. (*Biography of Mahommah G. Baquaqua . . . written and revised from his own words by Samuel Moore*, 1854. From the website "The Atlantic Slave Trade and Slave Life in the Americas: A Visual Record," <http://hitchcock.itc.virginia.edu/Slavery>.)

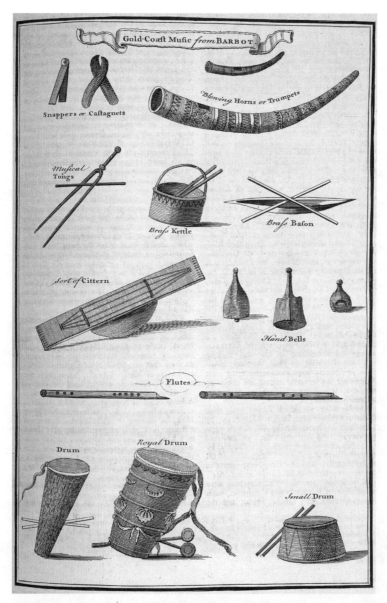

Seventeenth-century musical instruments from the Gold Coast, including "snappers or castagnets," horns, bells, drums, and flutes. (Jean Barbot, "A Description of the Coasts of North and South Guinea," in *A New General Collection of Voyages and Travels*, ed. Thomas Astley, 1745–47. Courtesy of Special Collections, University of Virginia Library.)

Table 5.1. Transatlantic Slave Trade Voyages from
the Gold Coast to British Colonies, 1650–1807

Destination	Number of Voyages from Gold Coast	Percentage of Total Voyages
Jamaica	623	51.0
Barbados	231	18.9
Other British Caribbean	236	19.3
Carolina	88	
Georgia	8	
Maryland	4	
Virginia	25	
Rhode Island	5	
USA Total	132	10.8
Grand total	1,222	100.0

Source: Calculated from Eltis et al., *The Trans-Atlantic Slave Trade Database.*

creation of separate ethnic organizations within the Irmandades da Mina in Rio de Janeiro.[11] Although the proportions of Igbo exported from the Bight of Biafra during the eighteenth century is debated among scholars,[12] American documents from eight different colonies dating from 1770 to 1827 (see tables 6.1, 6.3, and 6.4) indicate that the Igbo were a very large majority among ethnicities from the Bight of Biafra until the end of the eighteenth century and a smaller but still substantial majority during the nineteenth century.

Clustering of Africans shipped to the Americas from the Gold Coast is very clear. They were funneled into British Caribbean colonies, most heavily into Jamaica, from which they were less likely to be transshipped than Africans arriving from other coasts. The information about Atlantic slave trade voyages from the Gold Coast in *The Trans-Atlantic Slave Trade Database* is good. Among the 2,174 Atlantic slave trade voyages from this coast, 1,837 (84.5 percent) give their major selling regions in the Americas and 1,958 (90.1 percent) give the country in which the ship was registered. A large majority were ships of British registry (65.8 percent, n = 1,288), followed by those registered by the United States (14.6 percent, n = 285), the Dutch (8.3 percent, n = 162), and the French (7.6 percent, n = 149). The strong preference for Akan Africans in the British West Indies probably accounts for the much smaller number and percentage of transatlantic slave trade voyages from the Gold Coast arriving in the United States compared with Jamaica and other British islands.

If we consider that Akan peoples from the Gold Coast were highly esteemed in the colonial and national United States,[13] a surprisingly small percentage of Atlantic slave trade voyages arrived in South Carolina and Virginia from the Gold Coast: only 88 voyages (15.7 percent) in the case of the former and 25 (18.9 percent) in the case of the latter. In contrast, a total of 623 voyages (29.7 percent) arrived in Jamaica from the Gold Coast, where they were clustered over time: between 1701 and 1725, 96 voyages (50.5 percent), and between 1751 and 1775, 229 voyages (38.2 percent).[14]

We need to reduce the presence of Akan Africans in the United States, which has been overstated based to some extent on expressed preferences among masters as well as the large number of United States–registered Atlantic slave trade ships buying enslaved Africans in the Gold Coast, especially slavers from Rhode Island, whose rum was popular there. Although some of the Rhode Island African "cargoes" from the Gold Coast went to the United States, the vast majority went primarily to Jamaica and secondarily to Barbados. Although voyages from the Gold Coast were prominent in Dutch Suriname, a study over time indicates a wave pattern of Africans arriving from other coasts, especially from West Central Africa.

Thus the wave pattern involved in shipping African ethnicities, often to places where they were preferred, compensated for the growing linguistic diversity of Africans shipped across the Atlantic from Lower Guinea. Africans from the Slave Coast were clustered in French colonies, where their ethnicities were listed in greater detail than in the colonies of any other nation. Before 1810, speakers of the closely related Gbe language subgroup were exported from the Slave Coast in large numbers. They could understand each other, if not at once, then fairly quickly. They were listed in American documents as Gege, Fon, Dahomey, Arada, Aja, Mina-Popo, or simply as Mina. After 1780, Yoruba, Hausa, Chamba, and other peoples shipped down the Volta and from the Central Sudan region outnumbered the Gbe language subgroup speakers. Yoruba, listed in most Spanish documents in the Americas as Lucumí and in other Spanish documents and in Portuguese and French documents as Nago, were not Gbe language subgroup speakers. But they had ancient religious ties with the Gbe speakers, shared some of the same gods, and had interacted closely with them over the centuries through immigration, mutual conquest, and occupations. By the last two decades of the eighteenth century, increasing numbers of Yoruba were exported to the Americas as a result of the collapse of the Oyo Empire. In St. Domingue/Haiti in 1796 and 1797, the Nago/Yoruba outnumbered the Arada, the normal listing for Gbe language speakers in that colony.[15] It has recently been argued that the shift to the Yoruba from the Gbe language group speakers resulted from their demographic depletion over many decades, but this argument is not entirely convincing.[16] During the nineteenth century, most of the Yoruba, listed as Nago, ended up in Bahia, Brazil. They were also sent in substantial, possibly exaggerated numbers to Cuba, where they were listed as Lucumí.[17]

I WILL NOW demonstrate how crossing the Atlantic over time and place and using databases combined with more traditional documents can help answer some difficult questions about the identify of African ethnicities in the Americas. In particular, I want to deal with the thorny question of the ethnic and linguistic identities of Africans listed in documents in the Americas as members of the Mina nation or *casta*. When Africans were listed in American documents as "Mina," or sometimes as "Mine" in French documents, the meaning of the designation varied. Some Mina lived in the Slave Coast. Their ancestors were Akan speakers from the Gold Coast. They were sometimes bilingual, learning and using Gbe subgroup languages spoken on the Slave Coast. Robin Law has noted that the people of Little Popo in the western Slave Coast trace their origin to a specific migration from the Gold Coast beginning in about 1650,[18] but there are reasons to believe that they arrived earlier. In his book about African ethnicities first published in 1627, Alonso de Sandoval described the Mina as a *casta* largely indistinguishable from Gbe sublanguage group speakers. Sandoval was a Jesuit missionary who labored throughout his long career in Cartagena de Indias (now in Colombia), the major port of entry for all Africans brought into Spanish America. Many of these Africans arrived moribund. Sandoval's main concern was to communicate with them so he could save their souls by quickly instructing them in the Catholic faith and properly baptizing them before they died. This was, of course, why he focused heavily on language, relying on Africans as interpreters. He wrote that the Mina arrived in Cartagena de Indias after being transshipped from São Tomé. He linked the *casta* Mina with the Popos, Fulãos, Ardas, or Araraes, concluding that they were all one (*que todo es uno*). The Ardas or Araraes meant Allada, which was the dominant state on the Slave Coast until Dahomey conquered it in 1724. Sandoval makes it very clear that the *casta* Mina were part of the Gbe-speaking Africans from the Slave Coast: the Ewe, Aja, and Fon. Sandoval went to great lengths to make numerous distinctions among ethnicities often lumped together, for example, the Lucumí (Yoruba), and the Karabalí (Calabar). In both editions of his book (1627 and 1647), he stated that the slave trade between Cape Palmas and the kingdom of Popo was closed, specifically excluding the area in and around Elmina from this trade. When Alonso de Sandoval wrote in 1627 that the *casta* Mina was the same as the other Gbe language group speakers, there is little doubt that by the early seventeenth century there was, indeed, an ethnicity named Mina whose members identified themselves with or were identified as part of the Aja/Fon peoples of the Slave Coast and were Gbe sublanguage group speakers, although they most likely spoke Akan as well.[19] Sandra Greene has argued that immigrants and their cultural influence reached the Anlo, the Western Ewe, overwhelmingly from the Gold Coast to the west rather than from the Yoruba to the east, at least before 1730.[20]

The nation or *casta* Mina probably began to arrive in the Volta River basin quite early. It has been argued that they were displaced from near Elmina Fortress at the end of the sixteenth century and were therefore named Mina. But it is also possible that they were called Mina because they were skilled gold miners. They settled north of the Ga heartland located near the mouth of the Volta River on its west bank. They were described as excellent traders of salt, fish, gold, and slaves and became outstanding warriors, adopting the use of firearms pioneered by the Akwamu, whose armies were organized in large phalanxes to compensate for the inaccuracy of these weapons. These new military tactics based on European muskets and powder became widely adopted in the Gold Coast during the last half of the 1600s, displacing hand-to-hand combat as the decisive factor in warfare. Firearms purchased largely with gold began to arrive in the Gold Coast in huge quantities after 1650. Slave Coast polities became increasingly dependent on mercenary armies and troops from the Gold Coast, including the Mina of Little Popo.[21] With the rise of the Akwamu Empire after 1677, Ga as well as Mina were displaced to the east across the Volta River into the western Slave Coast and took refuge in Little Popo.[22]

Trade and settlement along the Slave Coast fluctuated to some extent as a result of war, with defeated parties often moving to some other stretch of the coast. The movement of people from the Gold Coast to Little Popo is only one such example. They were often groups of mercenary warriors who migrated to places where their services were in demand, functioning as separate armies as well as individual mercenaries. Mina armies were a major military force in the Slave Coast. Many of them were obviously captured and sold to the Americas. During the eighteenth century, the Akwamu Empire included Mina settlements on both sides of the Volta River that were subsequently incorporated into the Asante Empire. Mina were spread out along both banks of the Volta where they actively engaged in slave raiding. C. G. A. Oldendorp, who worked in the Danish West Indies between 1766 and 1768, called them Amina. He wrote that his informants were very reliable. He described the Amina as the most powerful nation east of the Gold Coast, saying that they were widely feared and highly militarized, armed with guns rather than bows and arrows. They were actively engaged in warfare to capture and enslave their neighbors, but enslaving activities sometimes broke out among themselves over disputed successions.[23] The Mina have been identified as one of several major subgroups of Ewe peoples currently living along the shores of the Mono River running along the border of Togo and Benin.[24]

The "nation" designation "Mina" or "Mine" is widely encountered in French, Spanish, and Portuguese documents in the Americas. Many Americanists who are not Brazilians or Brazilianists have widely assumed that Africans listed as Mina were brought from the Gold Coast via the fortress São Jorge da Mina (Elmina); or that they were Gold Coast slaves living near this port but perhaps exported from another port. Gabriel Debien, familiar with the rich French documents, did not make this mistake; he listed the Mina among slaves from the Slave Coast. Indeed, "Mina" was often an ethnic— not a port—designation. Many slaves designated as Mina were brought to the Americas from the Slave Coast, not from the Gold Coast, and were often speakers of the mutually intelligible Gbe dialects, which included Ewe, Aja, Fon (Dahomean), and Mahi. If many of the slaves designated Mina were indeed Gbe language group speakers, the linguistic and cultural fragmentation of Africans in the Americas was less extensive than previously believed.

Varying interpretations of the meanings of "Mina" illustrate the pitfalls of seizing on obvious, nominal similarities to identify African ethnicities. The word "mina" can be especially confusing. "Mina" means "mine" in Spanish and Portuguese, which no doubt explains the name of the settlement Elmina on the Gold Coast. The Brazilian province of Minas Gerais was the famous gold- and diamond-mining area of Brazil. Many slaves designated as Mina were brought to Minas Gerais, especially during the first half of the eighteenth century, the height of the gold and diamond rush. They came from a region in Africa that the Portuguese and the Brazilians called the Mina Coast. This designation used in Brazil did not mean Dutch-controlled Elmina. Rather, the Mina Coast referred to the coast east of Mina, particularly the Slave Coast.[25] As we have seen in chapter two, the "Mina Coast" as used in early Portuguese sources meant all of Lower Guinea. In Brazil, the term "Mina" was broadly used to designate Africans of various ethnicities who had been brought from this "Mina Coast." It has been recognized that in Brazil "Mina" had a very broad meaning and often meant any West African. But "Mina" often meant a specific ethnicity rather than a port or a region. Most Mina in Brazil were brought from the Slave Coast, although they or some of their ancestors had been immigrants from the Gold Coast. The Mina of Brazil were mainly Gbe language group speakers: Aja, Arada, Ewe, Fon, Mahi.

The assumption by some scholars that Africans listed in the Americas as Mina came from the Gold Coast and spoke Twi, an Akan language, has been persistent. In 1916, Fernando Ortiz identified slaves listed as Mina in Cuba as "People of the Slave Coast, southwest of Dahomey. Elmina was the oldest . . . slave trading post, which had been visited by Columbus before his voyage to America. A great number of Minas were dominated by their eastern neighbors the Asante and sold by them to the slave traders, according to Deniker. Their location is exact. In Cuba we had a cabildo Mina Popó from the Gold Coast, which further clarified their origin." [26]

Fernando Ortiz was a great pioneering scholar of the African diaspora. But his book was published almost a century ago. He relied on early, sometimes vague and inaccurate sources dealing with the geography of West Africa. This identification confuses the port of Elmina and the use of "Mina" as an ethnic term, which is still a very common problem in African diaspora studies. Ortiz's entry under "Popo" is somewhat clearer: "These blacks entered as *minas* or *mina-popos*. Grand Popo and Little Popo were towns on the shores of the Gold Coast [actually the Slave Coast], where a large-scale trade in slaves took place." [27]

Philip D. Howard's study of the Cabildos de Naciones in Cuba contains only one reference to a specific *cabildo* named Mina, the Cabildo Mina Guagui. [28] Gonzalo Aguirre Beltrán described "Guagui" as an early designation for some of the Hausa brought from the Slave Coast. Robin Law has a more convincing interpretation of "Mina Guigui," suggesting that it might be "Genyi," the indigenous name for the kingdom of Little Popo. "Gen" was the local name for "Ga," the indigenous name for Accra. The typonym "Accra" was derived from its Fante name. [29]

Aguirre Beltrán added to the confusion by exaggerating the role of Elmina as a Dutch port exporting Africans to the Americas. He claimed that the slaves listed in the Americas as Mina came from Elmina on the Gold Coast, and that Mina was a port, not an ethnic designation. Philip D. Curtin did not entirely clear up this confusion by saying, "For the Gold Coast, 'Mine,' the name most commonly found, is another shipping point, the ancient fort at Elmina, but the name had long been extended to mean any of the Akan peoples . . . (and in Brazil) almost anyone from West Africa, but more narrowly those from the Slave Coast on the Bight of Benin . . . In English usage (Coromanti) rather than Mina was used for Akan peoples generally." [30] According to Curtin, then, except in Brazil, "Mina" was considered a port designation, or else it referred to Akan generally and was synonymous with Coromanti in British colonies. Curtin did not discuss its meaning in French and Spanish documents in the Americas.

"Mina-Popo" was widely used in Brazil as well as in Cuba. The discussion of the meaning of "Mina" among Brazilian scholars and Brazilianists is nuanced, thanks in part to the early, insightful statements published by Nina Rodrigues in 1906. He cited E. Réclus's universal geography published in 1887. It explained that West Africans were known throughout Brazil as Minas. Rodrigues characterized this definition as very insufficient and called for more detailed archival research and a more sophisticated conceptualization.[31]

In order to clarify the meanings of "Mina" in different contexts, sources on both sides of the Atlantic over time and place are studied here. This includes changing patterns in the Atlantic slave trade along African coasts, enslaved Africans designated as Mina over time and place in lists of slaves in notarial documents, in lists of runaway slaves from maroon communities, in conspiracies and revolts against slavery, in Irmandades in Brazil and in Cabildos de Naciones in Cuba as well as in notarial documents and sacramental records. Chronology is crucial. Mina are found in large numbers in documents throughout the Americas. From the sixteenth through the mideighteenth century, most African slaves in Colombia were listed in notarial documents and reports of runaway slaves as Mina. In eighteenth-century notarial documents, the Arara followed the Mina in numeric importance, making it less likely that "Mina" in this context could have been a large, regional designation. It could have meant the Mina ethnicity in the Slave Coast, which was being distinguished from the Arara, another ethnicity from the Slave Coast. Or it could possibly mean that these Africans were listed for their skills as gold miners. The third most numerous Africans in these documents were listed as Carabalí, meaning Africans from the Bight of Biafra, probably mainly Igbo during this time period.[32]

Mina were found among runaway slaves in the Americas long before any significant number of Africans from the Gold Coast were likely to have arrived in the Americas. Runaway slave communities emerged as early as the 1530s near Cartagena de Indias. Colombia was an extremely rich gold-mining area and was settled very early. The terrain was mountainous, facilitating runaway communities. The Native American population resisted forced labor and became quickly depleted. The Spanish colonists no doubt needed the assistance of Africans knowledgeable about various techniques for panning, digging, and processing gold. During the last half of the sixteenth century, substantial numbers of Africans were working in mining. The many runaways among them were designated largely as Mina.[33] The first half of the sixteenth century was the height of the gold rush on the Gold Coast and of the sugar industry on the island of São Tomé. Enslaved Africans were being imported into the Gold Coast, and few if any of them were being shipped out.

In Colombia during the sixteenth century, Africans listed as Mina emerged as the most numerous, best armed, best led, and most uncompromising among the runaway slaves. Spanish colonial authorities spent the next 150 years trying to root them out. Pedro Mina was listed as the captain of the Mina *palenque* (fortified runaway slave community) consisting of sixty-five men, twenty-two women, and thirteen children. The Mina *palenque* had forty-eight firearms, while the Creole *palenque* was armed only with bows and arrows. The reliance on firearms among the Mina in the Americas co-incided in time with their incorporation into the military tactics of the Akwamu and the Mina in the Gold Coast/Slave Coast region and was prob-ably a carryover from Africa. The Mina runaways were much more distrust-ful of Spanish peace treaty offers and more reluctant to compromise than the Creole runaways. When the *palenque* of San Miguel was attacked by Span-ish troops in 1691, 450 men defended it. In 1691, Spanish authorities offered to give freedom to Mina and Creole slaves of the Palenque de María in re-turn for an agreement not to receive any more runaway slaves. The Mina runaways sabotaged this proposed treaty. In 1693, there were well-organized *cabildos* of Arara and Mina with their court of kings, treasurers, and "other pompous officials." The Mina were described as "extremely bad and barba-rous" because they killed themselves to avoid being subjected to slavery. In 1702, both the Mina, described as dangerous, and "strong slaves from Cape Verde" were prohibited from entering Spanish America.[34] In Venezuela dur-ing the eighteenth century, another Mina, Guillermo Ribas, led the *palenque* named Ocoyta. The Mina runaways were reported as being the most resistant to Christianity.[35]

In Santo Domingo in the Caribbean, a community of runaway slaves from the French part of the island was established in 1678 near the capital of the Spanish part of the island. It was named San Lorenzo de los Minas. This com-munity still exists and is now known by the abbreviated name Los Minas. The Spanish authorities provided them with a priest. But the archbishop, after visiting them in 1679, described them as "rude and short" in matters of God and the Holy Faith. In 1689, the French threatened to send a fleet to recap-ture them. In 1691, Governor Perez Caro favored demolishing San Lorenzo de los Minas because it attracted runaways from the French part of the island. He described them as "Barbarous blacks who kill each other and there is no way of teaching them or making them attend indoctrination or Church ser-vices." The governor's efforts to destroy this community failed, as did sub-sequent efforts throughout the eighteenth century. Complaints about resis-tance to Christianization continued. In 1740, the archbishop wrote that it was a population of blacks who had "what they call a church" made of wooden boards and palm leaves, badly placed "like things of blacks." Its population

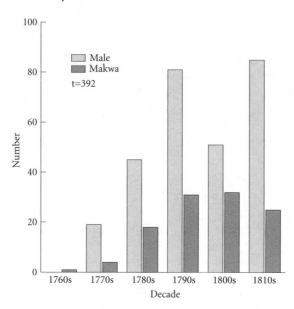

Figure 5.1.   Mina in Louisiana by Gender (1760s–1810s).
Calculated from Hall, *Louisiana Slave Database, 1719–1820.*

was 205 persons. Another effort to destroy this settlement failed in 1746. By then, they were providing military service to the Spanish colonial authorities. In 1768, they were cultivating garden crops, making cassava meal, and selling it in the capital. They established several other settlements in Santo Domingo: in the Santa Barbara district of its capital; in Pajarito, now Villa Duarte; and perhaps in Mendoza and other places.[36]

It is not surprising that African slaves recorded as Mina stood out in resisting slavery throughout the Americas. The unusually high proportion of males among them points to warriors. We have seen that Mina were prominent as mercenary soldiers and armies in the Slave Coast. Whether some of these mercenaries had been imported for this purpose along with the Akwamu and the Ga from the eastern Gold Coast and had settled in Keta and Little Popo or if they continued to arrive in the Slave Coast throughout the eighteenth century is not entirely clear. But Mina slaves arrived in the Americas during the eighteenth and early nineteenth centuries in growing numbers.

In 1791, Mina slaves at the Pointe Coupée Post in Louisiana were accused of conspiring to revolt in order to overthrow slavery. This event occurred shortly before the slave revolt began in St. Domingue/Haiti. The alleged conspirators' trial began in New Orleans in 1793. Two free black Mina were the official, sworn interpreters of the Mina language, which unfortunately is unidentifiable from the documents. One of these interpreters, Antonio/Antoine Cofi Mina, a member of the black militia, had been the recognized leader of the Mina community for the previous twenty years. Cofi is an Akan day name, and four among the accused were also named Cofi. Although these names were found among other ethnicities in Louisiana including Bamana and Nalo, "Cofi" was most clustered among Mina slave names. The name could have been passed down among Akan families with roots in the Gold Coast who had settled in the Slave Coast.

There was evidently a wide Mina network in Louisiana. Pointe Coupée was a rural post at a considerable distance upriver from New Orleans, where Antonio Cofi Mina lived. The Mina conspirators were finally all released because of the absence of attending witnesses and official interpreters during their original interrogations at Pointe Coupée in 1791. They claimed they were unable to understand or speak Louisiana Creole when they were first interrogated. Antonio Cofi Mina was later exiled to Cuba because of his involvement in the 1795 Pointe Coupée Conspiracy against slavery.[37]

The price of Mina slaves in Louisiana dropped precipitously during the first half of the 1790s. Although the weighted, mean sale price of Mina males (ages 15–40) was slightly higher (678.89) than that of the price of all of the eighteen most frequent African ethnicities in Louisiana (671.45), it was second to lowest between 1790 and 1794. But memory is short. By 1815, the price of Mina slaves was the highest among all African-born slaves.[38]

In Louisiana, Mina men asserted their family rights more vigorously than did slaves of any other origin. Little information about husbands and fathers was recorded in Louisiana documents after the French administration ended in 1769. Nevertheless, family information recorded in estate and sales documents during the Spanish period played a role in the assertion of the limited customary rights against family breakup when slaves were sold. In proportion to their numbers, Mina men were by far the most likely among all slaves, Creoles as well as Africans, to be recorded as married as well as fathers of children. Seven out of the eight Mina women recorded as having mates were married to Mina men. Mina men were 6.4 percent (n = 430) of males of identified African ethnicities. They were 11.5 percent (n = 21) of those recorded as husbands and 16.3 percent (n = 31) of the recorded fathers of children of African men.[39]

The Mina were recognized as a formal, organized community in Cuba. In 1794, the Cabildo Mina Guagui of Havana was given permission to "sponsor dances and other activities as stated in the Libros a Cabildos, as the government cautiously surveys its activities, performed by that nation . . . when it ostensibly buys things . . . [particularly] when it purchases the freedom of its enslaved members." The members of the Cuban Cabildos de Naciones elected their officials. They made loans, acquired property, and were financially responsible for their activities and obligations. The Cabildo de Mina was especially active. It sued and was sued in the courts. The Mina, the Mandingo, the Lucumí (Yoruba), the Ashanti, and the Carabalí each had their own *cabildo*. In 1811, Aponte, a respected leader of the Cabildo Shangó Tedum and a member of the Ogboni, the most powerful secret society of Yorubaland, plotted to overthrow the Spanish colonial government and abolish slavery and the slave trade. He enlisted the support of the Cabildo de Mandingo, the Cabildo de Ashanti, and the Cabildo de Mina Guagui led by Salvador Ternero who had been one of its presidents since 1794. Another conspiracy against Spanish rule, slavery, and the slave trade was organized in Bayamo, Cuba. This conspiracy took place concurrently with but was supposedly organized independently of the Aponte Conspiracy in Havana. The Bayamo conspiracy involved both the Mina and the Mandingo Cabildos de Naciones of Bayamo. Blas Tamayo and members of both of these *cabildos* were rounded up and executed. Others were exiled to prison in Florida.[40] In Cuba, the Mina Cabildos de Naciones were distinct from the Cabildos de Ashanti (Akan language group speakers from the Gold Coast). In Brazil as well as in Cuba they were sometimes referred to as Mina-Popo. Popo was an Ewe (recorded as "Gege" in Brazil) kingdom near the western end of the Slave Coast. Miguel Acosta Saignes's review of the literature about the Mina explains that at the start of the twentieth century Nina Rodrigues found the Mina tradition well preserved in Bahia. Africans there clearly distinguished between the Mina-Popo and the Mina-Ashanti (designated "Mina-Santes" in Bahia), noting that the Mina-Popo had crossed the Volta and occupied a small zone in the territory of the Ewe. Although the Mina were at times Nago/Yoruba in Brazil, they were normally Dahomeans, that is, Gbe language group speakers.[41]

A study of the Mina in Africa can tell us something about when and where they were located but less about who they were, how long they had been there, and what language or languages they spoke. There were Mina living in various places in the Slave Coast. During the 1720s, Des Marchais identified Mina ("Minois")) among the eight nationalities that he listed as being sold at Whydah. Robin Law has written that during this time "the Term 'Minois', i.e. those from Elmina or more generally from the Gold Coast, here probably refers to immigrants to Little Popo from the Gold Coast and still commonly called 'Minas' at this period."[42]

It is very unlikely that in the Portuguese, Spanish, and French colonies the "Mina" were slaves shipped from or near Elmina. They were most likely the *casta* Mina: usually Gbe sublanguage group speakers or bilingual speakers of Gbe and Akan languages. Ethnolinguistic evidence about their identity is strong. A Fon vocabulary, a language of the Gbe sublanguage group spoken on the Slave Coast, was recorded by Europeans early and in some detail. A standard missionary handbook containing Fon vocabulary with translations was published in 1658.[43] A Mina/Portuguese vocabulary was collected in Brazil in 1740 to help masters understand and therefore better control their slaves. First analyzed by Antonio da Costa Peixoto in 1945 and more recently by Olabayi Yai, Mina was in the view of both of these scholars a language almost identical with Fon. It is interesting to note that a vocabulary recorded in Brazil during the nineteenth century for the purpose of social control was by then Nago/Yoruba.[44] Although "Mina" generally had a broad coastal meaning in Brazil and some of the Africans designated as Mina were Akan speakers, the fact that the general Mina language was very close to Fon indicates a preponderance of Gbe language group speakers incorporated into the general designation "Mina" in Brazil. Enslaved Africans exported from the Slave Coast were heavily Gbe speakers during the eighteenth century and Nago/Yoruba speakers from the 1780s onward.

A study of transatlantic slave trade voyages indicates that it is extremely unlikely that the many Africans referred to as Mina in documents in the Americas could have come through Elmina. This post was first established by the Portuguese in 1483, a decade before the first Columbus voyage to the Americas. Gold and ivory — not slaves — were the major exports from this post. By 1540, the slave trade to Elmina had greatly diminished, and Africans were being sent to the northern coast of South America, where the Spanish colonists were eagerly seeking gold. Although the Dutch captured Elmina in 1637, the Dutch Atlantic slave trade continued to involve mainly piracy at sea. It is clear that by the early seventeenth century slaves of the *casta* Mina had arrived in Cartagena de Indias.

The Trans-Atlantic Slave Trade Database records few voyages bringing Africans to the Americas from Elmina, although some early voyages are no doubt missing from this database.[45] There is only one Portuguese voyage entered before 1650: a 1619 voyage stopping first in Sierra Leone (probably at the Portuguese slave trade post of Cacheu, where it collected its "cargo"), then the "Windward Coast," and then the Gold Coast, bringing seventy-one recorded slaves to Cartagena. There are no Dutch slave trade voyages of known African coastal origin before 1656 in this database. A recently published essay based on calculations from *The Trans-Atlantic Slave Trade Database* found that among voyages giving major ports of purchase of Africans sent to the Americas between 1676 and 1832, only fourteen voyages identified Elmina as the primary port of purchase, that is, only 1.3 percent of the voyages that left the Gold

Coast.[46] No Dutch voyages from Elmina were included in this database. Between 1675 and 1732, however, there were seventeen Dutch West India Company voyages that purchased slaves for the Americas in Elmina, and also four in Elmina/Lay and four in Elmina/Aja. Even if we add these omitted voyages as well as the seven voyages with Elmina as a secondary port of purchase that were included in *The Trans-Atlantic Slave Trade Database* and the 1,682 individual slaves sold by Dutch officials at Elmina to traders of various nations between 1741 and 1792, the number of Africans shipped from Elmina remains very small.[47]

Except for Suriname and a fairly brief occupation of parts of northeast Brazil, Dutch colonies in the Americas were trading posts rather than slave plantation societies. The percentage of Dutch Atlantic slave trade voyages entered into *The Trans-Atlantic Slave Trade Database* giving buying regions in Africa is relatively low: 558 voyages out of total of 1,227 (45.5 percent). The percentage of voyages giving both buying regions in Africa and selling regions in the Americas is even lower: 497 of 1,227 (40.5 percent). Many Dutch voyages continued to obtain Africans through privateering and piracy at sea. Many of them were probably unacknowledged in Dutch slave trade documents. Despite the weaknesses in the Dutch data, we can accept the patterns revealed about buying regions in Africa of voyages with known destinations in the Americas as a good sample. These calculations indicate that the Dutch slave trade focused primarily on West Central Africa (223 voyages, 44.9 percent) and secondarily on the Gold Coast (148 voyages, 29.8 percent), followed by the Bight of Benin/Slave Coast (118 voyages, 23.7 percent).

In sum, Africans recorded as Mina appeared very early in the Americas, long before there was a significant transatlantic slave trade from the Gold Coast. But Gold Coast Africans and other Africans skilled in the production and processing of gold could have been especially sought out for the gold-producing regions of northern Spanish America. After 1650, Africans from the Gold Coast were most likely to be found primarily in British America, where they were widely recorded as Coromanti. The Mina ethnic designation was ubiquitous in the Americas in French, Spanish, and Portuguese documents. Slaves designated as Mina were unusually influential in several important places in Latin America. They were prominent in runaway slave communities and in conspiracies and revolts against slavery in Cartagena, Brazil, Cuba, Santo Domingo, and Spanish Louisiana. They were well represented among Africans forming Irmandades, Cabildos de Naciones, and other mutual aid societies in Brazil and Cuba. Slave women recorded as Mina were the preferred mates of Portuguese men during the eighteenth-century gold rush in Brazil. In 1726, the governor of Rio de Janeiro wrote that African slaves exported from Whydah were reputed to have a special gift for discovering new gold deposits. "For this reason there is not a Mineiro who can live without a negress from Mina, saying that only with them do they have any luck."[48] It was obviously a matter of exploiting African skills rather than luck.

We have seen that Brazilians and Brazilianists have avoided the pitfall of defining slaves recorded in the Americas as Mina as Africans coming through the port of Elmina. Pierre Verger explained that the Mina Coast did not mean the Gold Coast post of Elmina but the coast east of Mina, although some Akan speakers from the Gold Coast were also in Brazil—in what proportions we do not know. In São Luis, Maranhão, the Casa das Minas is a Dahomean cult-house.[49] C. R. Boxer stated that most slaves listed in Brazil as Mina during the Brazilian gold rush of the first half of the eighteenth century were exported from Whydah and were mainly Yoruba. But this assumption is dubious. Boxer exaggerated the proportion of Nago/Yoruba exported from Whydah before 1780.[50] Although there were some Nago (Yoruba) exported to Brazil during the first half of the eighteenth century, they arrived in relatively small numbers. Their export began to spike during the 1780s, well after the height of the Brazilian gold rush.

Patrick Manning argues that almost all the Africans exported from the Bight of Benin before 1740 were Aja peoples, who were Gbe sublanguage group speakers, and they continued to be a substantial majority among Africans exported from the Bight of Benin until the 1780s, when increasing numbers of Yoruba and then Hausa were exported. Manning concludes that the Yoruba did not begin to outnumber of Gbe language speakers (Aja) before 1810. He maintains that especially after 1817 the number of Nago/Lucumí (Yoruba) exported to the Americas, by then mainly to Brazil and Cuba, had substantially increased.[51] Both Louisiana and St. Domingue data raise some questions about this argument. Aja peoples had close to even sex ratios, while males predominated on slave trade voyages. As we can see from table 5.2, the Aja/Fon/Arada were only 12.6 percent (n = 133) of the six most frequent ethnicities from the Bight of Benin recorded between 1720 and 1820. Their proportion dropped very substantially after 1770. The Nago/Yoruba substantially outnumbered them at 19.4 percent (n = 359). The proportion of Chamba coming from the Middle Belt was higher than that of either of these groups: 22.6% (n = 417); the Hausa, arriving late, were 7.2 percent (n = 133); the Edo 3.7 percent (n = 68). The Mina were by far the largest group: 34% (n = 628). Even if we assume that all the Mina were Aja by the eighteenth and early nineteenth centuries, the Aja were not even a majority, at least in Louisiana.

Who, then, were the Mina? The meaning of "Mina" clearly varied over time and place in the Americas. "Mina" often had a broad meaning in Brazil,

Table 5.2. Major Ethnicities from the Bight of Benin Found on Louisiana Estates, by Decade

	AJa/Fon/ Arada	Mina	Nago/ Yoruba	Edo	Chamba	Hausa	Total
1770s	20	12	8	—	11	2	53
	37.7%	22.6%	15.1%		20.8%	3.8%	5.0%
1780s	30	60	43	2	51	1	187
	16.0%	32.2%	23.0%	1.1%	27.3%	.5%	17.8%
1790s	46	112	68	18	87	25	356
	12.9%	31.5%	19.1%	5.1%	24.4%	7.0%	33.8%
1800s	22	93	26	9	44	19	213
	10.3%	43.7%	12.2%	4.2%	20.7%	8.9%	20.2%
1810s	15	113	22	2	38	53	243
	6.2%	46.5%	9.1%	.8%	15.6%	21.8%	23.1%
Total	133	390	167	31	231	100	1,052
	12.6%	37.1%	15.9%	2.9%	22.0%	9.5%	100%

Source: Calculated from Hall, *Louisiana Slave Database, 1719–1820*.

where the lingua geral da Mina arose from a merger of various Gbe languages spoken by the various ethnicities brought to Brazil from the Slave Coast. Its meaning in early Spanish American documents is unclear. The large number of very early listings makes it unlikely that they were from the *casta* Mina described as Gbe language speakers by Alonso de Sandoval in 1627. Nor were they likely to be from the Gold Coast, where the slave trade did not begin on a significant scale before 1650. Before 1650, "los Minas" could have simply been miners of various ethnicities. After 1650, the Mina-Popo in Brazil and in Cuba were more likely the Mina who had settled in Little Popo and elsewhere in the Slave Coast and had adopted a Gbe language. The Mina were clearly a particular ethnicity in various times and places in the Americas. A broad definition of Mina seems to be peculiar to Brazil and neighboring Spanish American colonies. The changing patterns of export of slaves of various ethnicities from the Slave Coast over time indicate that Africans recorded as Mina in Brazil before the early nineteenth century were most likely Gbe language group speakers. This was reflected in the general Mina language that was almost identical to Fon. We know that the Mina in both Louisiana and Cuba spoke a common language, but we do not know what that language was. During the last half of the eighteenth and the first half of the nineteenth century, the Mina of both Louisiana and Cuba were specific, self-identified, strong, well-organized, and assertive language and social communities. Africans listed as

Table 5.3.   Gender Balance among Major Ethnicities from the Bight of Benin
Recorded in Louisiana Documents, 1760–1820

Ethnicity		Male	Female	Total
Aja/Fon/Arada	Number	114	117	231
	% by gender	49.4%	50.6%	100.0%
	% within gender	9.4%	19.5%	12.8%
	% of all	6.3%	6.5%	12.8%
Chamba	Number	272	138	410
	% by gender	66.3%	33.7%	100.0%
	% within gender	22.5%	23.0%	22.7%
	% of all	15.0%	7.6%	22.7%
Hausa	Number	121	11	132
	% by gender	91.7%	8.3%	100.0%
	% within gender	10.0%	1.8%	7.3%
	% of all	6.7%	.6%	7.3%
Mina	Number	425	197	622
	% by gender	68.3%	31.7%	100.0%
	% within gender	35.2%	32.8%	34.4%
	% of all	23.5%	10.9%	34.4%
Nago/Yoruba	Number	239	110	349
	% by gender	68.5%	31.5%	100.0%
	% within gender	19.8%	18.3%	19.3%
	% of all	13.2%	6.1%	19.3%
Edo	Number	38	27	65
	% by gender	58.5%	41.5%	100.0%
	% within gender	3.1%	4.5%	3.6%
	% of all	2.1%	1.5%	3.6%
Total	Number	1,209	600	1,809
	% by gender	66.8%	33.2%	100.0%
	% within gender	100.0%	100.0%	100.0%
	% of all	66.8%	33.2%	100.0%

Source: Calculated from Hall, Louisiana Slave Database, 1719–1820.

Mina throughout the Americas were surely not invariably, or probably even
often, Africans who had lived near or been shipped through Elmina on the
Gold Coast. The meaning of "Mina" varied over time and place and by language of document, and the term sometimes could have meant "miner." But
"Mina" normally was either an ethnic or a coastal designation that, although
it included the Gold Coast, was often a specific ethnicity exported from the
Slave Coast.

CHAPTER SIX

Lower Guinea: The Bight of Biafra

The newly arrived [Igbo] find help, care, and example from those who have come before them.
—Moreau de St.-Méry, *Description topographique, physique, civile, politique, et historique de la partie française de l'isle de St. Domingue,* 1797

The Bight of Biafra is discussed here separately from the Ivory Coast, the Gold Coast, and the Slave Coast/Bight of Benin, the other regions also commonly considered part of Lower Guinea. Its geography, economy, and politics as well as the patterns of its transatlantic slave trade were distinct. The Bight of Biafra is located in the Niger delta and the Cross River valley. This region is now southeastern Nigeria. Extensive mangrove swamps made access by ocean-going vessels very difficult. Europeans did not get access to the interior until the mid-nineteenth century. Slaves were brought down to the coast by boats operating along creeks and lagoons. Well over 90 percent of the slaves from the Bight of Biafra were exported from three ports: Elem Kalabar (New Calabar), Calabar (Old Calabar) on the Cross River, and Bonny, which arose as the leading port during the eighteenth century. *The Trans-Atlantic Slave Trade Database* indicates that 85 percent of the voyages were British. The ships left mainly from Bristol and later from Liverpool. Despite the escalation of the British slave trade from the Bight of Biafra after 1740, only 7.7 percent (n = 43) of these voyages arrived in South Carolina from this coast.

The Atlantic slave trade from this region began early but got off to a slow start, rose during the late 1670s and 1680s, and escalated rapidly during the eighteenth century. It went from about 1,000 voyages a year during the first decade of the 1700s to 3,800 during the 1730s, 10,000 during the 1740s, 15,200 during the 1760s, and, at its peak, 17,500 during the 1780s. It continued well into the nineteenth century long after it was outlawed, bringing significant numbers of slaves to Cuba. Other patterns were unique as well. An unusually high proportion of females were sent to the Americas as slaves. Gross "coastal figures" conceal the sharply contrasting gender proportions among ethnicities exported from this region. High proportions of females were characteristic of the Igbo rather than of the other ethnicities—for example, Ibibio and Moko, who tended to be heavily male.

There appears to be a consensus among scholars that the Igbo occupation of the Niger delta was quite ancient. There was no oral tradition of migration from another region. Their creation myths explain that they came from the earth.[1] Archaeological evidence indicates more ancient human occupation and productive activities in Igboland than scholars have previously believed. A rock shelter at Afikpo revealed Stone Age tools and pottery some 5,000 years old. Yams were grown at least 3,000 years ago. Iron working is ancient, and bronze art is of the highest quality.[2]

The pioneer Nigerian historian Kenneth Dike convincingly argues that the Igbo were very heavily represented among slaves shipped across the Atlantic from the Bight of Biafra. He cites "scientific research" carried out by Captain John Adams between 1786 and 1800 and published in 1822. Adams wrote, "This place [Bonny] is the wholesale market for slaves, as not fewer than 20,000 are annually sold here; 16,000 of whom are members of one nation, called Heebo [Ibo], so that this single nation . . . during the last 20 years [exported no less] than 320,000; and those of the same nation sold at New Calabar [a delta port], probably amounted, in the same period of time, to 50,000 more, making an aggregate amount of 370,000 Heebos. The remaining part of the above 20,000 is composed of the natives of the Brass country . . . and also of Ibbibbys [Ibibios] or Quaws."[3]

Dike points out an ongoing process of creolization among the peoples living near the Atlantic Coast, which encompassed diverse peoples speaking various languages. He comments:

> It is broadly true to say that owing to their numerical superiority and consequent land hunger the Ebo migrants (enforced or voluntary) formed the bulk of the Delta population during the nineteenth century. They bequeathed their language to most of the city-states—to Bonny, Okrika, Opobo, and to a certain extent influenced the language and institutions of Old and New Calabar. But the population, which evolved out of this mingling of peoples, was neither Benin, nor Efik, Ibo nor Ibibio. They were a people apart, the product of the clashing cultures of the tribal hinterland and of the Atlantic community to both of which they belonged.[4]

In the Americas, the Igbo were the least endogamous among African peoples. The proportion of women among them was among the highest, and they married men of a variety of other ethnicities. This pattern of exogamous marriage among Igbo women seems to be true throughout the Americas.[5] The

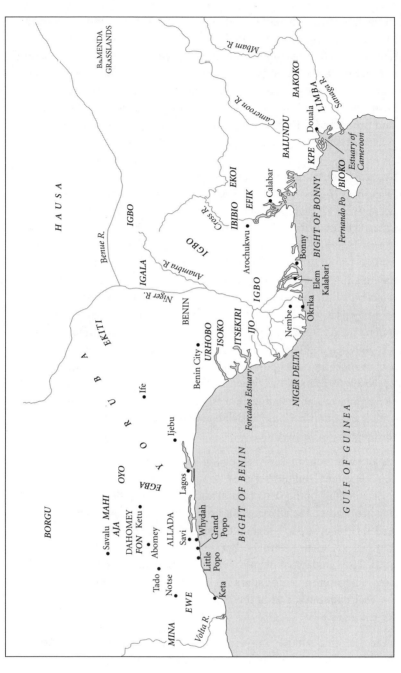

Map 6.1. Lower Guinea East, 1600–1900. Adapted from a map by E. J. Alagoa, in *UNESCO General History of Africa*, vol. 5, ed. B. A. Ogot (Berkeley: University of California Press, 1992); copyright © 1992 UNESCO.

Igbo, then, were least likely to remain as a separate enclave culture among Africans in the Americas.

In several other respects, the Bight of Biafra contrasts sharply with the coasts of Lower Guinea examined in the previous chapter. In the Bight of Biafra, Muslim influence arrived very late and was of minor importance. Highly centralized states were absent. The political structure was strong but segmented. Loose confederations maintained commercial and religious ties. The prestige of powerful oracles and some armed mercenaries enforced conformity and played an important role in obtaining slaves to ship across the Atlantic. Although large-scale warfare connected with state building was weak, slaves were "produced" through raids among villages, some kidnapping, legal proceedings, and religious rites.[6]

Which ethnicities were shipped out of the Bight of Biafra, when, and in what proportions? This is currently a hotly debated question. Some historians, mainly Americanists, believe that they were heavily Igbo, especially during the eighteenth century. Other historians, mainly Africanists, challenge this conclusion. In southern Nigeria, the denomination "Igbo" came to be associated with slave. The Aro, major slave traders in Igboland, "distinguished themselves from the more traditional Igbo groups. In addition, they strive to maintain ancient kinship, cultural and ethnic relationships with the Efik, Ibibio and Ekoi on the basis of trade, *ekpe*, inter-marriage and the original ethnic composition ties with various Aro settlements which are still found in these parts of non-Igbo areas."[7] But it is possible that some of these patterns have been read too far backward in time. Joseph Inikori remarks:

> It should be noted . . . that a pan-Igbo identity as we know it today did not exist during the Atlantic slave trade era. As Dike and Ekejiuba correctly observe, Igbo as an ethnic category is a twentieth-century development reluctantly accepted by several of the constituent groups on political and administrative grounds. As they put it, "during the period covered by our study (18th and 19th centuries), the now twelve million or more 'Igbo,' distributed over 30,000 square miles of territory east and west of the Niger, were variously referred to either as cultural groups . . . or by the ecological zone in which they were found. . . . Since Igbo was used at this time pejoratively to refer to the densely populated uplands, the major source of slaves and by extension to slaves, it is not surprising that many of these groups have been reluctant to accept the Igbo identity. The Aro were among the groups that did not consider themselves Igbo at the time. These facts of identity and socio-political organization are important in understanding the politico-military con-

ditions in Igboland that facilitated the procurement of captives for sale at the coastal ports."[8]

Americanists, however, cannot help but be impressed by the large numbers of Africans identified or self-identified as Igbo in American documents. We will see that in some times and places Igbo were clearly differentiated from Ibibio, Moko, Calabar, and Bioko, all ethnic designations from the Bight of Biafra. The Igbo "nation" or "casta" appears among several other ethnicities in Alonso de Sandoval's book dating from 1627. The Igbo were very significant in both numbers and proportions in slave lists created in eight different colonies in North America between 1770 and 1827. One could perhaps argue that "Igbo" was a name imposed by Europeans on Africans. But, as we have seen, Africans often identified their own ethnicities recorded in American documents. C. G. A. Oldendorp, a Moravian missionary who worked in the Danish West Indies in 1767 and 1768, interviewed an African in Pennsylvania who described himself as Igbo.[9] Deminster, a forty-year-old slave, identified his nation as Igbo when he testified about runaway slaves in Louisiana in 1766. L'Éveillé, a blacksmith, identified his nation as Igbo when he testified during the trial of the Pointe Coupée conspirators seeking to abolish slavery in 1795.

There were self-identifications of other ethnicities from the Bight of Biafra. Guela ran away from his master and was recaptured in 1737. He identified his nation as Bioko (native of the island of Fernando Po in the Gulf of Guinea). He explained that he had run away because his master beat him often and did not give him enough to eat. He had run away once before and came back voluntarily. His ears were cut off, and he was branded on the shoulder. In this case, and others, Africans from the Bight of Biafra were not simply lumped together as Igbo. Some were identified as Ibibio, Moko, Ekoi, Esan/Edoid, Bioko, and Calabar. The well-populated Bamenda grasslands northwest of the slave-trading ports supplied some enslaved Africans who were shipped out directly from the Cameroon River. Estimating the slave trade from the Cameroons poses many difficulties. It appears to have peaked between 1760 and 1776 and was always a tiny fraction of the slave trade from the Bight of Biafra ports. We have not found ethnicities from the Cameroons or the Bamenda grasslands recorded in American documents.[10]

It is clear that the vast majority of Africans from southeastern Nigeria and the Bight of Biafra found in American documents were recorded as Igbo. They were a heavy majority during the eighteenth century and a smaller majority during the nineteenth century. If we discuss the Igbo in the United States, the focus of the recently criticized work of Douglas B. Chambers,

Table 6.1 Numbers, Percentages, and Gender Balance of Igbo Compared with
Ibibio/Moko on Probated Estates in Guadeloupe, Louisiana, and St. Domingue/Haiti

	Igbo	Ibibio/Moko	Calabar
Guadeloupe	79.5% (n = 248)	20.5% (n = 64)	
(1770–89)	male 47% (n = 116)	male 63% (n = 40)	–
	female 53% (n = 132)	female 37% (n = 24)	
Louisiana	69.5% (n = 524)	11.0% (n = 82)	19.5% (n = 47)
(1719–1820)	male 54.8% (n = 287)	male 74.4% (n = 61)	male 59.9% (n = 88)
	female 45.2% (n = 237)	female 25.6% (n = 21)	female 40.1% (n = 59)
St. Domingue/	93.2% (n = 1,129)	6.8% (n = 83)	
Haiti	male 49.2% (n = 556)	male 65.1% (n = 54)	–
(1721–97)	female 50.8% (n = 573)	female 34.9% (n = 29)	

Sources: Calculated from Vanony-Frisch, "Les esclaves de la Guadeloupe"; Hall, *Louisiana Slave Database, 1719–1820*; and Geggus, "Sex Ratio, Age, and Ethnicity in St. Domingue."

Michael A. Gomez, and Lorena Walsh, we can affirm the assumption made
by those scholars that the Igbo represented a high portion of Africans from
the Bight of Biafra. They were reasonably likely to have identified their own
ethnicities. They were clustered in the Caribbean as well as in the Chesapeake. Some of the Africans exported from the Bight of Biafra were recorded
in American documents as Ijo, Ibibio, Moko, Ekoi, and Bioko, but they were
a very small minority before the nineteenth century.[11]

It is not possible to determine the approximate percentage of Igbo exported from the Bight of Biafra by studying transatlantic slave trade voyages
alone or by studying ethnicities recorded in any one colony in the Americas. Since some ethnicities were shipped from more than one coast, descriptions of Africans in American documents can tell us about the proportions of ethnicities recorded among enslaved Africans in particular times
and places in the Americas, but they cannot tell us from which coasts they
were shipped. Sex ratios among Africans shipped from various coasts cannot be extrapolated to ethnicities presumably shipped from these coasts. Nor
can sex ratios among ethnicities recorded in American documents be extrapolated to Africans shipped from a particular coast.[12] But information
about ethnicities listed in a significant number of colonies during the same
time period is more enlightening. Various ethnicities were exported from the
same ports, and their proportions changed over time. Enslaved Africans exported from Bonny were evidently most likely to be Igbo. During the early
eighteenth century, Bonny emerged as the major slave trading port on the

Olaudah Equiano, an Igbo, also known as Gustavas Vassa. (Olaudah Equiano, *The Interesting Narrative of the Life of Olaudah Equiano, or Gustavas Vassa, the African, Written by Himself,* 1789. From the website "The Atlantic Slave Trade and Slave Life in the Americas: A Visual Record," <http://hitchcock.itc.virginia.edu/Slavery>.)

Bight of Biafra. The latest studies by Lovejoy and Richardson indicate that by about 1730 Bonny already outpaced Old Calabar as a port in the Atlantic slave trade: at least forty years earlier than historians previously estimated. The early predominance of Bonny resulted from its superior financial structures, including the important role of pawnship there. There is a consensus that Bonny shipped mainly Igbo, indicating that Igbo were indeed prominent in the Atlantic slave trade to the Chesapeake as well as elsewhere after the 1720s. Lovejoy and Richardson's calculations on *The Trans-Atlantic Slave Trade Database* reveal that for the entire transatlantic slave trade 40.5 percent (n = 1,046) of voyages leaving the Bight of Biafra came from Bonny; 27.0 percent (n = 697) from Old Calabar; and 9.2 percent (n = 238) from Elem Kalabar (New Calabar). These data are likely to be reasonably complete and accurate since they were mainly British voyages. The documents are centrally located in large archives and studied by David Richardson. Lovejoy and Richardson state that voyages from Bonny were most heavily clustered between 1726 and 1820.[13]

"Calabar" appears occasionally in American documents but its meaning is uncertain. It might refer to Africans shipped from two slave-trading posts: Old Calabar or New Calabar. Or it could mean the Calabar Coast, which

Table 6.2. Enslaved Africans Shipped from the Three Major Ports of the
Bight of Biafra

| | Ports | | | Total Number |
Period	Bonny	Old Calabar	Elem Kalabari	of Slaves
Pre-1730	13.2%	63.8%	22.9%	(21,011)
1730–1779	58.2%	33.4%	8.4%	(209,563)
1780–1840	66.8%	21.9%	11.2%	(268,626)
1660–1840	61.0%	28.5%	10.5%	(499,200)
Total number	(304,309)	(142,393)	(52,498)	(499,200)

Sources: Adapted from Lovejoy and Richardson, "'This Horrid Hole,'" and Eltis et al., *The Trans-Atlantic Slave Trade Database*, calculated from 1,405 voyages.

would include Bonny and other ports as well. "Calabar" could also have been an ethnic designation. Dike referred to the "Kalabari" during the early nineteenth century as "a Delta people."[14] Oldendorp interviewed five slaves who described themselves as members of the Kalabari nation. They reported that they lived far up the Calabar River and that the Igbo were a very populous people who were their "neighbors and friends who share the same language with them."[15] In Cuba, Calabar (given as "Karabalí") was certainly a broad, coastal designation, not an ethnic one. Among slaves from the Bight of Biafra sold there between 1790 and 1880, 93.2 percent (n = 2,943) were listed as Karabalí, 5.8 percent (n = 183) as Bibi (meaning Ibibio), and only 1 percent (n = 32) as Ibo. These few references to specific ethnicities from the Bight of Biafra in Cuban sales documents were almost all from documents found in Santiago de Cuba, where St. Domingue/Haitian slave owners predominated.[16] "Calabar" was not found in documents in St. Domingue. Among Africans from the Bight of Biafra listed on probated estate documents dating from 1721 to 1797, David Geggus found that 90.7 percent (n = 1,129) were listed as Igbo, 6.6 percent (n = 83) as Ibibio/Bibi, and 2.7 percent (n = 33) as Moko and others.[17] There are many listings of Igbo in American documents dating from the eighteenth century. In Louisiana and elsewhere as well, the Ibibio/Moko were heavily male, in contrast to the Igbo who were about half female during the eighteenth century.

Some historians are questioning whether an Igbo identity existed at all before the twentieth century. They cite the work of Sigismund W. Koelle, a minister and linguist who interviewed recaptives from illegal slave trade voyages in Freetown, Sierra Leone, around 1850. They had been landed by British anti–slave trade patrols during the 1820s and 1830s. Although Koelle designated them as Ibo, he did so with a caveat: "Certain natives who have come from the Bight are called Ibos. In speaking to some of them respecting this name, I learned that they never had heard it till they came to Sierra Leone. In their own country they seem to have lost their general national name, like the Akus [Nago/Lucumí/Yoruba], and know only the names of their respective districts or countries. I have retained this name for the language, of which I produce specimens, as it is spoken in five of the said districts or countries."

Historians of Africa have effectively used Koelle's remarkable work. He was a careful scholar. He expressed his reservations about the reliability of his informants, pointing out that he interviewed them in English during the early 1850s. Most of them had been recaptured by British anti–slave trade ships and brought to Sierra Leone decades before. Among the six Igbo he interviewed, four had been in Sierra Leone for thirty years, one for twenty-four years, and one for eleven years after he was kidnapped from his home at the age of three. When Koelle wrote that the Igbo he interviewed had "lost their general national name," he implied that they previously had one.[18]

From this single ambiguous statement made late in the slave-trading era, transcendent conclusions have been drawn about all Africans throughout the Americas: for example, that all Africans were so isolated and immobilized that they were unaware that there were other Africans who were different from themselves. Therefore, terms for African ethnicities appearing in American documents arose not in Africa but rather in the Americas after slaves were first exposed to Africans unlike themselves. Maybe they called themselves something else. Maybe they did not fully understand their interrogators, or their interrogators did not fully understand them. Perhaps they could not remember too well. A word is an imperfect representation of reality. Regardless of which word they did or did not use to identify themselves in the past, it did not prevent them from considering themselves an internally related group different from others. In any case, Koelle's statement should not be extrapolated backward in time and to all African ethnicities. David Northrup has stated: "Some other 'nations' in Sierra Leone shared a common language. Speakers of the various dialects of Efik ('Calabar' in Sierra Leone), Hausa, Fulbe, Akan ('Kronmantee') of the Gold Coast, or Wolof came to use language as a way of distinguishing themselves from other Africans in Sierra Leone, even though no such national consciousness or political unity existed in their homelands."[19] This is a very broad generalization indeed. For example, the Wolof lived in developed, hierarchical states for many centuries before the Atlantic slave trade began and certainly identified themselves through common descent, history, law, politics, culture, and religion as well as language.

By the mid-nineteenth century, the designation "Igbo" might have had

more shame attached to it than in earlier times, when it was less clearly identified with "slave." The designation "Igbo" was recognized by Africans as well
as by Europeans long before the mid-nineteenth century, including by Alonso
de Sandoval in 1627. Sandoval did not discuss either numbers or percentages of African ethnicities arriving in Cartagena de Indias. Some of Sandoval's information about Africa and African ethnicities was obtained from reports and studies, mainly by Portuguese and Spanish missionaries stationed
in Africa. He does not always make clear which Africans he encountered in
Cartagena de Indias and which he obtained information about from other
sources. Although the vast majority of ethnicities he discussed were probably
brought to the Americas, some of them may never have been brought at all.
Nor can we assume that each ethnicity he mentioned was brought over in
the same proportions. In any case, Sandoval obviously was writing well before any significant number of African slaves arrived anywhere in the British
colonies.[20]

Nevertheless, some historians have concluded that the Igbo identified only
with their regions or villages and had no broader identity before they were
brought to the Americas, where the Igbo ethnic identity arose. This shaky
conclusion is then extrapolated to all Africans throughout the Americas at
all times and places. The Igbo were not as isolated as many historians claim.
Their "state" system and social organization did not conform to what Western scholars steeped in broad sociological constructions and delusions of
progress have looked for. It was not a weak, highly fragmented system. "Segmented" would be a better word.[21] Interviews of Igbo at Freetown during the
nineteenth century indicate that the "production" of slaves there involved
a high level of kidnapping of individuals, condemnation of "criminals" to
slavery, and raiding among villages.[22] Large-scale warfare in the course of
empire building was less common than in some other regions of Africa. But
the likelihood that Africans were isolated and immobilized in regions where
the transatlantic slave trade was active is slim. Ancient trade routes prolifer-
ated throughout Africa long before the Atlantic slave trade began.[23] Extensive trade networks over land, sea, lagoons, and rivers, mutual conquest and
empire building, and a normal process of creolization in Africa had long exposed Africans to many peoples besides their own. It is reasonable to generalize Boubacar Barry's description of the peaceful interactions and interpenetrations among African ethnicities long before the transatlantic slave
trade began. After it began, warfare, capture, and displacement of populations through flight and famine were endemic to the process of "producing"
slaves.

Documents generated in the Americas containing ethnicity listings point toward a heavy Igbo majority among those Africans shipped from the Bight of Biafra during the last half of the eighteenth century and a diminishing majority during the nineteenth century. Chambers, Gomez, and Walsh, writing about the African population in the British North American mainland during the eighteenth century, assumed that the vast majority of Africans arriving from the Bight of Biafra were Igbo. The highest estimate of Igbo or Igbo-speaking slaves was published by Chambers who claimed that it was "likely or at least possible" that they were 80 percent of the Africans arriving from the Bight of Biafra, although he has recently revised this estimate slightly downward.[24]

We do not have valid, direct evidence from the British mainland colonies because of the scant attention paid to African ethnicities in English-language documents. If we restrict ourselves to the eighteenth century, the most important time period for the United States, Chambers, Gomez, and Walsh's assumption of large numbers of Igbo in Virginia is supported by documents created on the American side of the Atlantic, but with some caveats. *The Trans-Atlantic Slave Trade Database* shows that voyages from the Bight of Biafra to Virginia took place early: 84 percent (n = 89) before 1750, 16 percent between 1751 and 1775 (n = 17), and none after that date. But voyages from Bonny where a high proportion of Igbo were exported began earlier than scholars previously believed.

We do not know the coastal origins or ethnicities of new Africans brought to the Chesapeake via the transshipment trade from the Caribbean, or perhaps via slave trade voyages organized and carried out by Chesapeake slave owners or would-be slave owners to buy Africans for their own use, or by pirates. But we do have rich African ethnicity information from documents from eight different colonies in the North American continent. Our most detailed and reliable ethnicity data generated in American documents date from between 1770 and 1827. French-language documents, especially notarial documents from St. Domingue, Guadeloupe, and Louisiana, are particularly rich and detailed about African ethnicities. Lists of slaves in French-language notarial documents list the Northwest Bantu language speakers including the Ibibio and the Moko as well as the Igbo in some detail over time. In Louisiana, the vaguer designation "Calabar" is listed as well. This evidence does not support the likelihood that Northwest Bantu language speakers of Efik dialects, the Ibibio, Moko, and Ijo were numerous in the Americas during the eighteenth century. They establish that the overwhelming majority of Africans living in the lower Niger delta sent to the Americas and recorded over time in surviving and studied American notarial documents were listed as Igbo, even if we exclude Africans listed as Calabar.

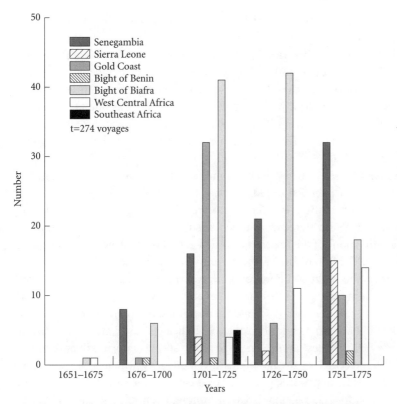

Figure 6.1.   Atlantic Slave Trade Voyages to Maryland and Virginia: Coasts of Origin over Time (1651–1775). Calculated from Eltis et al., *The Trans-Atlantic Slave Trade Database*. Voyages from "Windward Coast" added to Sierra Leone.

Unlike evidence from the African side, these American data collected from notarial documents allow for calculations of ethnic designations recorded over time and place and by gender, as well as much other information about enslaved Africans. For eighteenth-century St. Domingue/Haiti, David Geggus studied nearly 400 probate inventories in documents dating from between 1721 and 1797 that listed over 13,300 Africans. He found that the Igbo listed were 90.7 percent (n = 1,129) of Africans coming from the Bight of Biafra. There were very few, if any, Africans listed as Calabar in Geggus's sample.[25] For Guadeloupe, Nicole Vanony-Frisch studied and data-based all extant, legible probate inventories listing slaves between 1770 and 1789. She found that fully 37 percent of *all* Africans of identified ethnicities were listed as Igbo (n = 248). There were no Calabar listed in her sample.

In probate inventories in Louisiana between 1770 and 1789, Africans listed as Igbo were 78.6 percent (n = 81) of all identified Africans from the Bight of Biafra. Louisiana probate documents show that the Northwest Bantu language speakers, Ibibio and Moko, had a very high percentage of males: 88.9 percent. Africans listed as Calabar on Louisiana estate inventories between 1770 and 1789 were 84.6 percent male (n = 11). There was one male listed as Ekoi and another listed as Bioko, both runaways. Numbers for all non-Igbo were very small; those listed as Calabar were probably unlikely to be Igbo at this place and time.

As we have seen, the evidence from the American side of the Atlantic indicates that the proportion of Igbo exported from the Bight of Biafra during the eighteenth century was very high: probably as high as what Chambers, Gomez, and Walsh stated or assumed, even if we draw the very unlikely conclusion that none of the Africans recorded as Calabar in American documents were Igbo. The Ibibio and Moko, the only other numerically significant Africans from the Bight of Biafra found thus far in American documents, were overwhelmingly male. Louisiana documents show that the Igbo had a slight majority of females until 1790, and thereafter a slight majority of males.

Data in both Africa and the Americas indicate a substantially higher proportion of Northwest Bantu language group speakers during the nineteenth century. Nevertheless, the Igbo remained a majority, which is clearest on the American side in slave registration lists created in the British West Indies in preparation for general emancipation. Among the five islands listing African ethnicity information, four were former French colonies and the other was Trinidad, to which French Creole-speaking masters and slaves had migrated, largely from Martinique. These nineteenth-century British registration lists (1813–27) reflect varying percentages of Igbo in British West Indies islands ranging from a low of 51.8 percent for Trinidad and a high of 72.4 percent for St. Kitts. On all of these lists, the Igbo were a total of 57.9 percent (n = 4,312; t = 7,566) of Africans from the Bight of Biafra region.

Africans described in these British lists were later arrivals than Africans recorded in probate documents. In Louisiana, data from sales documents recording Africans arriving during a comparable period (1790–1820) contrasts with the data from Trinidad but is close to the data from St. Kitts. The proportion of Igbo in these Louisiana documents dropped very slightly from the earlier probate lists: from 78.6 percent to 75 percent. But the sex ratio among slaves listed as Calabar closely tracked the sex ratio among Igbo, which might make this slight drop more apparent than real. The "Calabar" sold after 1789 had a lower percentage of males (48.8 percent) than the Igbo (54.6 percent), while the Northwest Bantu speakers (Ibibio and Moko) con-

Table 6.3.   African Ethnicities from the Bight of Biafra on British West Indies
Registration Lists, 1813–1827

Location	Ethnicity				Total
	Igbo	Moko	Ibibio	Other	
Trinidad (1813)	2,863 (51.8%)	2,240 (40.6%)	371 (6.7%)	21 (.04%)	5,520
St. Lucia (1815)	894 (71.5%)	291 (23.3%)	59 (4.8%)	6 (.5%)	1,250
St. Kitts (1817)	440 (72.4%)	164 (27.0%)	–	4 (.05%)	608
Berbice (1819)	111 (61.0%)	64 (35.2%)	–	7 (3.8%)	182
Anguilla (1827)	4 (66.7%)	2 (33.3%)	–	–	6
Total	4,312 (57.9%)	2,529 (33.4%)	371 (5.0%)	38 (.005%)	7,566

Source: Calculated from Higman, *Slave Populations of the British Caribbean*, tables S3.1–S3.5.

tinued to have a very high percentage of males (81.5 percent). It is very likely
that at least some of these Africans sold as Calabar in Louisiana were indeed
Igbo. If we add some of the Calabar to the Igbo, it brings the Igbo to nearly 80
percent of Africans from the Bight of Biafra sold in Louisiana between 1790
and 1820.

Looking at the African side, the 1848 census of Freetown, Sierra Leone, reflects the African ethnicities of recaptives brought in by the British anti–slave
trade patrols. Among those who arrived from the Bight of Biafra (excluding
the 657 Hausa from the totals in order to compare Igbo with their non-Igbo
neighbors), we find 60.9 percent (n = 1,231) Igbo, 15.8 percent (n = 319) Efik,
and 23.3 percent (n = 470) Moko.[26] This census shows a large majority of Igbo.
In sum, the evidence presented here indicates a drop in the proportion of
Igbo exported during the nineteenth century and a rise in the proportion of
males among them. Nevertheless, the Igbo continued to be a substantial majority of enslaved Africans living in the lower Niger delta who were exported
to the Americas.

It is a truism in the historical literature that Igbo, especially Igbo males,
were not at all appreciated in the Americas, mainly because of their propen-
sity to run away and/or commit suicide. Igbo were, indeed, sometimes described as "refuse slaves" who were purchased in high percentages in Virginia
because the poverty of the slave owners left them no alternative.[27] But female
Igbo were valued as more emotionally stable than the men, physically attractive, and hard workers. If we look closer at marketing patterns and other data,
we see a strikingly different image of the Igbo in various regions of the Americas. In some places, they were especially prized. Colin Palmer's study of the
British *asiento* slave trade to the Spanish colonies (1700–1739) makes it clear
that Spanish purchasers, having the advantage of easy access to Mexican sil-

Table 6.4.　Africans from the Bight of Biafra Sold Independently of Probate
in Louisiana, 1790–1820

Ethnicity	Males	Females	Total	Percentage of Total
Igbo	112 (55%)	93 (45%)	205	75
Ibibio/Moko	22 (82%)	5 (19%)	27	10
Calabar	20 (49%)	21 (51%)	41	15
Total	154 (56%)	119 (44%)	273	100

Source: Calculated from Hall, *Louisiana Slave Database, 1719–1820.*

ver coins, bought only prime Africans, for whom they paid the highest prices. According to Palmer, "The Ibo . . . were considered tractable and hence were highly sought after by some of the slaveholders in America."[28]

When Igbo could not be bought to settle a new upland plantation in Jamaica, the manager explained that he did not buy other slaves because the Ibo were "that will answer best there."[29] In 1730, a Barbados merchant complained, "There has not [been] a Cargo of Ebbo slaves sold here [for] a long time and many people are Enquirering [sic] for them." Daniel Littlefield presents convincing evidence that Igbo women were uniquely valued by British slave traders along the African coast.[30]

We must be cautious about relying heavily on anecdotal evidence disparaging the Igbo. Most evidence comes from surviving documents written by large planters. Planters operating small units might have been more positive about the Igbo, but they rarely left documentation of their activities and opinions. We need more systematic evidence. Documents in Louisiana, for example, demonstrate a lack of enthusiasm for Igbo slaves. They were underrepresented in Louisiana before 1790, although a high proportion of voyages from the Bight of Biafra arrived in Jamaica and Cuba, both major Caribbean transshipment points for Africans brought to Louisiana during the Spanish period (1770–1803). A slave sale document in Louisiana explained that the seller did not know the nation of the newly arrived African figuring in the transaction, but he guaranteed he was not an Igbo.[31]

It is evident that after the United States took over Louisiana in late 1803, Africans from the Bight of Biafra were being smuggled into Louisiana in large numbers. Between 1804 and 1820, Igbo began to appear in higher proportions among all Africans and became one of the five most frequent ethnicities encountered in documents. Their mean age did not advance significantly over time, although the foreign maritime slave trade to Louisiana was illegal after 1803. They were more heavily male than during the eighteenth century. An insignificant number of Igbo (a total of nine) were listed as children. Although some of these Igbo could have been transshipped from Charleston before 1808, only six documented and databased transatlantic slave trade voyages arrived from the Bight of Biafra on the east coast of the United States (all at Charleston) between 1803 and 1807. On January 1, 1808, the foreign slave trade to the Untied States became illegal. Igbo were obviously among ethnicities actively smuggled into Louisiana as well as into Cuba long after the foreign slave trade was outlawed.[32]

Was this relative and absolute growth of the Igbo population in Louisiana because those who purchased them had no choice? The *Louisiana Slave Database* allows us to compare the prices paid for Africans of various ethnicities, male and female. A mixed picture emerges. The appendix of this book compares slave prices by ethnicity and gender in Louisiana and discusses the comparative reliability of the price date, including the complexities of inflation and the changing value of the variety of currencies in circulation.

Results for the Igbo are both surprising and anomalous. If Igbo men were despised and Igbo women prized, this is not reflected in prices during the Spanish period in Louisiana, when the mean price of Igbo men was highest among the most numerous ethnicities. The price of Igbo women was only 64 percent of the price of Igbo men, by far the greatest gap between male and female prices for any of these five ethnicities. Curiously, the pattern was entirely reversed during the early U.S. period as Louisiana quickly shifted from a "society with slaves" to a "slave plantation society," as Ira Berlin phrases it.[33] The mean price of Igbo men fell to last place. The mean price of Igbo women rose to 97.5 percent of that of Igbo men, by far the smallest gap between male and female prices within the same ethnicity during the early U.S. period. This reversal of the price gap between male and female Igbo is even more surprising because the gender price gap increased sharply among all other slaves sold.

The anomalous price trend among enslaved Igbo has several possible explanations. Igbo did not adjust to working in large slave gangs growing sugar or cotton. According to Michael Mullin, South Carolina slave owners considered Igbo unsuitable for rice production.[34] This could explain why they were not appreciated in South Carolina, where rice was the major export crop, and were more appreciated in Virginia, where tobacco reigned. During the early U.S. period in Louisiana (1804–20), sugar and cotton plantations displaced the varied indigo, rice, garden crop, tobacco, corn, cattle, meat, leather, naval stores, cypress and other timber production of the Spanish period. These products had usually been produced on small farms with relatively few slaves. The narrowing gap between male and female prices of Igbo in Louisiana might also have stemmed from the slave owners' growing acquaintance with their strengths and weaknesses, at least from the point of view of the masters. Igbo women were among the two African ethnicities whose women had the highest proportion of surviving children. They mated widely outside the Igbo group. By the early U.S. period, Igbo women without children might have been recent arrivals who had been separated from their children in Africa. Some of them might not have given birth to children in Louisiana as yet. Their buyers might have held out hope for their reproductive future. The other ethnicity with high reproductive results were the Wolof. During the Spanish period, the mean price of Wolof women was higher than that of Wolof men. Wolof women were sought out as mates in colonial Louisiana, where they were considered especially beautiful, intelligent, and elegant. But their relative mean price dropped during the early U.S. period along with that of almost all slave women except for the Igbo. Mandingo women demonstrated relatively low reproductive results. Between the Spanish and the early U.S. periods, Mandingo women dropped from third place to last place in the mean price of women among the most frequent ethnicities. Kongo women were numerous despite high male ratios, but their reproductive results were substantially lower than that calculated for women of any other African ethnicity, possibly because of a high abortion rate among them and/or the impact on their health and reproductive powers of the long trek from interior regions of Africa. The price gap between Kongo men and women diminished slightly from the Spanish to the early U.S. periods.

These price differentials point toward a substantial value placed on the reproductive powers of enslaved women. The price of women plummeted after age thirty-four, while the price of men remained stable until age forty. In regions like the Chesapeake, where natural reproduction of the slave population was a high priority, the Igbo were probably not "refuse" slaves but actually preferred. Because of the independent position and stance of Igbo women in Africa, their willingness to mate outside their ethnicity and to bear and raise children, their identification with small, local places, and their attachment to the land where their first child was born, they were well equipped to establish new communities on small estates where clear hierarchical structures were weak or absent. African Americans are likely to be descended directly from African women via the female line because they have many more white male than white female ancestors. In the United States, African mothers were reasonably likely to be Igbo or Wolof: a thesis that can eventually be tested through DNA studies.

The Igbo and their neighbors, then, have been neglected and unjustifiably depreciated in the historical literature about Africans in the Americas. There is no better way to conclude this chapter than by quoting from Dike:

> Perhaps the overriding genius of the Ibos, Ibibios, Ijaws, Ekoi, and Efiks and their political institutions lay in their extraordinary powers of adaptability — powers which they displayed time and again in the nineteenth century and throughout the period of the Atlantic slave trade in the face of the constantly changing economic needs of Europe. No less was their genius for trade. Dr. Talbot, a well-informed nineteenth-century observer living there, declared, "They are a people of great interest and intelligence, hard-headed, keen-witted, and born traders. Indeed, one of the principal agents here, a [European] of world-wide experience, stated that, in his opinion, the Kalabar [a delta people] could compete on equal terms with Jew or Christian or Chinaman."[35]

CHAPTER SEVEN

Bantulands: West Central Africa and Mozambique

> In no way would he make war, as it was the continual warfare which had
> already destroyed the kingdom, and also the Faith. Nor did the Congolese
> want any more troubles. They were already tired of being like beasts in the
> fields and wastelands: outraged, murdered, robbed and sold, and their rela-
> tives, wives and children killed on all sides.
> — Pedro IV, king of Kongo, 1710

The Atlantic slave trade in West Central Africa began very early and lasted
very late. It has been estimated that between 40 and 45 percent of enslaved
Africans brought to the Americas by the transatlantic slave trade were Bantu
language group speakers from West Central Africa.[1]

The west coast of Africa juts far out into the Atlantic Ocean and follows an
easterly course through the Niger delta. It then turns sharply south near the
equator and becomes a much narrower region called Central Africa. Bantu
language group speakers have lived in this region for thousands of years. In
this chapter, we will discuss West Central Africa, the region that supplied enslaved Africans to the Americas in staggering numbers throughout the entire
period of the transatlantic slave trade, and Mozambique in Southeast Africa
along the Indian Ocean, a region where the Atlantic slave trade began early
on a small scale and escalated during the late eighteenth and the nineteenth
centuries.

In many other regions of Africa deeply affected by the Atlantic slave trade,
Europeans were often confined to their fortresses or trading stations along the
coasts or short distances up navigable rivers; or they were forced to trade from
their ships anchored along the coast. In contrast, from the very beginning
of the Atlantic slave trade, Portuguese and Afro-Portuguese merchants, officials, soldiers, missionaries, and peddlers penetrated deeply into the interior
of the kingdom of Kongo and the Angolan hinterlands east of Luanda and
Benguela, the two major ports that they established on the coast of Angola.

During the many centuries before Portuguese caravels arrived off the coasts

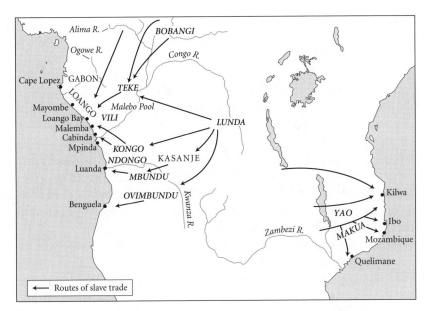

Map 7.1.   West and East Central Africa: Bantulands, 1500–1900. Adapted
from a map by Joseph E. Inikori, in *UNESCO General History of Africa*,
vol. 5, ed. B. A. Ogot (Berkeley: University of California Press, 1992);
copyright © 1992 UNESCO.

of West Central Africa in 1472, the region had been isolated from the trans-
Saharan camel caravan trade as well as the maritime trade routes along the
coast of East Africa.[2] When the Portuguese first arrived, they did not find
societies large and complex enough to support systematic trade—that is,
until 1483, when they reached the kingdom of Kongo. Its capital, Mbanza
Kongo, was located inland south of the Zaire (Congo) River. The kingdom of
Kongo had long-established internal trade routes, markets, and a shell currency (*nzimbu*). Portuguese trade with the kingdom of Kongo first involved
the exchange of copper bangles and ivory for Portuguese luxury goods and
the services of technical advisers. In 1486, the Portuguese settled the island of
São Tomé in the Gulf of Guinea and developed a sugar industry there. During
the 1490s, the Portuguese began to demand slaves to ship to São Tomé.

Joseph Inikori and Nicolás Ngou-Mve deny that slavery existed in West
Central Africa before the Portuguese arrived. Inikori argues that slavery in
Africa before the Atlantic slave trade was more like feudalism in medieval
Europe than like African slavery in the Americas—an opinion previously ex-
pressed by John Thornton with regard to the kingdom of Kongo.[3] Jan Vansina

explains that initially "dependents" in the kingdom of Kongo were sold. They were outsiders living in families and villages where clear-cut social distinctions were made based on lineage and descent in accordance with the principle that "people who lived together ought to be related to one-another."[4] Costa e Silva describes a transitory servile group, people of foreign origin captured in wars or raids, criminals alienated or removed from society, persons who had lost the protection of their own people. Their descendants were destined to be absorbed by the society.[5] Thus several prestigious historians have argued that West Central Africa had no experience with hereditary slavery or the export of slaves before the Portuguese arrived. The Atlantic slave trade from West Central Africa escalated after 1500 and increased sharply between 1520 and the late 1560s, when over 7,000 slaves per year were exported, mainly to the Gold Coast via São Tomé.[6]

In 1491, the king of Kongo embraced Christianity, was instructed in the faith, baptized, and adopted the Portuguese name João I. His successor, Alfonso I (1506–43), declared Christianity the official religion of the kingdom and sent some of his young subjects to Portugal for religious education. Portuguese officials, merchants, clerics, missionaries, and soldiers were stationed in the capital, Mbanza Kongo. The capital was renamed São Salvador.

West Central Africans suffered deeply from the early, direct, and continuous presence of the Portuguese and Brazilian maritime slave traders and the Afro-Portuguese originating in São Tomé and from the rivalry among the European powers involved in the Atlantic slave trade. The fragile, vulnerable polities of the kingdom of Kongo were fractured by rivalries among Portuguese officials, merchants, missionaries, fleets, soldiers, and settlers from the Iberian Peninsula as well as from São Tomé and Brazil and by itinerant traders (*pombeiros*) penetrating far into the interior. These intrusive factions promoted warfare in order to increase the supply of captives sent across the Atlantic as slaves. They intrigued and fought among themselves, recruiting West Central African clients to serve as allies against each other. The various orders of rival Catholic missions sent to Christianize the kingdom of Kongo and later Angola intrigued among themselves as well. Some of these missionaries made private fortunes in the slave trade. Although several rulers of the kingdom of Kongo expressed eloquent opposition to the slave trade, their objections had little impact in West Central Africa. John Thornton argues that it was not slavery and the slave trade that provoked the indignation of the kings of Kongo, but rather the flouting of their traditional rules and laws regulating enslavement and slavery.[7]

In 1568, the Jaga invaded the kingdom of Kongo. The Portuguese used—and some scholars have said created—the Jaga (described perhaps sensationally as cannibalistic mercenaries) to attack the kingdom of Kongo, forcing its rulers to seek Portuguese protection at the price of withdrawing their opposition to the slave trade. Although various African polities allied themselves with the Jaga, it has been argued that the Jaga were used primary by the Portuguese as an instrument of political control and expansion of their slave trade.[8] The Jaga terrorized the Kwanza River Valley between 1590 and 1640 and ultimately settled in several regions of Angola in polities named the Ovimbundu Kingdoms. Later rulers, including some in the Ovimbundu area, claimed this militaristic heritage, which was layered with magical beliefs.

By the mid-sixteenth century, Portugal began to focus away from the kingdom of Kongo to regions farther south. In 1575, Portugal established the port of Luanda under the illusion that this region was rich in silver, and Luanda emerged as a slave trade port directly under Portuguese control. Portugal invaded Luanda's hinterland to obtain captives from the wars it provoked. By 1622, the kingdom of Ndongo, under the rule of Ngola a Kiluanje, was carved out of the region south of the kingdom of Kongo with Portuguese backing. Having become well entrenched in Luanda and its hinterland, the Portuguese made Luanda the focus of their Atlantic slave trade and the major Atlantic slave trade port of West Central Africa. Over the centuries, Angola remained the major area from which Portuguese and Brazilian traders shipped enslaved Africans to the Americas.

The Dutch played the major role in undermining Portuguese control of the slave trade in Africa and spread it to new regions. Between 1580 and 1640, the crowns of Spain and Portugal were merged. The Dutch revolted against the Iberian kingdoms and challenged Portuguese rule all along the coast of Africa as well as in Brazil. As warfare among Portuguese and Dutch traders and their African clients escalated, African rulers and polities sometimes allied themselves with the Dutch: most notably the famous queen Nzinga and her northern neighbors defending the hinterland of Luanda from the Portuguese. Many captives of these wars were sold to the Portuguese slave traders at Luanda and ended up in Spanish America as well as in Brazil. After the Portuguese and the Dutch eventually signed a peace treaty, they left their African "allies" stranded.[9]

Between 1630 and 1654, the Dutch captured and held the sugar-producing province of Pernambuco in Brazil, and, from 1641 to 1648, they also had possession of Luanda. Although the African coastal origin of slaves brought to Dutch Brazil is not well documented, it is likely that the Dutch shipped substantial numbers from West Central Africa. Indeed, Luanda was captured by the Dutch mainly to supply slaves to their sugar plantations in Brazil. The Dutch could not ship enough slaves from Luanda because the Afro-

Portuguese retired to the Bengo River and to Massangano, a fortress on the Kwanza River, blocking the slave trade routes from the interior to Luanda. The Dutch had to resort mainly to the slave trade of the kingdom of Soyo and its port Mpinda on the Atlantic coast near the mouth of the Zaire (Congo) River. Africans shipped from Mpinda were largely Kikongo language group speakers. This trade was halted by warfare in 1642. In 1648, a Brazilian fleet expelled the Dutch from Luanda. In 1654, a Brazilian militia expelled them from Recife, the last Dutch stronghold in Brazil. Dutch traders exported about 2,064 enslaved West Central Africans between 1580 and 1639, 11,504 between 1640 and 1649 while they occupied Luanda, 785 between 1650 and 1659, and 7,337 between 1658 and 1674.[10] Because of the Brazilian role in expelling the Dutch from Brazil as well as from Luanda, their penetration of the Angola market with their popular rum, and the easy sail between West Central Africa and Brazil, Brazilians took over much of the slave trade from Luanda. It became largely a direct trade bypassing Portugal. Angola became to a great extent a Brazilian rather than a Portuguese colony.

There is no doubt that the early, continuous, active, and overwhelming presence of these intruders in West Central Africa and the recruitment of African clients by factions among them contributed heavily to extensive warfare, instability, famines, and depopulation. Surviving refugees migrated to remote, defendable places.[11] In 1657, a Portuguese army sided with the rivals of the Kongolese king Garcia, who had allied himself with the Dutch. The Portuguese invaded the kingdom of Kongo, routing its army and killing off most of its leadership at the Battle of Mbwila in 1665. Nevertheless, by 1670, the Portuguese were defeated, driven out, and did not return for 100 years. But, by 1689, the kingdom of Kongo was a spent force. It had become a poor, decentralized kingdom. Its capital, São Salvador, had disappeared. Its remaining Catholic missionaries left for Luanda, where many of them enriched themselves, often in the slave trade. A new generation of wealthy and highly competitive slavers fought over the legacy of the Catholic kingdom of Kongo of the early sixteenth century.

Between 1680 and 1715, there was constant, disruptive warfare. With widespread famine, the price of food sharply rose. Villages were burned, and their inhabitants fled. The kingdom of Kongo disintegrated amid unrelenting internal warfare. Many of the helpless Kongolese, nobles as well as commoners, were seized as slaves. They were sold to Luanda and later to the Vili traders, who funneled growing numbers of enslaved Africans from the Loango Coast into the Atlantic slave trade. Although there was some smuggling of slaves by northern European traders from smaller ports south of Luanda, Portugal and Brazil dominated at Luanda and its hinterlands and at Benguela,

the port it established south of Luanda. The northern European traders—
Dutch, English, and French—dominated along the Loango Coast north of the
Congo/Zaire River.

Several truly outstanding historians have studied the kingdom of Kongo
because of the unusually rich documentation, which includes reports by Portuguese officials and missionaries of several orders, along with correspondence between the kings of Kongo and the crown of Portugal. There are also
high-quality accounts by Dutch travelers and traders. Nevertheless, the continued impact of the kingdom of Kongo in Africa as well as in the Americas is not clear. By 1689, the kingdom of Kongo had collapsed and enslaved
West Central Africans were brought increasingly from regions farther north,
south, and east. Certainly, a substantial number of these Africans came from
the region of the old kingdom of Kongo or places influenced by it long after it
had disintegrated. But it seems reasonable to conclude that more West Central Africans arriving in North America during the seventeenth century were
Christianized than those arriving during the eighteenth century; most of the
latter came via the Loango Coast, where Christian missionary efforts were
late, extremely weak, and short lived, although substantial numbers of Christianized Angolans were being shipped via the Malebo Pool to the Loango
Coast for export to the Americas. When the Atlantic slave trade from the
Loango Coast became significant, it was controlled by the northern European powers—the Dutch, the French, and the English—who were less motivated to Christianize and baptize departing Africans than were the Portuguese and Brazilian slave traders. Yet, even in Luanda and the kingdom of
Kongo, indigenous African religious influence on Portuguese Catholicism remained strong.[12]

The slave trade along the Loango Coast got off to a very slow start. The
Dutch began trading there in 1595, but they did not buy slaves. They confined their purchases to ivory, cloth, and red dyewoods. By 1639, the Dutch
traders could only purchase 200 slaves annually at the port of Loango and 100
at Malemba. Between 1630 and 1670, the Vili ranged far and wide, trading a
variety of goods, but they became increasingly involved in the slave trade. By
the last quarter of the seventeenth century, a Dutch, an English, and a French
slave trade began to develop along the Loango Coast. The English became
active there after 1675 and the French after 1700. As late as 1702–3, it took nine
to ten months to collect a cargo of slaves along the Loango Coast, while at
Whydah on the Slave Coast it took only two to three months. Between 1706
and 1714, few ships came to the Loango Coast for slaves. The northern Europeans had to trade from ships at anchor. They were not allowed to establish
trading posts. But, by 1717, the slave trade started to increase.[13]

Chokwe Peoples, School of Muzamba, "Seated Chief-Musician Playing the Sansa (kaponya)," wood. (New Orleans Museum of Art: Bequest of Victor K. Kiam, 77.135.)

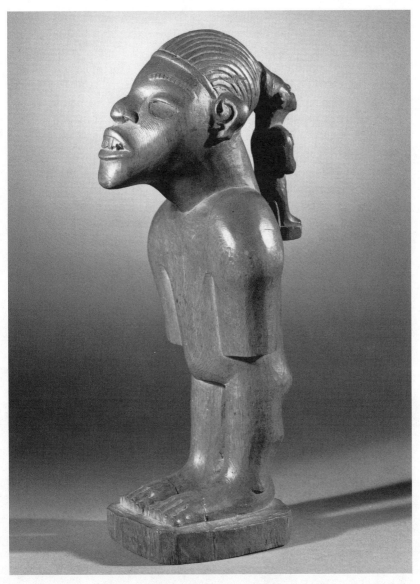

Kongo Peoples, "Magical Figure (nkisi)," wood, glass, late nineteenth
century. (New Orleans Museum of Art: Gift of Philip Thelin in memory of
his grandparents, Chief Justice of Switzerland and Madame Henri Thelin
Panchaud de Bottens, 94.213.)

During the eighteenth century, the northern European powers traded mainly along the Loango Coast while the Portuguese and Brazilians continued to focus on Angola. Since slave trade networks operated both above and below the Congo River, there was considerable overlap among African ethnic groups sold from Luanda, Angola, and the Loango Coast. Slave traders from the Loango Coast managed to cross the tumultuous Congo River at a few places. They penetrated south and west into Angola in their search for slaves. Nevertheless, Kongo speakers were sent mainly from the Loango Coast to North America and Kimbundu speakers (broadly designated as Angolans) to Brazil and to the southeast coast of Spanish America. West Central Africans brought to the Caribbean and the United States were mainly from the Loango Coast and were most likely closely related Kongo language group speakers.

The French dominated the Loango Coast slave trade throughout the eighteenth century until the outbreak of the French Revolution in 1789, which was followed closely by the slave uprising in St. Domingue/Haiti in 1791. In 1794, the French National Assembly ended slavery in all French colonies. British slave traders took over the port of Cabinda on the Loango Coast. During the last two decades of the eighteenth century and the long period of open, legal slave trade below the equator during the first half of the nineteenth century, there was a large, sustained spike in the Atlantic slave trade from Bantulands.

Our best estimate is that West Central Africans were about 45 percent of the enslaved Africans landed in the Americas. They were clustered most consistently in Brazil but in very substantial numbers throughout the Americas as well. The price of slaves in Brazil was generally lower than elsewhere, because voyages within the South Atlantic system were relatively short. Prices for West Central Africans were also relatively cheap due partially to the large number of enslaved West Central Africans "produced" by the holocaust resulting from the occupation by outsiders. Although the South Atlantic system of winds made for a quick, easy voyage from West Central Africa to southeastern Brazil, mortality was high. During the Atlantic crossing, the "cargo" remained the property of the Luanda-based, mainly Luso-African slave traders until it was sold in Brazil. The Portuguese and Brazilian maritime slave traders therefore were less motivated to try to reduce mortality, opting for tight packing of their victims, reduced food and water, and other deadly cost-saving measures.[14]

Voyages from West Central Africa to North America, the circum-Caribbean, and the north coast of South America took much longer than voyages from Upper and Lower Guinea. Because of greater distances and unfavorable winds and currents, these voyages required larger ships, bigger crews, and more supplies, resulting in higher shipping costs and higher disease and death rates among the "cargo" as well as the crew. Nevertheless, West Central Africans were brought in large numbers to almost all regions in the Americas during the entire transatlantic slave trade and were clustered over time and place, partially because of their ready availability, lower prices, and, except for those from Gabon, the lower incidence of revolt.[15]

We have seen that most West Central Africans brought to French and Spanish colonies in the Americas were recorded in documents as Kongo, while most West Central Africans brought to British colonies were recorded as Angolans. Although there were some other ethnic designations recorded for West Central Africans in the Americas, the use of broad identity designations on this scale is characteristic of West Central Africa alone and reflects the unique characteristics of this region, making for a fundamental unity among broad diversity.

Vili traditions hold that almost all the Kongo language group speakers, including those from the kingdom of Kongo as well as all the kingdoms along the Loango Coast, claimed common descent from the same woman, Nguunu. Because of shortages of land, her four sons migrated and formed new kingdoms. There were several kingdoms located along the Loango Coast. From north to south, they were the kingdoms of Mayumba, Chikongo, Loango, Kakongo, and Ngoyo. Their many dialects were not immediately mutually intelligible but nevertheless very closely related. Jan Vansina has reconstructed and roughly dated the great time depth and close interactions among West Central Africans using linguistic data. He has recently restated the fundamental linguistic and cultural unity of West Central Africans.[16]

During the late sixteenth century, Duarte Lopes wrote that Kongo and Kimbundu, the two major Bantu sublanguage groups spoken in West Central Africa, were as linguistically similar as Spanish and Portuguese. Alonso de Sandoval described Kimbundu dialects, despite their variations, as mutually intelligible. Thus language barriers among West Central Africans were weak. The speakers of the different tongues could learn to communicate with each other within a few weeks.

This pattern of fundamental unity amid diversity is a mirror of the general patterns of the societies of the region. Families were almost entirely matrilineal (calculating descent and providing for inheritance on the mother's side) and virilocal (living in the village of the father). The mbanza, the town or village, was the major polity and often the main basis for self-identification. The towns were generally sparsely populated. Social divisions were based on classes, occupational groups, households, or kin groups. Lineages were spread far and wide through exogamous marriage. Villages were grouped into districts ruled, at least in theory, by kings, whose powers were quite limited, and the level of autonomy of districts and villages was great. The rules of descent in these kingdoms sharply undermined their stability. After the death of a king, regents were not allowed, and any matrilineal descendant of a deceased king could claim the crown. Thus the number of possible candidates for king grew over time. In the kingdom of Kongo, efforts to change this pattern to primogeniture, by which only the eldest son of the king could succeed him, were opposed by the Portuguese and therefore unsuccessful.[17]

The geography of much of this region led to fragmentation as well. Many of the populated regions of the kingdom of Kongo consisted of deep forests, hills, and steep mountain slopes cut into ridges by streams and topped by high, cultivable plains. Small villages were located in places protected by high escarpments and difficult jungles. Small, but thickly populated islands in the Congo River remained independent of the kingdom of Kongo and paid no tribute.[18] During escalating warfare after the Atlantic slave trade began, women, children, and old people took refuge in these towns. Nicolás Ngou-Mve has discussed the correlation between the accelerating Atlantic slave trade and intensified warfare in West Central Africa. He counted in Kongo and Angola (Ndongo) nineteen wars between 1603 and 1607, sixteen between 1617 and 1620, six in 1626, and sixteen in 1641 and 1642. Of the 3,480 Portuguese soldiers that came into Luanda between 1575 and 1594, over 91 percent (n = 3,180) died.[19]

West Central Africans were agriculturists relying heavily on slash-and-burn agriculture. They were miners of iron, gold, and copper; metallurgists; potters and weavers; hunters and fishermen. By the early seventeenth century, they cultivated several varieties of corn brought in from the Americas by the Portuguese. Manioc (cassava) was not widely cultivated there before the eighteenth century. These food crops, especially manioc, were fairly easy to store and highly transportable. Other foods domesticated by Native Americans over several millennia were raised, including peanuts, sweet potatoes, and pineapples. The Native American crops helped compensate to some extent for the population loss caused by escalating warfare resulting largely from the Atlantic slave trade. Bananas, plantains, citrus fruits, beans, Benin pepper, yams, sugar cane, and palm trees for oil and light wine were other important crops. Food crops were cultivated almost entirely by women. While many Kongo slaves were likely to have been Christians or at least formally baptized before they were brought to the Americas, after the kingdom of Kongo disintegrated and Catholic missionaries fled to Angola, more Kongo were perhaps likely to practice less adulterated traditional Bantu religions. The presence of Christian missionaries along the Loango coast was very brief.

Patterns in Southeast Africa were different. Madagascar was a seminal re-

Nineteenth-century illustration of Bantu women cultivating the soil with hoes. (David and Charles Livingstone, *Narrative of an Expedition to the Zambesi and Its Tributaries; and of the Discovery of the Lakes Shirwa and Nyassa, 1858–1864*, 1865.)

gion for the Atlantic slave trade to English colonies, partially because of its important rice industry, a major source of the technology transfer of this crop to the Americas. But Mozambique was by far the major region in Southeast Africa from which enslaved Africans were imported. Its slave trade began with relatively small numbers and then escalated and lasted very late. During the Dutch occupation of Luanda (1641–48), the Portuguese focused on slaves from Mozambique. During the last half of the eighteenth century, French slavers populating the Mascarene Islands in the Indian Ocean (Mauritius and Réunion) were delighted to find high-quality and relatively inexpensive slaves being sold in Mozambique. French slave traders brought some of them to the Caribbean, overwhelmingly to St. Domingue (Haiti) during the last quarter of the eighteenth century. French slave traders brought 51 "cargoes" from Mozambique to St. Domingue. French voyages were 86.8 percent (t = 68) of voyages from Mozambique recorded in *The Trans-Atlantic Slave Trade Data-*

base for that quarter. It is certain that some of the slaves brought from Mozambique were transshipped from St. Domingue to Louisiana and probably to other colonies as well. After St. Domingue's slaves revolted in 1791, the slave trade from Mozambique became largely a Brazilian/Portuguese operation. After 1808, when the British outlawed the transatlantic slave trade north of the equator, Mozambique became an important source of Africans brought mainly to Rio de Janeiro, Brazil. Voyages from Mozambique were 16.1 percent (n = 250; t = 1,556) of the recorded voyages arriving in Rio de Janeiro between July 25, 1795, and December 31, 1830. The number of recorded slaves arriving from Mozambique between 1811 and 1830 was 68,846 (25 percent; t = 272,942). Thus, although there was a significant Atlantic slave trade from Mozambique, it began on a relatively small scale and developed late. French and British slave traders were very active in Mozambique between the 1850s and 1870s, collecting "contract workers" to ship to the Caribbean, but they were "produced" exactly in the way slaves were.

It is clear why the Atlantic slave trade from Southeast Africa lasted so late. The European anti–slave trade treaty system and anti–slave trade patrols began later than along the Atlantic Coast, and the treaty was inadequately enforced. Before the late nineteenth century, there were few anti–slave trade patrols in the Indian Ocean. Currents from the Congo River swept ships rounding the southern tip of Africa far out to sea, which in effect enabled them to avoid the coastal patrols. The ivory trade had produced the highest-quality ivory in Africa especially prized in India, but it was in decline. Hungry Brazilian, Portuguese, Cuban, Spanish, U.S., French, and Arab slave traders swarmed to Mozambique throughout most of the nineteenth century.

In contrast to the situation in West Central Africa, Portuguese control was weak in Mozambique. We have seen that as late as the 1820s the Portuguese were confined to the coast and were not allowed to enter the Makua or Yao territories.[20] After 1854, demand for "contract laborers" who were "produced" exactly the same way as slaves led to extensive slave raiding among the Makua. Its effect was devastating.

The peoples of Mozambique found that they were destroying each other to obtain a few prisoners to supply the Portuguese slave trade. For a time, they stopped the warfare, and the slave market at Mozambique Island was poorly populated. In 1857, although the Makua beat off the Portuguese by threatening to attack their settlements, subsequently the slave trade, euphemistically called trade in "contract workers," resumed with a vengeance.

Frederic Elton, the British consul at Mozambique during the 1870s, described this devastation:

The fear of slave-dealers' raids—their tracks are marked by many a burned and desolated settlement—has engendered a suspicious uneasiness among the villagers for so many years, that it has now become an innate feature of the Makua character, is marked upon their faces, and colors every action of their lives at the present day. No communication with a stranger or with an adjoining tribe is allowed without express permission from a "*baraza*" of chiefs. The Lomwé country, lying between Makuani and the Lake Nyassa, Mosembé, and Mwendazi, may not be visited under pain of capital punishment, without the headman of the subdivision of the tribe to which the intending traveler belongs referring for leave to higher authority. Tracks of land are purposely laid waste and desolated upon the frontiers, where armed scouts, generally old elephant hunters, continually wander, their duty being to report at the earliest moment any approach of strangers, who are invariably treated as enemies.[21]

Thus the large-scale Atlantic slave trade from Mozambique began and ended late. The three and a half centuries of unremitting export of slaves "produced" by endless warfare in West Central Africa and later in Mozambique played a major role in populating the Americas, both North and South.

Studying the patterns of introduction of this massive number of West Central Africans into the Americas over the centuries is far from simple. Many of them came from small villages and towns and identified most strongly with local places rather than broader, stratified polities. Their geographic and ethnic identifications are complicated by the use of broad and conflicting terminology by European slave traders as well as in documents created in the Americas. We have seen that British slave traders generally referred to all of West Central Africa as Angola and British colonists generally called all West Central Africans Angolans. French and Spanish documents tended to list all West Central Africans as Kongo. Brazilian documents often used names of ports to describe them. In early Peru, the term "Angola" was used, probably because the slaves there were coming overwhelmingly from Luanda. Except for some late-eighteenth- and early-nineteenth-century runaway slave advertisements in Jamaican newspapers that gave "Mungola" as a nation designation, notarial documents in Louisiana and St. Domingue that listed substantial numbers of Mondongue, and Mary Karasch's study of travelers' accounts from nineteenth-century Rio de Janeiro, we have relatively little information about specific ethnicities from West Central Africa in documents in the Americas. Nevertheless, it is reasonably safe to conclude that, regardless of the designations used by the British as opposed to the French, Spanish, and Portuguese, most of the Bantu speakers brought to North America and the Caribbean after 1700 were Kikongo language group speakers brought from the Loango Coast and most of those brought to Brazil were Kimbundu language group speakers brought from Angola. As was indicated earlier in this chapter, leading experts in history, anthropology, and linguistics assure us that West Central Africans shared very closely related languages and cultures.

It is hard to overestimate the numbers and the universal presence of West Central Africans throughout the Americas. Although they have often been discussed within the framework of slavery in Brazil, they were prominent in Spanish America after 1575 and thereafter almost everywhere in the Americas. The Brazilian sugar industry began to develop during the last few decades of the sixteenth century and became a major cornerstone of Portuguese wealth. Native American labor was used heavily during its early stages, but enslaved Africans proved to be more productive and somewhat easier to control. Increasing numbers of West Central Africans arriving on voyages from Luanda, Angola, diluted the clustering of Greater Senegambians in sixteenth-century Brazil and Spanish America. They began to arrive in large numbers by the 1590s and quickly became the main source of labor. Escalating Portuguese military action in Kongo and Angola, warfare between the Portuguese and the Dutch who recruited allies and clients among Africans to fight each other, and the introduction of rum by the Dutch during the 1640s at Mpinda and then by the Brazilians at Luanda fueled a growing export of enslaved Angolans to Spanish America as well as to Brazil.[22] The Portuguese *asiento* traffic to Spanish America between 1595 and 1640 brought in increasing numbers of Angolans. The vast majority of the slave trade voyages of identified coastal origin arriving in Veracruz, Mexico, came from Luanda, Angola, and a large minority of such voyages to Cartagena de Indias embarked from Luanda as well. Although during most of the sixteenth century the vast majority of enslaved Africans were brought to Spanish America from Greater Senegambia/Upper Guinea, by the late sixteenth century Luanda, Angola, rose in importance as an African port of origin for all of the Americas. During the seventeenth century, Kongo and Angola predominated in notarial documents in Costa Rica.[23] Africans arriving in eastern Cuba were overwhelmingly from Luanda for several reasons. When ships from Luanda were heading to Cartagena and Veracruz and their "cargo" was in precarious condition, they were sometimes unloaded and sold in Santiago de Cuba. Some of them were skilled copper miners and were used to develop the copper mines near Santiago.[24]

They worked on sugar estates and in silver mines in Mexico. Voyages arriving in the Río de la Plata, the Spanish American region along the South

Table 7.1.   Voyages to Cartagena de Indias and Veracruz
from Identified African Coasts, 1595–1640

Place of Departure	Cartagena de Indias	Veracruz	Total
Ríos de Guinea	4	—	4
Cape Verde Islands	24	6	30
Guinea	27	1	28
São Tomé	11	6	17
Angola	46	106	152
Arda (Allada)/Slave Coast	2	—	2
Calabar/Bight of Biafra	—	1	1
Total	114	120	234

Source: Calculated from Vila Vilar, *Hispanoamérica y el comercio de esclavos,* cuadros 3–5.

Atlantic coast directly below Brazil, came overwhelmingly from Angola as well. During the first half of the seventeenth century, West Central Africans entered Upper Peru from the east coast of Spanish America via the Rio de la Plata. This traffic brought in about 1,500 to 3,000 enslaved Africans from Angola each year. Traces of them are found in sale documents of slaves in Charcas, Bolivia, between 1650 and 1710. Those of identified African ethnicities were mainly West Central Africans (n = 51). Only seventeen were from Upper Guinea. The West Central Africans were heavily female (thirty-one females, twenty males), probably domestics.[25]

After Portugal regained its independence from Spain in 1640, the Portuguese monopoly of the maritime trade to Africa collapsed. By the early eighteenth century, the northern European slave traders in West Central Africa operated mainly along the Loango Coast stretching south from Mayombe through the coast north of the Congo River. They began importing substantial numbers of West Central Africans to their colonies in the Americas. The Loango Coast had exported few slaves during the seventeenth century and then grew slowly during the early eighteenth century.[26] Thereafter, this slave trade escalated, bringing enormous numbers of Kongo to the Caribbean and to the United States. Although the British usually called them Angolans, they were almost certainly mainly Kongo. Angola continued to supply Brazil with huge numbers of enslaved Africans during the eighteenth and nineteenth centuries.

West Central Africans were brought to the United States in large numbers.[27] During the decade of the 1730s, the majority of documented transatlantic slave trade voyages to South Carolina arrived from West Central

Africa. They were referred to as Angolans in documents recorded in South Carolina, but they were with little doubt overwhelmingly Kongo collected mainly along the Loango Coast by British slave traders. There were very few voyages from West Central Africa to South Carolina between 1740 and 1800, no doubt because of fears resulting from the Kongo-led Stono Uprising in 1739. Voyages from West Central Africa to South Carolina did not resume in significant numbers until a few years before the foreign slave trade to the United States was outlawed on January 1, 1808.

In Louisiana after 1770, Africans recorded as Kongo were most heavily clustered on estates in Orleans Parish and after 1803 in St. Charles Parish immediately upriver as well. Sugar plantations were booming in both parishes. The proportion of Kongo listed in documents spiked between 1800 and 1820. Shortly after the United States acquired the Louisiana Territory in late 1803, the foreign slave trade to Louisiana was outlawed. The illegal slave trade appears to have focused very heavily on West Central Africa, although some of the Kongo in Louisiana documents could have been transshipped legally from Charleston before 1808. Between 1801 and 1805, twenty-three voyages (41.1 percent of all voyages) arrived in South Carolina from West Central Africa. In 1806–7, 39 voyages (36.1 percent of all voyages) arrived from this region. Evidence from Louisiana documents after 1803 indicates that some of these Kongo Africans were transshipped there from Charleston.

The Kongo were less prominent farther up the Mississippi River, where Africans from the Bight of Benin and from Greater Senegambia continued to predominate through 1820. Many of the Kongo men—but none of the women—were ruptured from heavy lifting. The proportion of Kongo listed with family ties was substantially lower than among other African ethnicities. It appears that these smuggled Kongo, heavily male, were used for intense gang labor in the sugar industry. The percentage of males among the Kongo and the male/female price differential increased.[28]

During the nineteenth century, the proportion and numbers of peoples from Bantulands brought to the Americas grew sharply. When Britain signed treaties with Spain and Portugal in 1817 to end the transatlantic slave trade to the Americas in return for a substantial payment, Portugal reserved her right to continue the slave trade below the equator until 1830. Anti–slave trade patrols were not active below the equator before 1842. In 1826, after Brazil became independent, it signed a treaty with Britain to end its import of slaves in return for British recognition of the new nation's sovereignty. But the Atlantic slave trade to Brazil increased through 1850.[29] As a result, growing proportions of West Central Africans were brought to all regions of the Americas, further contributing to the clustering of Africans from this region.

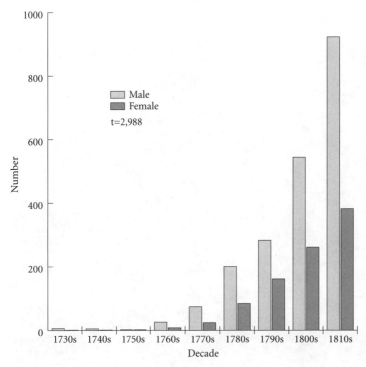

Figure 7.1.   Kongo in Louisiana by Gender (1730s–1810s).
Calculated from Hall, *Louisiana Slave Database, 1719–1820.*

The Kongo presence in Cuba during the nineteenth century has been under-stated, partially because some Cubans appear to be ashamed of the Kongo and more proud of the Yoruba. We have seen that in Mozambique the slave trade, euphemistically called the trade in "contract laborers," continued well into the last half of the nineteenth century.

Smuggling of enslaved Africans from all coasts continued throughout the nineteenth century. During the wars for Latin American independence (1808–21), piracy and slave smuggling escalated in the Caribbean, Florida, and the Gulf South of the United States. Anne Perotin Dumont described the pirates and smugglers as "corsaires de la liberté."[30] Regardless of this flattering desig-nation, they were deeply involved in smuggling slaves. Evidence from African ethnicities recorded in American documents indicates that many of the ships captured by pirates originated in West Central Africa and that smugglers had direct ties with West Central African suppliers. The smugglers' networks in-volved illicit traders to and from Cuba, Guadeloupe, and Florida. The Lafitte brothers, pirates operating from Barataria, Louisiana, and then from Gal-

Princess Madia, a Kongo woman who arrived in the United States in 1860, when the American slave ship she was aboard, *Wildfire*, was captured by the U.S. Navy near Key West, Florida. Because of the dignity of her bearing and the deference shown to her by some fellow captured slaves, *Wildfire*'s crew called her "princess." (*Harper's Weekly*, June 2, 1860.)

veston, Texas, smuggled new Africans into Louisiana during the early nineteenth century. Slave trade ships bringing new Africans to Cuba were their main targets.[31] It is clear that these ships were coming mainly from West Central Africa. After 1819 when the foreign slave trade to Cuba was outlawed by a treaty between Britain and Spain, the entrenched network of pirates became very active smuggling enslaved Africans into Cuba. Africans smuggled

Table 7.2.   West Central Africans in the British West Indies

Colony	Year	Total Identified Africans	West Central Africans
St. Kitts	1817	2,746	1,348 (49.1%)
St. Lucia	1815	2,638	602 (22.8%)
Trinidad	1813	13,398	2,569 (19.2%)
Berbice	1819	1,138	248 (21.8%)
Anguilla	1827	53	20 (37.7%)
Total		19,973	4,787 (24.0%)

Source: Calculated from Higman, *Slave Populations of the British Caribbean,* appendix, section 3.

into the north coast of the Gulf of Mexico were from the same ethnicities smuggled into Cuba: mainly Kongo, Igbo, and Ibibio. Table 2.2 (in chapter 2) demonstrates that the Kongo and the "Kalabarí" (Bight of Biafra) were 55 percent of the slaves sold in Cuba between 1790 and 1880. Surprisingly, the Lucumí (Yoruba) were only 9 percent. Manuel Moreno Fraginals's studies of African ethnonyms listed on Cuban sugar and coffee estates shows that the Lucumí/Yoruba rose from 8.22 percent (n = 354) of these ethnicities between 1760 and 1769 to 8.38 percent (n = 453) between 1800 and 1820 and then to 34.52 percent (n = 3,161) between 1850 and 1870. There are no data for the period between 1821 and 1849, when the Lucumí were no doubt beginning to be introduced in large numbers.

The same two African coasts, West Central Africa and the Bight of Biafra, became major sources of the slave trade to the British West Indies during the nineteenth century. Despite great distances and unfavorable winds and currents, one-fourth of the enslaved Africans introduced into five British West Indies colonies during the early nineteenth century were West Central Africans. They were referred to overwhelmingly as Kongo, obviously because these colonies had previously been French except for Trinidad, which, however, had been settled mainly from Martinique.

After 1830, anti–slave trade patrols recaptured even fewer Africans from Bantulands than from Upper or Lower Guinea because West Central Africa was not patrolled before 1842 and less effectively patrolled than Upper and Lower Guinea thereafter. Much information for the nineteenth century recorded in *The Trans-Atlantic Slave Trade Database* comes from ships captured by anti–slave trade patrols. Before 1830, these patrols operated legally only north of the equator,, which meant that the proportion of the nineteenth-century maritime slave trade from Upper and Lower Guinea, the patrolled areas, came to be overstated compared to those of West Central and Southeast Africa. Thus historians studying documented transatlantic slave trade voyages shipped to the Americas during the nineteenth century are likely to underestimate voyages originating in Central Africa. After the legal Atlantic slave trade ended, "emancipados" and "contract" laborers, in good part West Central Africans, continued to be introduced into the Caribbean in substantial numbers. East Central Africans, mainly from Mozambique, were taken to Brazil in large numbers before the legal slave trade ended there in 1830 and surely through 1850, when the Atlantic slave trade to Brazil was finally effectively suppressed.[32]

Thus the transatlantic slave trade from Bantulands began early, escalated over time, and lasted very late. With some overlap, Africans from Angola tended to be clustered along the east coast of South America — in Brazil, Uruguay, and Argentina — and the Kongo tended to be clustered in the Caribbean and surrounding coasts and in the United States. Thus Bantu Africans arrived in large and growing numbers everywhere in the Americas.

Implications for Culture Formation in the Americas

This book is only the beginning of the long, complex, challenging, but important task of restoring the severed links between Africa and the Americas. In order to understand the roots of cultures anywhere in the Americas, we must explore the pattern of introduction of Africans over time and place. It will, one hopes, lay the basis for a better-informed discussion of African cultural influences in various regions in the Americas. We can no longer be satisfied with simplistic, romanticized ideas about the identities of the African ancestors of African Americans. They were very unlikely to be speakers of Swahili. Nor were they likely to be Yoruba in the United States except in Louisiana. Even in Louisiana, the Yoruba were only about 4 percent of slaves of identified African ethnicities. The Yoruba were most prominent in nineteenth-century Bahia, Brazil.[1] Although the Yoruba/Lucumí were important in nineteenth-century Cuba, they arrived in large numbers late, much later than in Bahia, Brazil. It is possible that their presence and influence in Cuba has been overstated at the expense of the Igbo, the Ibibio, and especially the Kongo.

One of the glories of history is that it allows us to avoid overly abstract, static constructions blinding us to the richness and complexity of life. We need to study Africans in Africa and the Americas over time and place and avoid dealing with questions in isolation from broad patterns. The many millions of people dragged in chains from Africa to the Americas need to be rescued from the anonymity of generic Africans and studied as varied, complex peoples. This book argues that a significant number of Africans recorded in documents created in the Western Hemisphere identified their own ethnicities or those of other Africans. Despite the difficulties of identifying African ethnic designations recorded in various ways in several major languages in documents throughout the Americas and despite changing ethnic designations and identities over time on both sides of the Atlantic, these ethnic descriptions are key evidence linking Africans in Africa with Africans in the Americas.[2]

Conclusions from one place and time should not be extrapolated to all of Africa and the Americas. We need to place our questions within the framework of changing patterns over time and place and avoid broad generalizations projected backward in time. Studies of the nineteenth and twentieth centuries are most frequent because there is more available evidence and documentation. But with the exception of religion, worldview, and esthetic principles, the last two centuries are not always likely to reflect the more distant past. Patterns of creolization in Sierra Leone during the nineteenth century cannot be extrapolated to creolization in the Americas at all times and places.[3] Africans arriving in some regions in the Americas were not nearly as varied as Africans who were disembarked and resettled within a limited time period in Sierra Leone from recaptured ships. These recaptives were not slaves. If creolization meant Europeanization in Sierra Leone, it certainly meant no such thing in the Americas. Creolization was not the process of Africans melting into a European pot. Creolization was a continuum encompassing the entire population in American colonies with very heavy and sometimes quite specific African inputs. Africans landing in Sierra Leone during the nineteenth century learned English as the lingua franca. Africans landing in the circum-Caribbean learned Creole languages, which they or their forebears played a major role in creating and developing. Africans arriving in Brazil evidently created and learned the general Mina language of Brazil. It was based on Gbe languages during the eighteenth century and then on Nago/Yoruba languages with the influx of large numbers of speakers of the latter during the nineteenth century. Africanization was not a process affecting Africans and their descendants alone. The entire population was more or less Africanized in language use as well as in many other aspects of culture.

The impact of Africans on patterns of creolization varied greatly over time and among different places, depending on several factors. These include the patterns of introduction of Africans of particular regions and ethnicities; their gender proportions and their patterns of mating and parenting; how rapidly they began to reproduce themselves; the proportion and strength of the native American population; the extent of race mixture; whether the geography facilitated runaway slave communities; the economic, strategic, and military priorities of the colonizing powers; military and police uses of slaves; the extent and role of manumission; the labor demands of the major exports as the economy evolved; and policies of social control reflected in various European religious and legal traditions and institutions. But Europeans were not all-powerful, certainly not in matters of economy and culture. They, too, were strangers in a strange, dangerous, and hostile world. European power and control was often weak, especially during the early, most crucial stages of culture formation. Patterns of creolization differed throughout the Americas over time and place. In most places, the high percentage of males among Africans was a major factor limiting the possibility of creating ongoing, specific African enclave cultures. Some African ethnicities with high proportions of females—for example, the Igbo—had exogamous mating patterns and their reproductive rate was unusually high.

One of my quarrels with some specialists in African and transatlantic slave trade history involves their excessive attention to monolingual English-language sources. In English-language documents generated in the Americas, information about African ethnicities is rare. Newspaper advertisements and jailhouse records describing runaway slaves sometimes identify their ethnicities, but they do not necessarily reflect the ethnic composition of the slave population. For example, documents in English cannot shed much light on the proportions of Igbo in the slave population during the eighteenth and nineteenth centuries because Igbo ran away in higher proportions than others. Evidently, English-language documents generated in Africa, Atlantic slave trade documents, and other major sources translated into English do not help much either. David Northrup has stated: "There is little direct evidence of the origins of slaves, but it is possible to calculate the relative percentage of speakers of the major languages in the catchment basins of the region's major slaving ports and to adjust these purely topographical calculations with information about population densities and slaving operations."[4]

This approach raises some questions. First of all, we do not know the proportions of Africans from particular ethnicities shipped from the interior via these ports. We cannot assume that Africans of various ethnicities were being shipped out in proportion to where they lived. Our knowledge of trading and other patterns in the Bight of Biafra is limited by the fact that Europeans were confined to the coast until the mid-nineteenth century. The ambitious research project undertaken by David Eltis and G. Ugo Nwekoji might enlighten us about the proportion of Igbo captured by British anti–slave trade ships during the first few decades of the nineteenth century. Their project studies and databases the names and scarifications of Africans released from these voyages in Havana and in Sierra Leone. This appears to be a complex project, the results of which are not yet clear.[5]

By crossing the Atlantic, we can do better than that. African ethnicities recorded in particular places in the Americas do not allow us to draw conclusions about the numbers or proportions of a particular ethnicity exported from a particular African coast, especially since peoples brought from the interior were shipped to the Americas in increasing numbers and changing proportions over time. But we can speak with confidence about changing proportions of ethnicities appearing in descriptions of Africans in surviving documents generated in the Americas.

This book has demonstrated the value of combining the study of data from transatlantic slave trade voyages with descriptions of African ethnicities in documents from various times and places in the Americas. It establishes the value of databasing both types of information to allow for refined studies over time and place. The result is more subtlety in the questions asked and reasonably confidently answered. We can now begin to link Africans in Africa with Africans in the Americas.

I have argued here that for various cogent reasons Africans from particular regions and ethnicities were often clustered in the Americas. These reasons include the systems of winds and currents linking various African coasts with various regions in the Americas; traditional trade networks among European, Afro-European, American, and African buyers and sellers; the timing of the transatlantic slave trade involving increasing numbers of African coasts over the centuries; and the preferences of masters in American regions for particular African peoples. Africans from particular coasts and ethnicities often arrived in waves clustering them in specific places in the Americas.

African ethnicities arriving during the early, formative period of a particular place often continued to be preferred. These preferences were sometimes exercised energetically and effectively in the slave trade. As explained in chapter 3, the transshipment trade seems to have increased clustering as preferences among buyers were further implemented. Supply factors were certainly crucial. David Geggus argues that St. Domingue planters were reluctant to employ West Central Africans on sugar estates.[6] Gabriel Debien argues that West Central Africans were clustered on coffee estates because those estates were created later when the Atlantic slave trade had shifted heavily toward West Central Africa.[7] In Louisiana, the growth of the sugar industry in Orleans and St. Charles parishes coincided with an escalating, massive influx of West Central Africans into the transatlantic slave trade. They were clustered perhaps not so much by choice as by availability in places where demand for labor on sugar estates increased sharply.

What do these findings imply for culture formation in the Americas? Let us turn briefly to Suriname, relied on heavily in the influential Mintz-Price thesis. By collapsing the time span in their study of the transatlantic slave trade to Suriname, Mintz and Price concluded that Africans arrived as an incoherent crowd whose particular cultural identities and characteristics disappeared almost immediately after they landed in the Americas. They then generalized this finding to all of the Americas and dismissed the significance of particular African regional cultures and ethnicities in the formation of Afro-American cultures everywhere. But the Mintz-Price thesis does not even apply to Suriname, where there was a Gold Coast phase and then an almost entirely West Central African phase during the third quarter of the eighteenth century. Africans were never an incoherent crowd, not even in Suriname. The Mintz-Price thesis is insightful when it argues that African American cultures and Creole languages were formed early and had an ongoing impact on those who came after. Roger Bastide argues, in contrast, that those who arrived late and in large numbers exerted the preponderant cultural influence. The Bastide thesis tends to be an ahistorical, static approach to culture formation, tracing contemporary "survivals" to contemporary ethnicities and regions in Africa.[8] There is no doubt that massive late arrivals of Africans from particular regions and ethnicities impacted the existing cultures in an ongoing process of creolization. But the influence of those who came first maintained an edge by creating the earliest Afro-Creole languages and cultures to which newcomers had to adjust to a significant extent.

There is much to be learned from the Mintz-Price thesis. It makes important arguments having genuine validity: that Creole languages and cultures formed quickly and that African cultures were not preserved in a pickled form in the Americas but were subjected to the process of creolization over time. But these early cultures were not simply abstract, African American cultures. They were quite distinct regional cultures, which developed in response to an array of factors, including the patterns of introduction of Africans over time from various regions and the clustering of various African ethnicities arriving from Africa in waves. The earliest Africans often had a continuing and decisive influence on their Creole descendants, on Africans who arrived later, and on the wider society. David Geggus argues that in St. Domingue the early impact of Africans brought from the Bight of Benin explains the extensive, deeply rooted, resilient voodoo religion in Haiti, which still survives strongly and continues to evolve and change.[9] Between 1725 and 1755, 39.4 percent of Atlantic slave trade voyages arriving in St. Domingue came from the Bight of Benin, bringing in a large number of Aja/Fon/Arada/Ewe along with their vodun gods. In Martinique during this same period, 48.7 percent of Atlantic slave trade voyages arrived from the Bight of Benin. These Africans understood each other's languages well. Scholars have recently stressed Kongo influence on Haitian voodoo.[10] These interpretations are not contradictory. They are based on the massive introduction of West Central Africans during the last half of the eighteenth century and the very substantial impact of those peoples on the ongoing process of the creolization of religion in St.

Domingue. The creolization of religion followed a different course in Cuba, where the Bantu impact was more direct and unadulterated. To the present day, Palo Mayombe, a traditional Kongo faith, has had a strong influence in Cuba and among Cuban immigrants to the United States and the circum-Caribbean. In Cuba, although Yoruba gods and Santeria are often stressed, Kongo influences in folklore and religion are powerful as well. Religious influences from the Bight of Biafra are reflected in Afro-Cuban religious beliefs and practices, stemming from the significant introduction of Karabalí into nineteenth-century Cuba. Candomble in Brazil reflects the massive introduction of Nago/Lucumí/Yoruba during the late eighteenth and nineteenth centuries, especially in Bahia.[11]

In sum, the process of creolization in the Americas varied greatly over time and place, depending on the many varying factors discussed above. Creolization in Africa differed sharply from creolization in the Americas. As in most places in the world, it was an internal process as peoples from various ethnicities met and mingled as immigrants, conquerors and conquered, traders and consumers. European and Afro-European influence was important near the Atlantic coast in Africa, but that influence on the enslaved Africans sent to the Americas should not be exaggerated. As we have seen, after the Atlantic slave trade began, the Portuguese lançados played a major role in creolization along coasts, rivers, and other trading centers in Africa where they were allowed into or could force access to the interior. Portuguese-based Creole languages developed in São Tomé and in the Cape Verde Islands. Portuguese and Cape Verde merchants brought Cape Verde Creole to the Upper Guinea coast. In Upper Guinea, the early Afro-Portuguese established themselves in trading enclaves. But Mandingo continued to be the major language for communication and trade. In his book first published in 1627, Alonso de Sandoval wrote, "The Wolofs, Berbesies [Serer], Mandingas [Mandingos], and Fulos [Fulani] can ordinarily understand each other, although their languages and ethnicities [castas] are diverse, because of the extensive communication all of them have had with the damnable sect of Muhammed, no doubt to the great confusion of the Christians. . . . Among them the Mandinga are innumerable, being spread throughout almost all the Kingdoms, and thus knowing almost all the languages."[12] In 1735, Mandingo ("Mundingoe") was still described as the most common language spoken throughout Greater Senegambia, followed by Portuguese Creole, the language best known by Britons.[13]

In the Americas, creolization was a more radical process. The economies and cultures were based on decisive Native American influences, especially in the highlands of Latin America, but just about everywhere else as well. Europeans and Africans arriving in the Americas were strangers in a strange world.

It was a violent, insecure place where survival was often more important than prejudice. As a result, the most adaptive cultural elements from four continents were embraced, although their non-European derivation has never been adequately acknowledged. This radical biological and cultural cross-breeding is the basic strength of the Americas.

Culture formation varied from place to place. Each American region has to be examined separately over time to discern the prevailing patterns of introduction of various African peoples and their influences on the formation of culture in the ongoing process of creolization. This is not a simple task. It requires much new research using documents currently known and others still to be discovered. It requires a reasonable level of subtlety and sophistication and an open mind. It will not do to collapse time in simple, aggregate counts of transatlantic slave trade voyages to various places in the Americas. The transshipment trade in newly arrived Africans must be given due weight. The most frequent ethnicities must be disaggregated and studied. If one can identify in documents the presence of significant numbers of African ethnicities at different times and places, that information should be databased to allow for comparative, relational studies. Much work remains to be done before we can arrive at confident answers. Although the French Archives Coloniales in Aix-en-Provence has a huge collection of bound volumes of notarial documents from St. Domingue listing African ethnicities, the data there still remain to be thoroughly studied. Rich documentation about African ethnicities can be found in courthouses and archives throughout Cuba. The destruction of Brazilian documents involving slavery has been greatly exaggerated; important ones continue to exist throughout Brazil.[14]

Improved conceptualization and methodologies and new research are necessary for studies of the United States. Historians who have excessive faith in surviving documents no doubt neglect the transshipment trade from the Caribbean to the British mainland colonies as well as to Caribbean colonies of other nations. More knowledge about the transshipment trade from the Caribbean during the eighteenth century could alter the accepted wisdom about the rate of natural growth among slaves in British North America and the low proportions of Africans within the slave population during the eighteenth century. Except for slaves arriving with their masters from Barbados when Carolina was first colonized, it is not credible that the slave trade from the Caribbean brought significant numbers of Caribbean-born slaves. Slaves transshipped from the Caribbean were surely overwhelmingly African-born, very likely new arrivals from Africa. Many African foremothers and forefathers in the United States arrived no doubt on documented and undocumented voyages from the Caribbean. Anglophone historians need to widen their focus and become more proficient in the use of documents and the historical literature in other languages. Scholars who study the African diaspora in the Americas, regardless of their native tongue, need to learn how to create and use relational databases.

African cultures were neither preserved nor pickled. They should not be treated as static or viewed in isolation from each other either in Africa or in the Americas or from Creole cultures in formation. Specific African regional cultures and ethnicities should no longer be invisible as important factors contributing to the formation of Afro-American cultures and indeed to the formation of wider cultures in the Americas.

Prices of Slaves by Ethnicity and Gender in Louisiana, 1719–1820

The price data in my *Louisiana Slave Database* have their strengths and their weaknesses. Their greatest strength is the massive amount of price information they provide. Excluding records derived from Atlantic slave trade voyages that have no price information, they contain 45,369 records (49.4 percent) with individual price given; 37,466 records (40.7 percent) with group price given; and 9,186 records (10 percent) with no price given. Differential prices of slaves over time by origin or ethnicity, racial designation, gender, age, and skills can be calculated. Each record represents an individual described in a document, researched and entered from unpublished manuscript sources in French, Spanish, and English. Almost all of these documents are housed in libraries, archives, and courthouses throughout Louisiana.[1] Complete source information, with the exact date and location of the original document, was included in each record. Almost all extant documents were studied. The *Louisiana Slave Database* consists of 100,600 records. Among them, 8,645 concern individuals who arrived on transatlantic slave trade voyages and do not supply much information about them. There are 113 fields, which contain comparable information, and 19 recoded fields in the SPSS Slave.sav file. These files can be downloaded free of charge from <http://www.ibiblio.org/laslave>. This website supplies a search engine that greatly facilitates its use, but it does not contain all of the fields. Scholars wishing to make calculations on these databases should download the SPSS.sav versions of the *Louisiana Slave Database* as well as the *Louisiana Free Database*, which contains records of more than 4,000 slaves described in manumission documents.

Price studies can tell us a great deal about comparative social and economic history. Only slaves had prices placed on the value of their production and reproduction over their lifetimes. Price data for a particular time and

Table A.1.   Slaves Sold Independently of Probate in Louisiana, 1770–1820

	Mean Price: Males	Mean Price: Females	Female Price as Percentage of Male Price
Spanish Period (1770–1803)	605.91 (n = 3,043)	541 (n = 1,998)	89
Early U.S. Period (1804–1820)	827.40 (n = 6,457)	662.11 (n = 5,426)	80

Source: Calculated from Hall, *Louisiana Slave Database, 1719–1820.*
Note: Total records: 16,924. Individuals ages 15–34 only.

place have limited value until they can be compared with price data in other times and places. But comparisons have no value at all unless the price data for the particular place are themselves valid. The *Louisiana Slave Database* contains enough computerized price data to go beyond global prices, allowing for valid price comparisons of subgroups within the slave population. Differential prices of slaves over time by origin or ethnicity, racial designation, gender, age, and skills can be calculated and studied. All prices were collected and computerized because the greater the number of total records included, the larger is the sample for each subgroup.

Tables A.1–A.3 compare mean prices of slaves when prices for each individual were given. Calculating individual prices alone reduces the price of females compared to males inventoried because women sold with children and/or mates were eliminated. While this fact reveals the high value placed on the reproductive powers of women, it does not tell us enough about the price of women who had children and/or mates included with them in group prices. Recalculating group prices would certainly increase the valid numbers for each subgroup of the slave population. At this stage, this is a serious but correctable problem. Patrick Manning developed a coding system consisting of over 100 codes for various combinations of groups of slaves recorded in the *Louisiana Slave Database*, but these data have not been coded because of the cost, time, and labor involved. Manning's coding formulas can be supplied to any scholar who wishes to undertake this task using the descriptions of the group supplied in the records and creating price conversion formulas. Such a project would certainly increase the valid numbers for each subgroup of the slave population. The *Louisiana Slave Database* touches on a great many aspects of slavery, and unfortunately I had to set limits on what it could accomplish. But it is an eminently flexible tool, which can be customized by the user and/or revised and reissued very quickly and inexpensively.

Table A.2.   Mean Sale Price of the Five Most Frequently Found African Ethnicities
in Louisiana

	Spanish Period (1770–1803)			Early U.S. Period (1804–1820)			
Ethnicity	Male	Female	Female Price as Percentage of Male Price	Male	Female	Female Price as Percentage of Male Price	Total
Kongo	544.16 (n = 188)	452.11 (n = 84)	83	767.72 (n = 454)	622.49 (n = 194)	81	920
Igbo	644.70 (n = 23)	415.88 (n = 24)	64	682.15 (n = 47)	604.66 (n = 29)	97.5	123
Mandingo	553.97 (n = 72)	449.45 (n = 33)	81	712.72 (n = 72)	532.14 (n = 43)	75	220
Mina	580.63 (n = 49)	561.45 (n = 20)	97	873.88 (n = 32)	699.82 (n = 28)	80	129
Wolof	605.85 (n = 71)	642.82 (n = 22)	106	824.29 (n = 42)	637.43 (n = 21)	77	156

Source: Calculated from Hall, *Louisiana Slave Database, 1719–1820.*
Note: Total records: 1,548. Individuals ages 15–34.

The documents that I consulted are multilingual. Between 1719 and 1820, Louisiana was ruled by France, then Spain, and then the United States. Several types of currency circulated during all three periods. I had to resolve the problem of comparable prices listed in various currencies. In 1985, Robert A. Rosenberg, then director of the Edison Papers at Rutgers University, developed a price conversion formula from comparable prices that I had found in documents from the Pointe Coupée Post during the Spanish period (1770–1803). This formula has been applied in the field that makes automatic calculations of common denominator prices. It is valid for the overwhelming majority of prices and, with very few exceptions, has been used for the entire database. The formulas is: 5 livres = 1 piastre (in French) or peso (in Spanish); 1 pound of indigo marchande = 1 piastre or 1 peso; 1 piastre gourde sonante de Mexique (in French) or peso fuerte (in Spanish) = 1.75 piastres or pesos. For the early U.S. period (1804–20), the dollar was calculated as the same as the piastre or peso and brought quite credible results. In a very few cases, the gourde was listed as the currency in documents from the early U.S. period, but the recalculation formula results were not credible, so the common denominator price was changed by hand in these few cases. The original currency information was listed in the comments field.

Table A.3.   Mean Price of Slaves by Ethnicity and Gender Inventoried on
Estates in Louisiana over Time

Decade	Ethnicity	Male			Female		
		Number	Mean	Standard Deviation	Number	Mean	Standard Deviation
1770s	Bamana	7	282.66	26.904	3	266.67	61.101
	Chamba	5	306.00	39.749	2	280.00	113.137
	Kongo	37	259.00	95.596	9	246.67	107.703
	Igbo	8	248.75	71.602	7	320.00	40.15
	Mandingo	18	297.78	87.753	5	312.00	45.497
	Mina	9	263.33	99.624	4	245.00	88.506
	Nago/Yoruba	3	250.00	50.000	2	225.00	35.355
	Wolof	9	235.56	107.251	5	288.00	57.619
	Total	96	267.53	87.310	37	277.03	75.824
1780s	Bamana	28	425.54	172.333	7	385.71	146.385
	Chamba	23	424.35	149.691	7	491.43	199.368
	Kongo	89	400.84	164.215	31	398.55	150.162
	Igbo	16	552.81	161.637	13	289.38	179.691
	Mandingo	51	485.82	224.805	20	396.50	155.200
	Mina	32	435.00	178.163	12	408.33	160.728
	Nago/Yoruba	30	368.93	195.919	11	409.09	128.799
	Wolof	23	437.83	185.985	22	368.64	173.714
	Total	449	339.89	129.071	135	280.57	132.214
1790s	Bamana	48	371.15	132.244	3	336.67	197.569
	Chamba	46	340.15	143.318	17	318.00	107.740
	Kongo	119	331.76	125.443	41	279.12	126.721
	Igbo	25	290.60	135.803	9	206.67	131.909
	Mandingo	70	342.86	135.883	23	289.35	100.638
	Mina	69	349.35	104.526	11	309.09	191.139
	Nago/Yoruba	38	399.79	105.058	17	286.76	194.767
	Wolof	34	378.47	151.891	14	256.86	141.116
	Total	449	339.89	129.071	135	280.57	132.214
1800s	Bamana	39	497.31	235.542	2	300.00	353.553
	Chamba	38	473.03	196.109	23	323.91	160.163
	Kongo	121	517.04	192.192	48	437.19	159.484
	Igbo	22	492.73	187.011	12	264.17	188.316
	Mandingo	68	479.41	196.800	32	405.63	204.655
	Mina	41	502.63	230.314	22	418.18	189.326
	Nago/Yoruba	31	476.45	206.051	12	281.67	218.334
	Wolof	23	534.78	158.426	10	320.60	151.728
	Total	474	502.32	199.196	161	378.70	188.163

Table A.3.   Continued

Decade	Ethnicity	Male			Female		
		Number	Mean	Standard Deviation	Number	Mean	Standard Deviation
1810s	Bamana	45	420.22	261.008	7	511.43	316.882
	Chamba	38	420.39	282.715	11	328.64	187.538
	Kongo	377	650.63	326.512	102	571.96	273.692
	Igbo	42	622.62	284.391	18	486.11	291.954
	Mandingo	92	520.60	337.975	20	312.00	193.951
	Mina	76	660.86	512.788	15	440.33	244.894
	Nago/Yoruba	20	567.50	307.483	4	375.00	217.945
	Wolof	47	659.04	305.485	15	432.00	294.690
	Total	737	606.20	350.170	192	495.36	276.715

Source: Calculated from Hall, *Louisiana Slave Database, 1719–1820.*

Prices and calculations and recalculations dating from the Spanish (1770–1803) and early U.S. periods (1804–20) are trustworthy. But prices for the French period (1723–69) are of limited reliability, and the sample is very small compared to the samples from the Spanish and the early U.S. periods. There are, first of all, fewer records, and, among these, there are fewer individual prices because of the prohibition in the Code Noir on separating mother, father, and children under fourteen years of age when slaves were sold. This prohibition was effectively enforced in French Louisiana, and slave families were, in fact, inventoried and sold together. Except for children, there was relatively little numeric age information, probably because they were often Africans who did not know or could not communicate their numeric age. There are few records for the decade of the 1720s, and most years are entirely missing for the decade of the 1750s. The year 1758 is fairly well represented in the number of records, but they come from very few documents and include one large estate inventory of over 200 slaves. The prices for 1758 appear to be seriously inflated because of wartime conditions. French-period prices were not only inflated; they fluctuated wildly after 1735, when King Louis XV authorized the issuance of paper currency for Louisiana.[2] Louisiana currency was depreciated from an already depreciated Martinique currency. In 1741, the rate of depreciation for Martinique currency was explained: "We advise that the currency in use in Martinique is weak, divisible in piastres, like reaux, reaux and a half and that the piastre of weight is called gourde or round and is worth there 33 percent more than the said currency in use. The calculations made by M. Demuere in the account he rendered to M. du Conge is 165 piastres 4 reaux for the sum of 993 livres which at 33 percent above is reduced to 111 piastres of weight."[3]

Dividing 993 by 165, we arrive at approximately 6 livres for 1 piastre. Although the conversion rate of 6 livres to 1 piastre is mentioned in several documents, during the French period the official conversion rate was 4 to 1. By 1752, 3,300 livres in letters of exchange was worth 4,950 livres in Martinique,[4] or 1.5 Martinique livres for 1 livre in letters of exchange. By 1767, the value of colonial bills in Louisiana was fluctuating wildly in the face of abandonment of the colony by France and late and feeble assertion of authority by Spain. While the official exchange rate was stated to be as high as 4 livres to 1 piastre gourde and as low as 8 to 1 in several documents dating from 1767 and 1769, Louisiana colonial bills were, in fact, at times refused outright; barter was resorted to; or payment was made in letters of exchange payable in Europe or else in Mexican silver coins.[5] In July 1767, 6,344 livres 1 sol 3 deniers in colonial bills was worth 933 piastres in letters of exchange in Europe, or 6.8 livres in Louisiana colonial bills to 1 piastre in letters of exchange.[6] In February 1767, a letter of exchange for 200 pounds sterling drawn by Mr. Voix, merchant at La Rochelle, on Charles Ogebrie in London, endorsed by S. Maxent, merchant in New Orleans, converted at the rate of approximately 28 livres per 1 pound sterling.[7] Thus currency had no clear or stable value in Louisiana between 1735, when Louis XV authorized paper currency for the colony, until Spain established effective control in 1770 and introduced substantial numbers of Mexican silver coins. The conversion rate from livre to piastre (or peso) was 5 to 1, and from piastre or peso to Mexican silver piastre (recorded as piastre gourde sonante de Mexique or peso fuerte) it was 1.75 to 1 and remained stable.

While the calculations presented here are confined to lower Louisiana during our target time period, interesting comparisons can eventually be made with other slave societies throughout the Americas. It is essential to database any sophisticated price study in order to select subgroups on which to make calculations. Comparative studies of the internal structure of slave prices by age, gender, origin, skills, and ethnicity can show contrasts in the extent to which persons of various subgroups in the slave population were valued in accordance with time and place. Prices for children and elderly slaves in both Cuba and Brazil were low. In contrast, prices for children and old people appear to be surprisingly high in Louisiana. The gap between male and female prices in Louisiana grew during the early U.S. period. There was a sharp contrast in mean prices by gender among identified African ethnicities. The mean price of women of certain ethnicities was close to and sometimes higher than that of men of the same ethnicity despite a clear, overall trend of higher mean prices for men.

Scholars interested in asking their own questions of these databases can consult them using a search engine for some of the major fields. For complete calculations, one can download the database files free of charge in several different software packages along with detailed explanations about how they were created and how they can be used by clicking on the following website: <http://www.ibiblio.org/laslave>.

Notes

PREFACE

1. Du Bois, *The Negro*, 155–56; J. E. Harris, *Global Dimensions of the African Diaspora*.

2. For a recent study of the demography of the slave trades in Africa, see Manning, *Slavery and African Life*.

3. For a good summary, see Daget, "Abolition of the Slave Trade."

4. Hall, *Social Control in Slave Plantation Societies*, 131–35, 150.

5. Sundiata, *From Slaving to Neoslavery*. For a good summary of African "contract" laborers during the nineteenth century, see Lovejoy, *Transformations in Slavery*, 151–52.

6. For the Berlin Conference of 1885, see "Timeline of Slavery," in *Macmillan Encyclopedia of World Slavery*, ed. Finkelman and Miller, 2:981.

7. Hochschild, *King Leopold's Ghost*, especially 281–83; Sundiata, *Black Scandal*.

8. Lovejoy, *Transformations in Slavery*, 141.

CHAPTER ONE

1. *Kitab tabakat al-uman*, 36–37. Unless otherwise indicated this and all subsequent translations from French, Spanish, and Portuguese are by the author.

2. Niane, "Relationships and Exchanges," 614–34 (quote on 616–17). For an enlightening discussion of the limitations of the available historical record of this trade, see Austen, "Trans-Saharan Slave Trade"; and Niane, "Mali and the Second Mandingo Expansion," 119–23. For a discussion that ignores the early south Saharan thrust of the Almoravids and the impact of black African political and military leadership in Moorish Spain — a biased discussion of Almoravid rule relying heavily on Christian sources — see Fletcher, *Moorish Spain*, 105–18.

3. Niane, "Relationships and Exchanges," 620.

4. Costa e Silva, *A manilha e o libambo*, 133.

5. *Sevilla a comienzos del siglo XII*, para. 56, pp. 98–100.

6. For their racist interpretations, see Hitte, *History of the Arabs*, 540–45; and Dozy, *Spanish Islam*, 702, 721–23.

7. I will always be grateful to Dra. Concepción Muedra, a Catalonian refugee

from the Spanish Civil War living in Mexico, who introduced me to some of this fascinating literature when I studied with her in 1962–63 at Mexico City College (now the University of the Americas). She was reported to be the first woman who received a Ph.D. in history in Spain.

8. Codera, *Decadencia y desaparición de los Almoravids en España*, 190–217; Hulal al Mawsiyya, *Colección de crónicas árabes*, 95.

9. Niane, "Relationships and Exchanges," 618.

10. Shakundi, *Elogio del Islam español*, 98.

11. For the obscure and plagiaristic origins of credit for rhythmic notation in music scores in early Renaissance Europe, see Maitland, *Grove's Dictionary of Music and Musicians*, 2:100–102.

12. Sandoval, *Naturaleza*, 45.

13. Blackburn, *The Making of New World Slavery*; Wood, *Origins of American Slavery*, 10.

14. Landers, *Black Society in Spanish Florida*; Hanger, *Bounded Lives, Bounded Places*.

15. For scholarship combating these myths, see Hall, *Social Control in Slave Plantation Societies*, 96–107; Knight, *Slave Society in Cuba during the Nineteenth Century*; Rout, *The African Experience in Spanish America*; Helg, *Our Rightful Share*.

16. Manning, *Slavery and African Life*.

17. Eltis, *The Rise of African Slavery in America*, 261. For a more nuanced discussion, which contradicts his own conclusion, see ibid., table I-1 (p. 9) and pp. 29–56, where he includes the British born in America in his total of 300,000 English immigrants.

18. For a stimulating discussion of state power and enslavement comparing Europe and Africa, see Inikori, "The Struggle against the Slave Trade."

19. Eltis, "Europeans and the Rise and Fall of African Slavery in America"; Eltis, *The Rise of African Slavery in America*, 1–28, 267–73 (quote on 4).

20. Davis, "Looking at Slavery from Broader Perspectives."

21. Hall, *Africans in Colonial Louisiana*, 23, 25, 26.

22. Thornton, *Africa and Africans in the Making of the Atlantic World*; Eltis, *The Rise of African Slavery in America*.

23. Harms, *River of Wealth, River of Sorrow*, 148–53.

24. For medieval times, see Gomez, "Medieval Western Sudan."

25. Moore, *Travels into the Inland Parts of Africa*.

26. Law, *Ouidah*, 149.

27. Northrup, "A Collection of Interviews Conducted in Southeastern Nigeria in 1972–1973."

28. Cited in Vansina, *Kingdoms of the Savanna*, 52–53.

29. Thornton, "African Political Ethics and the Slave Trade."

30. Boahen, "The States and Cultures of the Lower Guinea Coast," 409.

31. Barry, "Senegambia from the Sixteenth to the Eighteenth Century."

32. Thornton, *Warfare in Atlantic Africa*, 4, 128.

33. M. A. Klein, "Senegambia."

34. For a vivid description of the first Portuguese raid for slaves in Senegambia by the chronicler Gomez Eannes de Azurara, see Conrad, *Children of Gold's Fire*, 5–11.

35. Lovejoy, *Transformations in Slavery*.

36. Akinjogbin, *Dahomey and Its Neighbours*, 18, 19.

37. Law, *Ouidah*, 50. Akinjogbin, *Dahomey and Its Neighbours*, 73–81, argues that Dahomey wanted to bring the Atlantic slave trade to an end. In *The Slave Coast of West Africa*, 300–308, Law contends that Dahomey was interested in protecting her own people but not other peoples from the Atlantic slave trade.

38. For the Dahomean conquest of the coast, see Akinjogbin, *Dahomey and Its Neighbours*, 64–100; Law, *The Slave Coast of West Africa*, 278–97.

39. Lovejoy, "Ethnic Designations of the Slave Trade," 27, citing Oliveira.

40. See the detailed discussion in chapter 2.

41. For the importance of rum during the eighteenth and early nineteenth centuries in Angola, see Miller, *Way of Death*, 466–67.

42. Niuelaut e P. Moortamer para o Conselho do Brasil, Maio de 1642, in Jadin, *L'Ancien Congo et l'Angola, 1639–1655*, 1:294.

43. Curto, *Alcool e escravos*. For a shortened English version dealing only with Luanda and its hinterland, see Curto, *Enslaving Spirits*.

44. Calculated from Eltis et al., *The Trans-Atlantic Slave Trade Database*.

45. Coughtry, *Rhode Island and the African Slave Trade*, 103–42.

46. Quoted in Brooks, *Eurafricans in Western Africa*, 307.

47. Inikori, "West Africa's Seaborne Trade"; communication from Joseph E. Inikori, 2003.

48. Portuando Zúñiga, *Entre esclavos y libres de Cuba colonial*, 44–57.

49. Costa e Silva, *A manilha e o libambo*, 816.

50. All these skills were found among African-born slaves in Louisiana. Hall, *Louisiana Slave Database*; Hall, *Louisiana Free Database*; Bowser, *The African Slave in Colonial Peru*, 125–46. For the skills Africans brought to early Brazil, see H. S. Klein, *African Slavery in Latin America and the Caribbean*, 42. For a discussion of African medical and herbal skills, see Galvin, "The Creation of a Creole Medicine Chest in Colonial South Carolina."

51. Cateau and Carrington, *Capitalism and Slavery Fifty Years Later*.

52. Inikori, *Africans and the Industrial Revolution in England*.

CHAPTER TWO

1. Moreno Fraginals, "Africa in Cuba."

2. Aguirre Beltrán, *La población negra de México*; Lockhart, *Spanish Peru*, 173. For a summary for the French West Indies, see Debien, "Les origines des esclaves des Antilles" and "Les origines des esclaves des Antilles (conclusion)."

3. Palmer, *Slaves of the White God.*

4. Niane, "Introduction"; Talbi, "The Spread of Civilization in the Maghrib and Its Impact on Western Civilization."

5. Blackburn, *The Making of New World Slavery*; Thomas, *The Slave Trade.*

6. Inikori, "Unmeasured Hazards of the Atlantic Slave Trade."

7. Curtin, *The Atlantic Slave Trade*, 268 (table 77); Inikori, "The Known, the Unknown, the Knowable and the Unknowable"; Inikori, "Africa in World History," 82; Thomas, *The Slave Trade*, 809, 862.

8. Barry, "Senegambia from the Sixteenth to the Eighteenth Century"; Moreno Fraginals, "Africa in Cuba"; Vila Vilar, "The Large-Scale Introduction of Africans into Veracruz and Cartagena."

9. Eltis et al., *The Trans-Atlantic Slave Trade Database.*

10. Eltis, *Rise of African Slavery in America*, 244–46; Law and Strickrodt, *Ports of the Slave Trade.*

11. Studer, *La trata de negros*; Garcia Florentino, *Em costas negras*, 23.

12. Barry, *La Sénégambie du XVe au XIXe siècle.*

13. Brooks, *Eurafricans in Western Africa*, 293–94.

14. Aguirre Beltrán, *La población negra de México*, 119.

15. Armah et al., "Slaves from the Windward Coast"; Debien, *Les esclaves aux Antilles françaises*, 45, 46, 67.

16. Geggus, "Sex Ratio, Age, and Ethnicity"; Vanony-Frisch, *Les esclaves de la Guadeloupe*, 32.

17. Higman, *Slave Populations of the British Caribbean.*

18. Brooks, *The Kru Mariners.*

19. Gomez, *Exchanging Our Country Marks*; Littlefield, *Rice and Slaves*; Chambers, *Jamaican Runaways.*

20. Reis, "Ethnic Politics among Africans in Nineteenth-Century Bahia."

21. Howard, *Changing History*, 27, 37, 39, 74.

22. For some exceptionally useful sacramental records with rich information about African ethnic designations, see Tardieu, "Origins of the Slaves in the Lima Region in Peru."

23. Soares, *Devotos da cor*, 80, 83–84.

24. Buhnen, "Ethnic Origins of Peruvian Slaves"; Brooks, *Eurafricans in Western Africa*, 167.

25. Soares, *Devotos da cor*, 78, 92–93, 201–30.

26. Lovejoy, "Ethnic Designations of the Slave Trade." For a careful, sophisticated discussion of the various meanings of racial and ethnic designations of slaves in Brazilian documents, see Karasch, *Slave Life in Rio de Janeiro*, 3–28.

27. Medeiros, "Moçambicanizaçao dos escravos saídos pelos portos de Moçambique"; Alpers, " 'Moçambiques' in Brazil."

28. *African Ethnonyms and Toponyms.* For a discussion of their recent study of recaptives in Sierra Leone and Havana, see Eltis and Nwokeji, "The Roots of the

African Diaspora," and "Characteristics of Captives Leaving the Cameroons for the Americas, 1822–1837."

29. Hall, *Louisiana Slave Database*. Recoded in the SPSS.sav file supplied in the CD publication and the website as the recoded field AFREQ.

30. Records of the Superior Council of Louisiana, 1738:04:11, 1743:09:09:06, Louisiana Historical Center, New Orleans; Original Acts Pointe Coupée Parish, December 6, 1802, New Roads, La. This information can also be found in the comments fields of the records under these dates and places in Hall, *Louisiana Slave Database*.

31. An inappropriate term used throughout Mullin, *Africa in America*.

32. For conflicts among children of co-wives, see Niane, *Sundiata*. For the Segu "Bambara" state, see Hall, *Africans in Colonial Louisiana*, 42–45. For West Central Africa, see Vansina, *Kingdoms of the Savanna*, 139–40; and Miller, *Kings and Kinsmen*, 128–73.

33. Costa e Silva, *A manilha e o libambo*, 153.

34. Calculated from Eltis et al., *The Trans-Atlantic Slave Trade Database*.

35. Geggus, "Sex Ratio, Age, and Ethnicity." For the Kongo identity of slaves described in South Carolina documents as "Angola," see Thornton, "African Dimensions of the Stono Rebellion." Calculated from Hall, *Louisiana Slave Database*.

36. Gomez, "African Identity and Slavery in America."

37. Calculated by Chambers from his *Jamaican Runaways*.

38. Harms, *River of Wealth, River of Sorrow*, 111–42.

39. Karasch, *Slave Life in Rio de Janeiro*.

40. Le Page du Pratz, *Histoire de la Louisiane*, 1:342–45.

41. Acosta Saignes, *Vida de los esclavos negros en Venezuela*, 152–53.

42. Inikori, "West Africa's Seaborne Trade."

43. Niane, "Introduction"; Niane, "Relationship and Exchanges among the Different Regions."

44. Rodney, *How Europe Underdeveloped Africa*.

45. Procédure criminelle contre la nommée Celeste de Jacob Beam et le nommé Urbin nègre (Criminal procedures against the named Celeste of Jacob Beam and the named black man Urbin), Original Acts Opelousas Post, March through June 1802, Louisiana State Archives, Baton Rouge.

46. Diouf, *Servants of Allah*, 60, 78, 87, 180.

47. Gomez, "African Identity and Slavery in America."

48. Mintz and Price, *An Anthropological Approach to the Afro-American Past*.

49. Palmié, "Ethnogenetic Processes and Cultural Transfer."

50. For relational databases published on CDs and websites and in publications using unpublished databases, see the database section of the bibliography.

51. Twelfth Report of the Secretary-General on the United Nations Organization Mission in the Democratic Republic of the Congo, October 18, 2002. The report blames multinational corporations from several countries, including the United States, for robbing billions of dollars of natural resources from this country while

provoking genocidal warfare there. Two and a half million lives were lost there over the past few years.

52. Diop, "A Methodology for the Study of Migrations."

53. Barry, *La Sénégambie du XVIème au XIXième siècle*, 35.

54. These records can be recoded easily and included among Africans of unknown ethnicities, or their ethnicities can be extrapolated from their names if the user of the *Louisiana Slave Database* so wishes; Philip D. Morgan, *Slave Counterpoint*, 454.

55. Communication from Dr. Ibrahima Seck, November 1999.

56. Hall, *Africans in Colonial Louisiana*, 359–61.

57. Communication from David Geggus.

CHAPTER THREE

1. For the first discussion of the wave pattern in transatlantic slave trade voyages, see Chambers, "Eboe, Kongo, Mandingo," 2, 5, 11, 13. For a discussion published several years later, see Eltis, Richardson, and Behrendt, "Patterns in the Transatlantic Slave Trade, 1662–1867." For a recently published study, see E. M. G. Harris, *The History of Human Populations*, 2:93–182, 305–408.

2. Debien, *Les esclaves aux Antilles françaises*, 59.

3. Higman, *Slave Populations of the British Caribbean*, 127.

4. Pierson, *Black Yankees*, cited in Gomez, *Exchanging Our Country Marks*, 26–27.

5. Costa e Silva, *A manilha e o libambo*. 318.

6. Ibid., 320–21; Brooks, *Eurafricans in Western Africa*, 292.

7. Menard and Schwartz, "Why African Slavery?".

8. For the early *lançados* in the Cape Verde Islands and Upper Guinea, see Costa e Silva, *A manilha e libambo*, 229–80. For a study of the Afro-Portuguese in Angola during later centuries, see Miller, *Way of Death*, 245–83.

9. Brooks, *Eurafricans in Western Africa*, 89–93; Costa e Silva, *A manilha e o libambo*, 244.

10. Heywood, "Portuguese into African."

11. Merlet, *Autour du Loango*, 9; Eltis, *The Rise of African Slavery in America*, 188.

12. Richardson, "Shipboard Revolts."

13. Costa e Silva, *A manilha e o libambo*, 153, 207–8, 269; Alvarez, *Ethiopia Minor*, cited in Brooks, *Eurafricans in Western Africa*, 75. For continued resistance to the slave trade in Upper Guinea, see Rashid, "'A Devotion to Liberty at Any Price,'" and Hawthorne, "Strategies of the Decentralized."

14. Oriji, "Igboland, Slavery, and the Drums of War," 129.

15. Elton and McLeod, "English Consuls at Mozambique during the 1850s and 1870s," cited in Alpers, *Ivory and Slaves*, 223–27.

16. For a collection of essays about resistance to slavery and the slave trade in Africa, see Diouf, *Fighting the Slave Trade*.

17. For the role of pawnship in credit, see Lovejoy and Richardson, " 'This Horrid Hole.' "

18. Florentino, *Em costas negra*, 240.

19. Verger, *Trade Relations between the Bight of Benin and Bahia*.

20. Brooks, *Landlords and Strangers*, 231–32.

21. Hall, *Africans in Colonial Louisiana*, 124.

22. R. K. Kent, "Madagascar and the Islands of the Indian Ocean." 864. A number of voyages from Madagascar to Virginia were omitted from *The Trans-Atlantic Slave Trade Database*. See Donnan, *Documents Illustrative of the History of the Slave Trade to America*, 4:183–85, 188–204.

23. Littlefield, *Rice and Slaves*.

24. For a good summary of the literature about the African origins of techniques of rice cultivation, including emphasis on Madagascar during the early stages of rice cultivation in America, see Gomez, *Exchanging our Country Marks*, 40–41. For a fine, detailed study of the transfer of African techniques of rice cultivation to America but which largely discounts Madagascar, see Carney, *Black Rice*. For an argument discounting the influence of African technology on rice cultivation in America, see Morgan, *Slave Counterpoint*, 182–83.

25. Estimated numbers and percentages of slaves landed would be smaller than in voyages coming from other African coasts. Voyages from Upper Guinea generally involved smaller ships bringing fewer Africans.

26. Costa e Silva, *A manilha e o libambo*, 816.

27. Portuando Zúñiga, *Entre esclavos y libres de Cuba colonial*, 44–57.

28. Records of the Superior Council of Louisiana, October 7, 1730, Document no. 1, Louisiana Historical Center, New Orleans. This slave had arrived on the *Duc de Noailles* on March 15, 1728.

29. Le Page du Pratz, *Histoire de la Louisiane*, 1:333–34.

30. Translated in Hall, *Social Control in Slave Plantation Societies*, 20–21.

31. Littlefield, *Rice and Slaves*, 115–73.

32. Palmer, *Human Cargoes*, 29, 97, 99 (table 9).

33. Eltis, *The Rise of African Slavery in America*, 224–57 (quote on 244).

34. Hall, "Myths about Creole Culture in Louisiana"; Hall, *Africans in Colonial Louisiana*, 58, 179, 180, 284; Walsh, "The Chesapeake Slave Trade."

35. Hall, "In Search of the Invisible Senegambians."

36. Records of the Superior Council of Louisiana, May 6 and May 10, 1768, contract between Evan Jones of Pensacola and Durand Brothers; declaration by Captain Peter Hill. Records of the Superior Council of Louisiana, 1768.05.10.02, Louisiana Historical Center, New Orleans.

37. LaChance, "Politics of Fear."

38. Papeles Procedentes de Cuba, December 31, 1786, Legajo 575, folio 89, Archivo Général de Indias, Seville, Spain.

39. Papeles Procedentes de Cuba, January 24, 1793, Comercio de negros, Legajo 101, folio 572, Archivo Général de Indias, Seville, Spain.

40. Calculated from Hall, *Louisiana Slave Database*.

41. LaChance, "Politics of Fear." Prohibition of the import of slaves to Louisiana was, indeed, enforced, as reflected in the growing mean ages and the evening-out of gender balances among slaves in Louisiana during the 1790s. Calculated from Hall, *Louisiana Slave Database*.

42. Calculated from Hall, *Louisiana Slave Database*, and Eltis et al., *The Trans-Atlantic Slave Trade Database*.

43. Lovejoy and Richardson, " 'This Horrid Hole.' "

CHAPTER FOUR

1. For an excellent discussion of the regional terminology used in the early Portuguese chronicles of voyages down the West African coast during the fifteenth century, see Soares, *Devotos da cor*, 37–62.

2. Thomas, *The Slave Trade*, 174.

3. Records of the Superior Council of Louisiana, April 24, 1737, contract between Jacques Coustillas and George Amelot, New Orleans, April 24, 1737, Louisiana Historical Center, New Orleans.

4. Rodney, *A History of the Upper Guinea Coast*. Hair, "Ethnolinguistic Continuity on the Guinea Coast," argues for the stability of ethnicities from early contact with Europeans to the present day. But he recognizes that his argument does not preclude cultural and linguistic interpenetration among these peoples. Barry, *Senegambia and the Atlantic Slave Trade*, discusses the peaceful interactions and interpenetrations among ethnicities in Greater Senegambia.

5. Buhnen, "Ethnic Origins of Peruvian Slaves."

6. Elbl, "The Volume of Early Atlantic Slave Trade."

7. Franco, *Negros, mulatos y la nación dominicana*, 5–61.

8. Brooks, *Landlords and Strangers*, 238–40.

9. Costa e Silva, *A manilha e o libambo*, 788–89.

10. Miller, *Way of Death*, 322, 493, 503, 574.

11. For the best recent summary of the African coastal origin of enslaved Africans brought to Spanish America between 1533 and 1580, see Castillo Mathieu, *Esclavos negros en Cartagena*, 23–38.

12. Vila Vilar, *Hispanoamérica y el comercio de esclavos*, 273–99.

13. Curtin, "Remarks"; Vila Vilar, "The Large-Scale Introduction of Africans into Veracruz and Cartagena."

14. Franco, *Negros, mulatos y la nación dominicana*, 5–61.

15. Quoted in Tardieu, "Origins of the Slaves in the Lima Region," 51–52.

16. Vila Vilar, *Hispanoamérica y el comercio de esclavos*.

17. Brooks, *Eurafricans in Western Africa*, 76.

18. Vila Vilar, *Hispanoamérica y el comercio de esclavos*, 122–3; Crespo, *Esclavos negros en Bolivia*, 36; Mellafe, *La introducción de la esclavitud negra en Chile*, 240–49.

19. Bowser, *The African Slave in Colonial Peru*, 37.

20. Vila Vilar, *Hispanoamérica y el comercio de esclavos*, 221–22.

21. Buhnen, "Ethnic Origins of Peruvian Slaves." For an excellent discussion of rice cultivation in Upper Guinea, see Rodney, *A History of the Upper Guinea Coast*, 20–22.

22. Sandoval, *De instauranda Aethiopum salute*, 110–11.

23. Boulègue, *Les luso-africains de Sénégambie*, 67–68; Costa e Silva, *A manilha e o libambo*, 243–44.

24. Brooks, *Eurafricans in Western Africa*, 108–9.

25. Creel, *"A Peculiar People"*; Walsh, "The Chesapeake Slave Trade."

26. Walsh, *From Calabar to Carter's Grove*, 55.

27. Pelletan, *Mémoire sur la colonie du Sénégal*, 93–94; Brooks, *Eurafricans in Western Africa*, 292.

28. Pelletan, *Mémoire sur la colonie du Sénégal*, 93–94.

29. Higman, *Slave Populations of the British Caribbean*, 442–58 (tables S3.1–3.6).

30. Vydrine, *Manding-English Dictionary*, 77–79. In his enlightening discussion of various interpretations of the Mande language group and mutual intelligibility among various ethnicities, Vydrine criticizes the prevailing "underestimation of closeness of Mande languages" (7–11). See also Bazin, "Guerre et servitude à Ségou."

31. Curtin, *Economic Change in Pre-colonial Africa*, 179.

32. Biloxi on the coast of the Gulf of Mexico and Balize at the mouth of the Mississippi River. Caron, " 'Of a Nation Which Others Do Not Understand.' "

33. For various peoples identified as "Bambara" in Senegal, see Hall, *Africans in Colonial Louisiana*, 42–44, 112, 288–89; for the French transatlantic slave trade to Louisiana, see ibid., 35 (fig. 2), 60 (table 2), 381–99.

34. Hall, *Africans in Colonial Louisiana*, 112; for the Spanish period, see 400–406. Subsequent studies of patterns of the Atlantic slave trade in Senegambia during the 1720s indicate that this figure was probably too low. See Searing, *West African Slavery and Atlantic Commerce*.

35. Lamiral, *L'Affrique et le peuple affriquain*, 184.

36. Records of the Superior Council of Louisiana: 1764.09.05.02, Confrontation between nègre Louis dit Foy and nègresse Comba; 1764.09.10.01, Interrogation under Torture of Louis dit Foy by Judge Foucault; 1764.09.04.01, Testimony of Comba, slave of the Capuchins.

37. Original Acts Avoyelles Parish, June 8, 1799, document no. 331, Avoyelles Parish, Marksville, La. Recorded in Hall, *Louisiana Slave Database*.

CHAPTER FIVE

1. Boahen, "The States and Cultures of the Lower Guinean Coast."

2. Wondji, "The States and Cultures of the Upper Guinea Coast," 377.

3. Boahen, "The States and Cultures of the Lower Guinean Coast," 401 (fig. 14.1).

4. Ryder, *Benin and the Europeans*, 2.

5. Costa e Silva, *A manilha e o libambo*, 344.

6. Law, *The Slave Coast*, 9.

7. Soares, *Devotos da cor*, 80.

8. David Northrup, "Igbo and Myth Igbo."

9. Vydrine, *Manding-English Dictionary*.

10. For a discussion of language use, mutual intelligibility, and designations of languages spoken on the Slave Coast, see Law, *The Slave Coast, 21–23*.

11. Soares, *Devotos da cor*, 78, 91–93, 201–30. "Mahi" was spelled "Maki" in Brazil.

12. Northrup, "Igbo and Myth Igbo."

13. Wax, "Preferences for Slaves in Colonial America."

14. Calculated from *The Trans-Atlantic Slave Trade Database*.

15. Michael A. Gomez has reported that among 14,167 enslaved persons found listed in documents in St. Domingue/Haiti in 1796 and 1797 by Gabriel Debien, 6,188 were Africans with ethnicity information recorded, some of whom could be divided into the following categories: Kongo (1,651), Nago (736), Arada (544), Igbo (519), "Bambara" (24), Hausa (124), "Senegals" (probably Wolof, 95), Susu (67), "Poulards" (26), Mandinka (26), "Malles" (3). Gomez, "African Identity and Slavery in America."

16. E. M. G. Harris, *The History of Human Populations*, 2:128.

17. For the state of denial about the substantial Kongo presence in Cuba, see Landers, "Central African Presence in Spanish Maroon Communities." For the Nago-Yoruba in Brazil, see Reis, "Ethnic Politics among Africans in Nineteenth-Century Bahia."

18. According to Law, those known today in Africa as being of Mina ethnicity are located near the mouth of the Mono River and are speakers of one of the Gbe languages, although they trace their ancestry to Akan-speaking boatmen who emigrated from the Gold Coast during the seventeenth century. See Law, *The Slave Coast*, 25–26.

19. Sandoval, *Un tratado sobre la esclavitud* (1627 ed.), 122–23, 139, 413; Sandoval, *Naturaleza* (1647 ed.), 29, 58–59.

20. Greene, "Cultural Zones in the Era of the Slave Trade."

21. Law, *The Slave Coast*, 228–29.

22. Costa e Silva, *A manilha e o libambo*, 808–10.

23. Law, *The Slave Coast*, 228; Oldendorp, *History of the Mission of the Evangelical Brethren*, 162–65.

24. Awoonor, *Guardians of the Sacred Word*, 13. I thank Ibrahima Seck for calling this citation to my attention. The *Rand McNally New Millennium World Atlas Deluxe*, a CD-ROM publication, lists Mina and Ewe as distinct ethnicities speaking different languages in Togo.

25. Verger, *Flux et reflux de la traite des nègres*, 7, 10. Robin Law believes, however, that the "Mina Coast" as understood in Brazil did, in fact, include parts of the Gold Coast as well as the Slave Coast; email from Robin Law, June 25, 2000.

26. Ortiz, *Los negros esclavos*, 53.

27. Ibid., 33, 35.

28. Howard, *Afro-Cuban Cabildos*, 27, 37, 39, 74.

29. Aguirre Beltrán, *La población negra de México*, 124.

30. Ibid., 127. Curtin, *Atlantic Slave Trade*, 185–86, 208–9; email from Robin Law, August 4, 2004.

31. Rodrigues, *Os Africanos no Brasil*, 41–42. Oldendorp, *History of the Mission of the Evangelical Brethren*, 162–65.

32. Gutiérrez Azopardo, *Historia del negro en Colombia*, 18. This historian interprets Mina as Africans from the Gold Coast coming through the San Jorge de Mina post.

33. Díaz López. *Oro, sociedad y economia*, 194–95.

34. Castillo Mathieu, *Esclavos negros en Cartagena*, 110. The author of this book describes the Mina as Akan speakers coming from the Gold Coast.

35. Arrazola, *Palenque*, 194–95; Landers, "Cimarron Ethnicity and Cultural Adaptation in the Spanish Domains," 38–42.

36. Blanco, *Los negros y la esclavitud*, 165–68.

37. For a full discussion of both of these conspiracies, see Hall, *Africans in Colonial Louisiana*, 316–74.

38. For various currencies used, formulas for conversion to common denominator prices, and tables showing mean prices by ethnicity and gender over time, see the appendix.

39. Calculated from Hall, *Louisiana Slave Database*.

40. Howard, *Changing History*, 27, 37, 39, 74; the excerpt from this document is translated by Howard on p. 27.

41. Acosta Saignes, *Vida de los esclavos negros en Venezuela*, 152–53.

42. Law, *The Slave Coast*, 189.

43. Hair, "An Ethnolinguistic Inventory of the Lower Guinea Coast," 230.

44. Peixoto, *Obra nova de lingua geral de Mina*; Yai, "Texts of Enslavement."

45. *The Trans-Atlantic Slave Trade Database*.

46. Eltis, Lovejoy, and Richardson, "Slave Trading Ports."

47. Postma, *The Dutch in the Atlantic Slave Trade*, 78–83, 149, 297, 355–61, and 373–76.

48. Boxer, *The Golden Age of Brazil*, 165.

49. Verger, *Flux et reflux de la traite des nègres*, 7, 10; Pereira, *A Casa das Minas*.

50. Boxer, *Golden Age of Brazil*, 175–76.

51. Manning, *Slavery, Colonialism, and Economic Growth In Dahomey*, 30, 31. For an interpretation emphasizing inland rather than coastal populations, see Inikori, "Sources of Supply for the Atlantic Slave Exports."

CHAPTER SIX

1. Afigbo, *Ropes of Sand*, 1–30, 77–79.

2. Alagoa, "Fon and Yoruba," 447–48.

3. Dike, *Trade and Politics in the Niger Delta*, 38, quoting Adams, *Sketches Taken during Ten Years Voyages to Africa between the Years 1786 and 1800*.

4. Dike, *Trade and Politics in the Niger Delta*, 30.

5. For example, see Hall, "African Women in Colonial Louisiana."

6. Dike, *Trade and Politics in the Niger Delta*, 19–46; Lovejoy, *Transformations in Slavery*, 59–60.

7. Dike and Ekejiuba, *The Aro of South-eastern Nigeria*, 326–27.

8. Inikori, "The Development of Entrepreneurship in Africa," 78 n. 44.

9. Brown, "From the Tongues of Africa," 49–50.

10. Austen and Derrick, *Middlemen of the Cameroons Rivers*, 5–47.

11. Northrup, "Igbo and Myth Igbo."

12. Inikori, "Sources of Supply for the Atlantic Slave Exports."

13. Lovejoy and Richardson, " 'This Horrid Hole.' "

14. Dike, *Trade and Politics in the Niger Delta*, 46.

15. Brown, "From the Tongues of Africa," 49–50.

16. Statistics are from the database constructed and used for Bergad, Iglesias García, and Barcia, *The Cuban Slave Market*. I am grateful to Fé Iglesias for giving me a copy of this database.

17. Calculated from Geggus, "Sex Ratio, Age, and Ethnicity."

18. Koelle, *Polyglotta Africana*, 7–8.

19. Northrup, *Africa's Discovery of Europe*, 131.

20. This documentation can be found in the original 1627 and 1647 editions of the Sandoval book and the facsimile publication of the 1627 edition.

21. Dike, *Trade and Politics in Nigeria*, 19–46.

22. Northrup, *Trade without Rulers*, 79–80.

23. Niane, "Relationships and Exchanges."

24. Gomez, *Exchanging Our Country Marks*; Walsh, *From Calabar to Carter's Grove*; Chambers, " 'My Own Nation' "; Chambers, "The Significance of Igbo in the Bight of Biafra Slave Trade."

25. Communication from David Geggus, September 2002.

26. Curtin, *The Atlantic Slave Trade*, 245 (table 71).

27. For a review of the literature citing negative perceptions about the Igbo, see Gomez, "A Quality of Anguish: The Igbo Response to Enslavement in America." Walsh, *From Calabar to Carter's Grove*, 79–80.

28. Palmer, *Human Cargoes*, 29.

29. Mullin, *Africa in America*, 26.

30. Littlefield, *Rice and Slaves*, 20, 26, 72–73.

31. Original Acts Pointe Coupée Parish, May, 1787, document no. 1571, vente d'esclave, Monsanto à LeDoux, New Roads, La.

32. Hall, "In Search of the Invisible Senegambians."

33. Ira Berlin, *Many Thousands Gone*. For a much earlier application of this methodology to slavery in America, see Hall, *Social Control in Slave Plantation Societies*.

34. Mullin, *Africa in America*, 23.

35. Dike, *Trade and Politics in Nigeria*, 45–46.

CHAPTER SEVEN

1. Heywood, *Central Africans and Cultural Transformations in the American Diaspora*, 1–20.

2. J. E. Harris, *Global Dimensions of the African Diaspora*.

3. Inikori, "Slavery in Africa and the Trans-Atlantic Slave Trade." Ngou-Mve, *El Africa bantú en la colonización en México*; Thornton, *The Kingdom of Kongo*, 22.

4. Vansina, *Paths in the Rainforests*, 200–201.

5. Costa e Silva, *A manilha e o libambo*, 369.

6. Miller, "Lineages, Ideology, and the History of Slavery in Western Central Africa," 41.

7. Thornton, *The Kingdom of Kongo*. 74–96; Thornton, "African Political Ethics and the Slave Trade."

8. Ngou-Mve, *El Africa bantú en la colonización de México*, 62–65.

9. Thornton, *Africa and Africans in the Making of the Atlantic World*, 110.

10. Miller, "Central Africa during the Era of the Slave Trade," 64–69.

11. Vansina, *Kingdoms of the Savanna*, 129–33.

12. For patterns over time and place, see Thornton, "Religious and Ceremonial Life in the Kongo and Mbundu Area," and Heywood, "Portuguese into African." For a discussion of the brief and frustrating career of Christian missionaries on the Loango Coast, see Martin, *The External Trade of the Loango Coast*, 48.

13. Martin, *The External Trade of the Loango Coast*, 56, 79, 80, 118.

14. Miller, *Way of Death*.

15. Richardson, "Shipboard Revolts."

16. Vansina, foreword to *Central Africa and Cultural Formations*, xi, xv; Vansina, *Paths in the Rainforests*.

17. Vansina, *Kingdoms of the Savanna*, 139–40.

18. Thornton, *The Kingdom of Kongo*, 6–15.

19. Vansina, *Kingdoms of the Savanna*, 37–69; Ngou-Mve, *El Africa bantú en la colonización de México*, 58, 59.

20. Alpers, *Ivory and Slaves*, 209.

21. Elton and McLeod, "English Consuls at Mozambique during the 1850s and 1870s," cited in Alpers, *Ivory and Slaves*, 223–27.

22. Ngou-Mve, *El Africa bantú en la colonización de México*.

23. Cáceres Gómez, *Negros, mulatos, esclavos y libertos*.

24. Duncan and Meléndez, *El negro en Costa Rica*, 19; Portuando Zúñiga, *Entre esclavos y libres de Cuba colonial*, 44–57.

25. Vila Vilar, *Hispanoamérica y el comercio de esclavos*, 122–23; Crespo R., *Esclavos negros en Bolivia*, 36.

26. Hilton, *The Kingdom of Kongo*, 148, 169. For a detailed chronology of West Central Africa from the thirteenth century through 1887, see Merlet, *Autour du Loango*, 133–53.

27. For the most recent, best informed discussion of the coastal origin of enslaved

Africans brought to the United States, including to Louisiana, see Gomez, *Exchanging our Country Marks*, 28, 29 (tables 2.6, 2.7).

28. Calculated from Hall, *Louisiana Slave Database*.

29. Daget, "The Abolition of the Slave Trade," 67.

30. Dumont, *Être patriotique sous les tropiques*.

31. Taylor, "The Foreign Slave Trade in Louisiana after 1808"; Hendrix, "The Efforts to Reopen the African Slave Trade in Louisiana."

32. For the Caribbean, see Schuler, *Alas, Alas Kongo*.

CONCLUSION

1. Reis, "Ethnic Politics among Africans in Nineteenth-Century Bahia."

2. Individual biographies are coming to the fore, some of them supported by the work of the Harriet Tubman Resource Centre directed by Paul E. Lovejoy at York University in Toronto, Canada. For a fine recent study, see Law and Lovejoy, *The Biography of Mahommah Gardo Baquaqua*. For a good summary of accounts by other enslaved Africans, see Northrup, *Africa's Discovery of Europe*, 107–15.

3. A questionable methodology used in Northrup, *Africa's Discovery of Europe*, 122–35.

4. Northrup, "Igbo and Myth Igbo," 9.

5. Eltis and Nwokeji, "The Roots of the African Diaspora."

6. Geggus, "Sugar and Coffee Cultivation."

7. For an enlightening discussion of the ethnic denomination Kongo and of other West Central Africans in the French West Indies, including the Mondongue, see Debien, *Les esclaves aux Antilles françaises*, 41, 49–52.

8. Bastide, *Les Amériques noires*.

9. Geggus, "The French Slave Trade"; Laguerre, *Voudou and Politics in Haiti*.

10. Vanhee, "Central African Popular Christianity."

11. Reis, "Ethnic Politics among Africans in Nineteenth-Century Bahia."

12. Sandoval, *De instauranda Aethiopum salute*, 91, 335.

13. Brooks, *Eurafricans in Western Africa*, 228.

14. For a synopsis of recently studied lists of slaves in Brazil giving African ethnic designations, see Lovejoy, "Ethnic Designations of the Slave Trade," 26–29 (tables 1.5–1.8).

APPENDIX

1. Hall, *Louisiana Slave Database*. For details, see the entry in the bibliography under "Published Databases."

2. Parsons Collection, September 14, 1735, Edict of Louis XV, 3D102, mislabeled, University of Texas Library, Austin.

3. Records of the Superior Council of Louisiana, 1741:11:23:01, Louisiana Historical Center, New Orleans.

4. Hurson to the Ministry of the Colonies, September, 1752, in Collection Moreau de St.-Méry, Ser. F3 90, fols. 70–71, Archives d'Outre-Mer, Aix-en-Provence, France.

5. Records of the Superior Council of Louisiana, various documents showing comparable prices: 1767.03.27.01, 1767.04.02.01, 1767.09.14.02, 1767.08.22.02, 1767.01.22.01, 1767.02.09.01, 1768.05.18.03, 1769.01.18.03, 1769.05.01.08, 1769.07.15.01, Louisiana Historical Center, New Orleans.

6. Ibid., 1767.07.07.04.

7. Ibid., 1767.02.04.01.

Bibliography

MANUSCRIPT COLLECTIONS

Aix-en-Provence, France
   Archives d'Outre Mer
   Collection Moreau de St.-Méry, Ser. F3
Austin, Texas
   University of Texas Library
   Parsons Collection
Baton Rouge, Louisiana
   Louisiana State Archives
   Original Acts Opelousas Post
Marksville, Louisiana
   Original Acts Avoyelles Parish
New Orleans, Louisiana
   Louisiana Historical Center
   Louisiana State Museum
   Records of the Superior Council of Louisiana
      The first four digits represent the year; the next two digits represent the month;
      the next two digits represent the day; and the last two digits represent the
      document number for that date. Thus 1767.03.27.01 represents March 27, 1767,
      document no. 1.

New Roads, Louisiana
   Original Acts Pointe Coupée Parish
Seville, Spain
   Archivo Général de Indias
   Papeles Procedentes de Cuba
   Comercio de negros, Legajo 101, folio 572
   Correspondencia de la Intendencia con la Aduana, 1786–87, Legajo 575, folio 89.

PUBLISHED DATABASES

Eltis, David, David Richardson, Stephen D. Behrendt, and Herbert S. Klein,
   eds. *The Trans-Atlantic Slave Trade: A Database on CD-ROM*. Cambridge:

Cambridge University Press, 1999. (Cited in the notes as Eltis et al., *The Trans-Atlantic Slave Trade Database*.)

Hall, Gwendolyn Midlo. *Louisiana Slave Database, 1719–1820*. In *Databases for the Study of Afro-Louisiana History and Genealogy, 1719–1860: Computerized Information from Original Manuscript Sources: A Compact Disk Publication*, edited by Gwendolyn Midlo Hall. Baton Rouge: Louisiana State University Press, 2000.

WEB DATABASES WITH SEARCH ENGINES

Hall, Gwendolyn Midlo. *Louisiana Slave Database, 1719–1820*. Available with a search engine for the most important fields at <www.ibiblio.org/laslave>. Available with a search engine at <www.ancestry.com>.

———. *Louisiana Free Database, 1719–1820*. Available with a search engine at <www.ancestry.com>.

Both of the Hall databases that are on the Web can be downloaded free of charge in several different software packages from <www.ibiblio.org/laslave>.

DATABASE IN PRESS

Chambers, Douglas B. *Jamaican Runaways: A Compilation of Fugitive Slaves, 1718–1817*. CD-ROM. Madison: African Studies Program Publication Series, University of Wisconsin, forthcoming.

PUBLISHED WORKS CONSTRUCTED FROM UNPUBLISHED DATABASES

Bergad, Laird W., Fé Iglesias García, and María del Carmen Barcia. *The Cuban Slave Market, 1790–1880*. Cambridge: Cambridge University Press, 1995.

Florentino, Manolo Garcia. *Em costas negras: Uma história do tráfico atlântico de escravos entre a Africa e o Río de Janeiro, séculos XVIII e XIX*. São Paulo: Companhia das Letras, 1997.

Florentino, Manolo Garcia, and José Roberto Góes. *A paz das senzalas: Familias escravas e tráfico atlântico*. Rio de Janeiro: Civilização Brasileira, 1997.

Vanony-Frisch, Nicole. "Les esclaves de la Guadeloupe à la fin de l'ancien régime." *Bulletin de la Société d'Histoire de la Guadeloupe*, nos. 63–64 (1985).

BOOKS, CHAPTERS, AND ARTICLES CITED

Acosta Saignes, Miguel. *Vida de los esclavos negros en Venezuela*. Valencia, Venezuela: Vadell Hermanos, Editores, 1984.

Adams, Captain John. *Sketches Taken during Ten Voyages to Africa between the Years 1786 and 1800*. London: 1822, 38. Cited in Dike, *Trade and Politics in the Niger Delta*, 29.

Afigbo, A. E. *Ropes of Sand: Studies in Igbo History and Culture*. Oxford: Oxford University Press, 1981.

African Ethnonyms and Toponyms: Report and Papers of the Meeting of Experts Organized by Unesco in Paris, 3–7 July, 1978. Paris: UNESCO, 1984.

Aguirre Beltrán, Gonzalo. *La población negra de México*. Rev. ed. Mexico, D.F.: Fondo de Cultura México, 1972.

Akinjogbin, I. A. *Dahomey and Its Neighbours, 1708–1818*. Cambridge: Cambridge University Press, 1967.

Alagoa, E. J. "Fon and Yoruba: The Niger Delta and the Cameroon." In *UNESCO General History of Africa*, vol. 5: *Africa from the Sixteenth to the Eighteenth Century*, edited by B. A. Ogot, 434–52. Berkeley: University of California Press, 1992.

Alpers, Edward A. *Ivory and Slaves: Changing Patterns of International Trade in East Central Africa to the Later Nineteenth Century*. Berkeley: University of California Press, 1975.

———. " 'Moçambiques' in Brazil: Another Dimension of the African Diaspora in the Atlantic World." Paper presented at the conference Enslaving Connections: Africa and Brazil during the Era of the Slave Trade, York University, October 12–15, 2000. To be published in *Africa and America: Interconnections during the Slave Trade*, edited by José C. Curto and Renée Soulodre-LaFrance.

Alvarez, Manuel. *Ethiopia Minor and a Geographical Account of the Province of Sierra Leone (c. 1615)*. Translated and edited by P. E. H. Hair. Liverpool: Department of History, University of Liverpool, 1990. Cited in Brooks, *Eurafricans in Western Africa*, 75.

Armah, Ayi Kwei, Adam Jones, and Marion Johnson. "Slaves from the Windward Coast," *Journal of African History* 21 (1980): 17–34.

Arrazola, Roberto. *Palenque: primer pueblo libre de América*. Cartagena, Colombia: Ediciones Hernandez, 1970.

Austen, Ralph A. "The Trans-Saharan Slave Trade: A Tentative Census." In *The Uncommon Market: Essays in the Economic History of the Atlantic Slave Trade*, edited by Henry A. Gemery and Jan S. Hogendorn, 23–76. New York: Academic Press, 1979.

Austen, Ralph A., and Jonathan Derrick. *Middlemen of the Cameroons Rivers: The Duala and their Hinterlands c. 1600–c. 1960*. Cambridge: Cambridge University Press, 1999.

Awoonor, K. *Guardians of the Sacred Word: Ewe Poetry*. New York: Nok Publishers, 1974.

Bastide, Roger. *Les Amériques noires: Les civilisations africaines dans le Nouveau Monde*. Paris: Payot, 1967.

Barry, Boubacar. *La Sénégambie du XVe au XIXe siècle: Traite negrière, Islam et conquête coloniale*. Paris: L'Harmattan, 1988.

———. *Senegambia and the Atlantic Slave Trade*. Translated by Ayi Kwei Armah. Cambridge: Cambridge University Press, 1998.

———. "Senegambia from the Sixteenth to the Eighteenth Century: Evolution of the Wolof, Sereer and 'Tukuloor.' " In *UNESCO General History of Africa*, vol. 5: *Africa from the Sixteenth to the Eighteenth Century*, edited by B. A. Ogot, 262–99. Berkeley: University of California Press, 1992.

Bazin, Jacques. "Guerre et servitude à Ségou." In *L'Esclavage en Afrique précolo-niale*, edited by Claude Meillassoux, 135–81. Paris: Maspero, 1975.

Bergad, Laird W., Fé Iglesias García, and María del Carmen Barcia. *The Cuban Slave Market, 1790–1880.* Cambridge: Cambridge University Press, 1995.

Berlin, Ira. *Many Thousands Gone: The First Two Centuries of Slavery in North America.* Cambridge, Mass.: Harvard University Press, 1998.

Blackburn, Robin. *The Making of New World Slavery: From the Baroque to the Modern, 1492–1800.* London: Verso, 1997.

Blanco, Larranzabal. *Los negros y la esclavitud.* Santo Domingo, Dominican Republic: Julio D. Postigo e hijos, 1975.

Boahen, A. A. "The States and Cultures of the Lower Guinean Coast." In *UNESCO General History of Africa*, vol. 5: *Africa from the Sixteenth to the Eighteenth Century*, edited by B. A. Ogot, 399–433. Berkeley: University of California Press, 1992.

Boogaart, Ernst van den, and Peter Emmer, "The Dutch Participation in he Atlantic Slave Trade, 1596–1650." In *The Uncommon Market: Essays in the Economic History of the Atlantic Slave Trade*, edited by Henry A. Gemery and Jan S. Hogendorn, 353–76. New York: Academic Press, 1979.

Boulègue, Jean. *Les luso-africains de Sénégambie.* Paris: Université de Paris I, Centre de recherches africaines, 1989.

Bowser, Frederick P. *The African Slave in Colonial Peru, 1524–1650.* Stanford: Stanford University Press, 1974.

Boxer, C. R. *The Golden Age of Brazil, 1695–1750.* Berkeley: University of California Press, 1962.

Brooks, George E. *Eurafricans in Western Africa: Commerce, Social Status, Gender, and Religious Observance from the Sixteenth to the Eighteenth Century.* Athens, Ohio: Ohio University Press, 2003.

———. *The Kru Mariners in the Nineteenth Century: An Historical Compendium.* Newark, Del.: Liberian Studies Association in America, 1972.

———. *Landlords and Strangers; Ecology, Society, and Trade in Western Africa, 1000–1630.* Boulder, Colo.: Westview Press, 1993.

Brown, Soi-Daniel W. "From the Tongues of Africa: A Partial Translation of Oldendorp's Interviews." *Plantation Society in the Americas* 2, no. 1 (1983): 37–61.

Buhnen, Stephan. "Ethnic Origins of Peruvian Slaves (1548–1650): Figures for Upper Guinea," *Paideuma* 39 (1993): 57–110.

Cáceres Gómez, Rina. *Negros, mulatos, esclavos y libertos en la Costa Rica del siglo XVII.* México, D.F.: Instituto Panamericano de Geografía e Historia, 2000.

Carney, Judith A. *Black Rice: The African Origin of Rice Cultivation in America.* Cambridge, Mass.: Harvard University Press, 2001.

Caron, Peter. " 'Of a Nation Which Others Do Not Understand': Bambara Slaves and African Ethnicity in Colonial Louisiana, 1718–60." *Slavery and Abolition* 18 (1997): 98–121.

Castillo Mathieu, Nicolás del. *Esclavos negros en Cartagena y sus aportes léxicos.* Bogotá: Instituto Caro y Cuervo, 1982.

Cateau, Heather, and S. H. H. Carrington, eds. *Capitalism and Slavery Fifty Years Later: Eric Eustace Williams—A Reassessment of the Man and His Work.* New York: Peter Lang, 2000.

Chambers, Douglas B. "Eboe, Kongo, Mandingo: African Ethnic Groups and the Development of Regional Slave Societies in Mainland North America, 1700–1820." Working Paper no. 96–14, International Seminar on the History of the Atlantic World, 1500–1800, Harvard University, September 1996.

———. " 'My Own Nation': Igbo Exiles in the Diaspora." *Slavery and Abolition* 18, 1 (1997): 72–97.

———. "The Significance of Igbo in the Bight of Biafra Slave Trade: A Rejoinder to Northrup's 'Myth Igbo.' " *Slavery and Abolition* 23, 1 (2002): 101–20.

Codera y Zaidín, Francisco. *Decadencia y desaparición de los Almoravids en España.* Zaragoza: Tip. de Comas hermanos, 1899.

Conrad, Robert Edgar. *Children of Gold's Fire.* Princeton: Princeton University Press, 1984.

Costa e Silva, Alberto da. *A manilha e o libambo: A Africa e a escravidão, de 1500 a 1700.* Rio de Janeiro: Editora Nova Fronteira, 2002.

Coughtry, Jay. *Rhode Island and the African Slave Trade.* Philadelphia: Temple University Press, 1981.

Creel, Margaret Washington. *"A Peculiar People": Slave Religion and Community-Culture among the Gullahs.* New York: New York University Press, 1988.

Crespo R., Alberto. *Esclavos negros en Bolivia.* La Paz: Academia Nacional de Ciencias de Bolivia, 1977.

Curtin, Philip D. *The Atlantic Slave Trade: A Census.* Madison: University of Wisconsin Press, 1969.

———. *Economic Change in Pre-colonial Africa: Senegambia in the Era of the Slave Trade.* Madison: University of Wisconsin Press, 1975.

———. "Remarks." In *Comparative Perspectives on Slavery in New World Plantation Societies,* edited by Vera Rubin and Arthur Tuden, 202–4. New York: New York Academy of Sciences, 1977.

Curto, José C. *Alcool e escravos: O comércio luso-brasileiro do álcool em Mpinda, Luanda e Benguela durante o tráfico atlântico de escravos (c. 1480–1830) e o seu impacto nas sociedades da Africa Central Ocidental.* Lisbon: Editora Vulgata, 2002.

———. *Enslaving Spirits: The Portuguese-Brazilian Alcohol Trade at Luanda and Its Hinterland, c. 1550–1830.* Leiden: Brill Academic Publishers, 2003.

Daget, Serge. "The Abolition of the Slave Trade." In *UNESCO General History of Africa,* vol. 6: *Africa in the Nineteenth Century until the 1880s,* edited by J. F. A. Ajayi, 64–89. Berkeley: University of California Press, 1989.

Davis, David Brion. "Looking at Slavery from Broader Perspectives." *American Historical Review* 105, no. 2 (April 2000): 452–66.

Debien, Gabriel. *Les esclaves aux Antilles françaises (XVIIe–XVIIIe siècles)*. Basse-Terre and Fort-de-France: Société d'Histoire de la Guadeloupe et de la Martinique, 1974.

————. "Les origines des esclaves des Antilles." *Bulletin de IFAN*, ser. B, 23, nos. 3–4 (1961): 363–87.

————. "Les origines des esclaves des Antilles (conclusion)." *Bulletin de IFAN*, ser. B, 29, nos. 3–4 (1967): 536–58.

Díaz López, Zamira. *Oro, sociedad y economia: El sistema colonial en la Gobernación de Popayán: 1533–1733*. Bogotá: Banco de la República, 1994.

Dike, Kenneth Onwuka. *Trade and Politics in the Niger Delta, 1830–1885: An Introduction to the Economic and Political History of Nigeria*. Oxford: Clarendon Press, 1956.

Dike, Kenneth Onwuka, and Felicia Ekejiuba. *The Aro of South-eastern Nigeria, 1650–1980*. Ibadan: University Press Limited, 1990.

Diop, Cheikh Anta. "A Methodology for the Study of Migrations." In *African Ethnonyms and Toponyms*, 86–109.

Diouf, Sylviane. *Servants of Allah: African Muslims Enslaved in America*. New York: New York University Press, 1998.

————, ed. *Fighting the Slave Trade: West African Strategies*. Athens, Ohio: Ohio University Press, 2003.

Donnan, Elizabeth, ed. *Documents Illustrative of the History of the Slave Trade to America*. 4 vols. Washington, D.C.: Carnegie Institution of Washington, 1930–35.

Dozy, Reinhart. *Spanish Islam*. Translated by Francis Griffin Stokes. London: Frank Cass, 1972.

Du Bois, W. E. B. *The Negro*. 1915. Reprint, Philadelphia: University of Pennsylvania Press, 2001.

Dumont, Anne Pérotin. *Être patriotique sous les tropiques: La Guadeloupe, la colonisation et la Révolution, 1789–1794*. Basse-Terre: Société d'histoire de la Guadeloupe, 1985.

Duncan, Quince, and Carlos Meléndez. *El negro en Costa Rica*. San José: Editorial Costa Rica, 1981.

Elbl, Ivana. "The Volume of the Early Atlantic Slave Trade, 1450–1521." *Journal of African History* 38 (1997): 31–75.

Eltis, David. "Europeans and the Rise and Fall of African Slavery in America: An Interpretation." *American Historical Review* 98, no. 5 (1993): 1399–1423.

————. *The Rise of African Slavery in America*. Cambridge: Cambridge University Press, 2000.

Eltis, David, Paul E. Lovejoy, and David Richardson. "Slave Trading Ports: Towards an Atlantic-Wide Perspective." In *Ports of the Slave Trade (Bights of Benin and Biafra)*, edited by Law and Strickrodt, 12–34.

Eltis, David, and G. Ugo Nwokeji. "Characteristics of Captives Leaving the Cameroons for the Americas, 1822–1837." *Journal of African History* 43 (2002): 191–210.

————. "The Roots of the African Diaspora: Methodological Considerations in the Analysis of Names in the Liberated African Registers of Sierra Leone and Havana." *History in Africa* 29 (2002): 365–79.

Eltis, David, David Richardson, and Stephen D. Behrendt. "Patterns in the Transatlantic Slave Trade, 1662–1867: New Indications of African Origins of Slaves Arriving in the Americas." In *Black Imagination and the Middle Passage*, edited by Maria Diedrich, Henry Louis Gates Jr., and Carl Pedersen, 21–32. New York: Oxford University Press, 1999.

Elton, Frederic, and Lyons McLeod. "English Consuls at Mozambique during the 1850s and 1870s." Cited in Alpers, *Ivory and Slaves*, 223–27.

Finkelman, Paul, and Joseph C. Miller, eds. *Macmillan Encyclopedia of World Slavery*. 2 vols. New York: Simon and Schuster, 1998.

Fletcher, Richard. *Moorish Spain*. Berkeley: University of California Press, 1993.

Florentino, Manolo Garcia. *Em costas negras: Uma história do tráfico atlântico de escravos entre a Africa e o Río de Janeiro, séculos XVIII e XIX*. São Paulo: Companhia das Letras, 1997.

Florentino, Manolo Garcia, and José Roberto Góes. *A paz das senzalas: Familias escravas e tráfico atlântico*. Rio de Janeiro: Civilização Brasileira, 1997.

Franco, Franklin J. *Negros, mulatos y la nación dominicana*. Santo Domingo: Editora Nacional, 1969.

Galvin, Mary L. "The Creation of a Creole Medicine Chest in Colonial South Carolina." In *Creolization in the Americas*, edited by David Buisseret and Steven G. Reinhardt, 63–98. College Station: Texas A&M University Press, 2000.

Geggus, David. "The French Slave Trade: An Overview." *William and Mary Quarterly*, 3rd ser., 58, no. 1 (January 2001): 119–38.

————. "Sex Ratio, Age, and Ethnicity in the Atlantic Slave Trade: Data from French Shipping and Plantation Records." *Journal of African History* 30 (1989): 23–44.

————. "Sugar and Coffee Cultivation in St. Domingue and the Shaping of the Slave Labor Force." In *Cultivation and Culture; Work Process and the Shaping of Afro-American Culture in the Americas*, edited by Ira Berlin and Philip Morgan, 73–98. Charlottesville: University of Virginia Press, 1993.

Gomez, Michael A. "African Identity and Slavery in America." *Radical History Review* 75 (1999): 111–20.

————. *Exchanging Our Country Marks: Transformation of Identities in the Colonial and Antebellum South*. Chapel Hill: University of North Carolina Press, 1998.

————. "Medieval Western Sudan." In *Macmillan Encyclopedia of World Slavery*, edited by Finkelman and Miller, 2:942–44.

————. "A Quality of Anguish: The Igbo Response to Enslavement in America." In *Trans-Atlantic Dimensions of Ethnicity in the American Diaspora*, edited by Paul Lovejoy and David Trotman, 82–95. London: Continuum Press, 2003.

Greene, Sandra E. "Cultural Zones in the Era of the Slave Trade: Exploring the Yoruba Connection with the Anlo-Ewe." In *Identity in the Shadow of Slavery*, edited by Paul E. Lovejoy, 86–101. London: Continuum, 2000.

Gutiérrez Azopardo, Ildefonso. *Historia del negro en Colombia: Sumisión o rebeldía?* Bogotá: Editorial Nueva América, 1980.

Hair, P. E. H. "Ethnolinguistic Continuity on the Guinea Coast." *Journal of African History* 8, no. 2 (1967): 247–68.

Hall, Gwendolyn Midlo. *Africans in Colonial Louisiana: The Development of Afro-Creole Culture in the Eighteenth Century*. Baton Rouge: Louisiana State University Press, 1992.

————. "African Women in Colonial Louisiana." In *The Devil's Lane: Sex and Race in the Early South*, edited by Catherine Clinton and Michele Gillespie, 247–62. New York: Oxford University Press, 1997.

————. "In Search of the Invisible Senegambians: the Louisiana Slave Database (1723–1820)." In *Saint-Louis et l'esclavage, Actes du symposium international sur la traite négrière à Saint-Louis du Sénégal et dans son arrière-pays* (Saint-Louis, 18, 19 et 20 décembre 1998), edited by Djibril Samb, 237–64. Dakar: Institut Fondamental d'Afrique Noir [IFAN], 2001.

————. "Myths about Creole Culture in Louisiana: Slaves, Africans, Blacks, Mixed Bloods, and Caribbeans." *Cultural Vistas* 12, no. 2 (Summer 2001): 78–89.

————. *Social Control in Slave Plantation Societies: A Comparison of St. Domingue and Cuba*. Baltimore: Johns Hopkins Press, 1971.

Hanger, Kimberly S. *Bounded Lives, Bounded Places: Free Black Society in New Orleans, 1769–1803*. Durham, N.C.: Duke University Press, 1997.

Harms, Robert W. *River of Wealth, River of Sorrow: The Central Zaire Basin in the Era of the Slave and Ivory Trade, 1500–1891*. New Haven: Yale University Press, 1981.

Harris, E. M. G. *The History of Human Populations: Migration, Urbanization, and Structural Change*. 2 vols. Westport, Conn.: Praeger, 2003.

Harris, Joseph E. *Global Dimensions of the African Diaspora*. Washington, D.C.: Howard University Press, 1982.

————. "The Dynamics of the Global African Diaspora." In *The African Diaspora*, edited by Alusine Jalloh and Stephen E. Maizlish, 7–21. College Station: Texas A & M University Press, 1996.

Hawthorne, Walter. "Strategies of the Decentralized: Defending Communities from Slave Raiders in Coastal Guinea-Bissau, 1450–1815." In *Fighting the Slave Trade: West African Strategies*, edited by Sylviane A. Diouf, 132–69. Athens, Ohio: Ohio University Press, 2003.

Helg, Aline. *Our Rightful Share: The Afro-Cuban Struggle for Equality, 1886–1912*. Chapel Hill: University of North Carolina Press, 1995.

Hendrix, James Paisley, Jr. "The Efforts to Reopen the African Slave Trade in Louisiana." *Louisiana History* 10 (1969): 97–123.

Heywood, Linda M. "Portuguese into African: The Eighteenth-Century Central

African Background to Atlantic Creole Cultures." In *Central Africans and Cultural Transformations*, edited by Heywood, 91–116.

———, ed. *Central Africans and Cultural Transformations in the American Diaspora*. Cambridge: Cambridge University Press, 2002.

Higman, B. W. *Slave Populations of the British Caribbean, 1807–1834*. Baltimore: Johns Hopkins University Press, 1984.

Hilton, Anne. *The Kingdom of Kongo*. Oxford: Clarendon Press, 1985.

Hitte, Philip K. *History of the Arabs*. London: Macmillan, 1937.

Hochschild, Adam. *King Leopold's Ghost: A Story of Greed, Terror, and Heroism in Colonial Africa*. Boston: Houghton Mifflin, 1998.

Howard, Philip A. *Changing History: Afro-Cuban Cabildos and Societies of Color in the Nineteenth Century*. Baton Rouge: Louisiana State University Press, 1998.

Hulal al Mawsiyya. *Colección de crónicas árabes de las dinastias Almorávides, Almohade y Benimerin*. Translated by Ambrosio Huici-Miranda. Tetuan: Editora Marroqui, 1951.

Inikori, Joseph E. "Africa in World History: The Export Slave Trade from Africa and the Emergence of the Atlantic Economic Order." In *UNESCO General History of Africa*, vol. 5: *Africa from the Sixteenth to the Eighteenth Century*, edited by B. A. Ogot, 74–112. Paris: UNESCO, 1992.

———. *Africans and the Industrial Revolution in England*. Cambridge: Cambridge University Press, 2002.

———. "The Development of Entrepreneurship in Africa: Southeastern Nigeria during the Era of the Trans-Atlantic Slave Trade." In *Black Business and Economic Power*, edited by Alusine Jalloh and Toyin Falola, 41–79. Rochester, N.Y.: University of Rochester Press, 2002.

———. "The Known, the Unknown, the Knowable and the Unknowable: Evidence and the Evaluation of Evidence in the Measurement of the Trans-Atlantic Slave Trade." Unpublished paper presented at the Williamsburg Conference on the Trans-Atlantic Slave Trade Database, September 1998.

———. "Slavery in Africa and the Trans-Atlantic Slave Trade." In *The African Diaspora*, edited by Alusine Jalloh and Stephen E. Maizlish, 39–72. College Station: Texas A&M University Press, 1996.

———. "The Sources of Supply for the Atlantic Slave Exports from the Bight of Benin and the Bight of Bonny (Biafra)." In *De la traite à l'esclavage: Actes du Colloque international sur la traite des Noirs, Nantes, 1985*, edited by Serge Daget, 2:26–43. Nantes: Centre de recherche sur l'histoire du monde atlantique, 1988.

———. "The Struggle against the Slave Trade: The Role of the States." In *Fighting the Slave Trade: West African Strategies*, edited by Sylviane A. Diouf, 170–98. Athens, Ohio: Ohio University Press, 2003.

———. "The Unmeasured Hazards of the Atlantic Slave Trade: Sources, Causes and Historiographical Implications." In *From Chains to Bonds*, edited by Dou Dou Diène, 86–102. Paris: UNESCO, 2001.

———. "West Africa's Seaborne Trade, 1750–1850: Volume, Structure and Implications." In *Figuring African Trade*, edited by Liesegang, Pasch, and Jones, 50–88.

Jadin, Louis. *L'Ancien Congo et l'Angola, 1639–1655*. 3 vols. Brussels: Institut historique belge de Rome, 1975.

Karasch, Mary C. *Slave Life in Rio de Janeiro, 1808–1850*. Princeton: Princeton University Press, 1987.

Kent, R. K. "Madagascar and the Islands of the Indian Ocean." In *UNESCO General History of Africa*, vol. 5: *Africa from the Sixteenth to the Eighteenth Century*, edited by B. A. Ogot, 849–94. Paris: UNESCO, 1992.

Kitab tabakat al-uman (*Livre des catégories des nations*). Attributed to Sa'id ibn Ahmad, al-Andalusi. Translated by Régis Blachère. Paris: Larose, 1935.

Klein, Herbert S. *African Slavery in Latin America and the Caribbean*. Oxford: Oxford University Press, 1986.

Klein, Martin A. "Senegambia." In *Macmillan Encyclopedia of World Slavery*, edited by Finkelman and Miller, 2:944–47.

Knight, Franklin W. *Slave Society in Cuba during the Nineteenth Century*. Madison: University of Wisconsin Press, 1970.

Koelle, S. W. *Polyglotta Africana*. 1854. Reprint, edited, with an introduction, by P. E. H. Hair. Graz, Austria: Akademische Druck- und Verlagsanstalt, 1963.

LaChance, Paul. "The Politics of Fear: French Louisianians and the Slave Trade, 1786–1809." *Plantation Societies in America* 1 (1979): 162–97.

Laguerre, Michel. *Voudou and Politics in Haiti*. London: Macmillan, 1989.

Lamiral, Dominique Harcourt. *L'Affrique et le peuple affriquain considérés sous tous leurs rapports avec notre commerce & nos colonies . . .* Paris: Dessenne, 1789. Cited in Gabriel Debien, "Les origines des esclaves aux Antilles," *Bulletin de l'Institut français d'Afrique noir*, ser. B, 23 (1961): 363–87.

Landers, Jane. *Black Society in Spanish Florida*. Urbana: University of Illinois Press, 1999.

———. "The Central African Presence in Spanish Maroon Communities." In *Central Africans and Cultural Transformations*, edited by Linda M. Heywood, 227–42. Cambridge: Cambridge University Press, 2002.

———. "Cimarron Ethnicity and Cultural Adaptation in the Spanish Domains of the Circum-Caribbean, 1503–1763." In *Identity in the Shadow of Slavery*, edited by Paul Lovejoy, 30–54. London: Continuum, 2000.

Law, Robin. *Ouidah: The Social History of a West African Slaving "Port," 1727–1892*. Athens, Ohio: Ohio University Press, 2004.

———. *The Slave Coast of West Africa, 1550–1750*. Oxford: Oxford University Press, 1991.

Law, Robin, and Paul E. Lovejoy, eds. *The Biography of Mahommah Gardo Baquaqua: His Passage from Slavery to Freedom in Africa and America*. Princeton: Markus Weiner Publishers, 2001.

Law, Robin, and Silke Strickrodt, eds. *Ports of the Slave Trade (Bights of Benin and Biafra)*. Stirling: Centre of Commonwealth Studies, University of Stirling, 1999.

Le Page du Pratz, Antoine Simone. *Histoire de la Louisiane*. 3 vols. Paris: Lambert, 1758.

Liesegang, G., H. Pasch, and A. Jones, eds. *Figuring African Trade: Proceedings of the Symposium on the Quantification and Structure of the Import and Export and Long Distance Trade in Africa, 1800–1913* [St. Augustine, January 3–6, 1983]. Berlin: D. Reimer, 1986.

Littlefield, Daniel C. *Rice and Slaves: Ethnicity and the Slave Trade in Colonial South Carolina*. Baton Rouge: Louisiana State University Press, 1981.

Lockhart, James. *Spanish Peru, 1532–1560: A Colonial Society*. Madison: University of Wisconsin Press, 1968.

Lovejoy, Paul E. "Ethnic Designations of the Slave Trade and the Reconstruction of the History of Trans-Atlantic Slavery." In *Trans-Atlantic Dimension of Ethnicity in the African Diaspora*, edited by Paul E. Lovejoy and David V. Trotman, 9–42. London: Continuum, 2003.

———. "Kola in the History of West Africa," *Cahiers d'Etudes africaines* 20, 1–2 (1980), 97–134.

———. *Transformations in Slavery: A History of Slavery in Africa*. Rev. ed. Cambridge: Cambridge University Press, 2000.

Lovejoy, Paul E., and David Richardson. " 'This Horrid Hole': Royal Authority, Commerce and Credit at Bonny, 1690–1840." *Journal of African History* 45, 3 (2004): 363–92.

Maitland, J. A. Fuller, ed. *Grove's Dictionary of Music and Musicians*. Philadelphia: Theodore Presser, 1918.

Manning, Patrick. *Slavery and African Life: Occidental, Oriental, and African Slave Trades*. Cambridge: Cambridge University Press, 1990.

———. *Slavery, Colonialism, and Economic Growth in Dahomey, 1640–1960* (Cambridge: Cambridge University Press, 1982).

Martin, Phillis M. *The External Trade of the Loango Coast, 1576–1870: The Effects of Changing Commercial Relations on the Vili Kingdom of Loango*. Oxford: Clarendon Press, 1972.

Medeiros, Eduardo. "Moçambicanizaçao dos escravos saídos pelos portos de Moçambique." Paper presented at the conference Enslaving Connections: Africa and Brazil during the Era of the Slave Trade, York University, October, 12–15, 2000. To be published in *Africa and America: Interconnections during the Slave Trade*, edited by José C. Curto and Renée Soulodre-LaFrance.

Meillassoux, Claude, ed. *L'esclavage en Afrique précoloniale*. Paris: Maspero, 1975.

Mellafe, Rolando. *La introducción de la esclavitud negra en Chile: Tráfico y rutas*. 1958. Reprint, Santiago de Chile: Editorial Universitaria, 1984.

Menard, Russell, and Stuart B. Schwartz. "Why African Slavery? Labor Force Transitions in Brazil, Mexico, and the Carolina Lowcountry." In *Slavery in the*

Americas, edited by Wolfgang Binder, 89–114. Würzburg: Königshausen und Neumann, 1993.

Merlet, Annie. *Autour du Loango, XIVieme–XIXieme siècle: Histoire des peuples du sud-ouest du Gabon du temps du royaume de Loango et du "Congo français."* Libreville/Paris: Centre culturel français Saint-Exupéry (SEPIA), 1991.

Miller, Joseph C. "Central Africa during the Era of the Slave Trade, c. 1490s–1850s." In *Central Africans and Cultural Transformations in America*, edited by Linda M. Heywood, 21–69. Cambridge: Cambridge University Press, 2002.

———. *Kings and Kinsmen: Early Mbundu States in Angola*. Oxford: Clarendon Press, 1976.

———. "Lineages, Ideology, and the History of Slavery in Western Central Africa." In *Ideology of Slavery in Africa*, edited by Paul Lovejoy, 40–71. Beverly Hills: Sage Publications, 1981.

———. *Way of Death: Merchant Capitalism and the Angolan Slave Trade, 1730–1830*. Madison: University of Wisconsin Press, 1988.

Mintz, Sidney, and Richard Price. *An Anthropological Approach to the Afro-American Past: A Caribbean Perspective*. Philadelphia: Institute for the Study of Human Issues, 1976. Republished under the title *The Birth of African-American Culture: An Anthropological Perspective*. Boston: Beacon Press, 1992.

Moore, F. *Travels into the Inland Parts of Africa*. London: E. Cave, 1738. Cited in Brooks, *Eurafricans in Western Africa*, 228–29.

Moreno Fraginals, Manuel. "Africa in Cuba: A Quantitative Analysis of the African Population in the Island of Cuba." In *Comparative Perspectives on Slavery in New World Plantation Societies*, edited by Vera Rubin and Arthur Truden, 187–201. New York: New York Academy of Sciences, 1977.

Morgan, Philip D. *Slave Counterpoint: Black Culture in the Eighteenth-Century Chesapeake and Lowcountry*. Chapel Hill: University of North Carolina Press, 1998.

Mullin, Michael. *Africa in America: Slave Acculturation and Resistance in the American South and the English Caribbean, 1736–1831*. Urbana: University of Illinois Press, 1992.

Ngou-Mve, Nicolás. *El Africa bantú en la colonización en México*. Madrid: Consejo Superior de Investigaciones Científicos, 1994.

Niane, D. T. "Introduction." In *UNESCO General History of Africa*, vol. 4, *Africa from the Twelfth to the Sixteenth Century*, edited by D. T. Niane, 1–14. Berkeley: University of California Press, 1984.

———. "Mali and the Second Mandingo Expansion." In *UNESCO General History of Africa*, vol. 4, *Africa from the Twelfth to the Sixteenth Century*, edited by D. T. Niane, 117–71. Berkeley: University of California Press, 1984.

———. "Relationships and Exchanges among the Different Regions." In *UNESCO General History of Africa*, vol. 4, *Africa from the Twelfth to the Sixteenth Century*, edited by D. T. Niane, 614–34. Berkeley: University of California Press, 1984.

————. *Sundiata: An Epic of Old Mali*. Translated by G. D. Pickett. London: Longmans, 1965.

Northrup, David. *Africa's Discovery of Europe, 1450–1850*. New York: Oxford University Press, 2002.

————. "A Collection of Interviews Conducted in Southeastern Nigeria in 1972–1973." Unpublished.

————. "Igbo and Myth Igbo: Culture and Ethnicity in the Atlantic World, 1600–1850." *Slavery and Abolition* 21, no. 3 (December 2000): 1–20.

————. *Trade without Rulers: Pre-colonial Economic Development in South-eastern Nigeria*. Oxford: Clarendon Press, 1978).

Oldendorp, C. G. A. *C. G. A. Oldendorp's History of the Mission of the Evangelical Brethren on the Caribbean Islands of St. Thomas, St. Croix, and St. John*. Edited by Johann Jakob Bossard [Bossart]. Translated by Arnold R. Highfield and Vladimir Barac. Ann Arbor, Mich.: Karoma Publishers, 1987.

Oriji, John N. "Igboland, Slavery, and the Drums of War and Heroism." In *Fighting the Slave Trade: West African Strategies* edited by Sylviane A. Diouf, 121–31. Athens, Ohio: Ohio University Press, 2003.

Ortiz, Fernando. *Los negros esclavos*. Havana: Editorial de Ciencias Sociales, 1996.

Palmer, Colin. *Human Cargoes: The English Slave Trade to Spanish America, 1700–1739*. Urbana: University of Illinois Press, 1981.

————. *Slaves of the White God: Blacks in Mexico, 1570–1650*. Cambridge, Mass.: Harvard University Press, 1976.

Palmié, Stephan. "Ethnogenetic Processes and Cultural Transfer in Afro-American Slave Populations." In *Slavery in the Americas*, edited by Wolfgang Binder, 337–64. Würzburg: Königshausen und Neumann, 1993.

Peixoto, Antonio da Costa. *Obra nova de lingua geral de Mina*. Edited by Luis Silveira. Lisbon: República Portuguesa, Ministério das Colónias, Divisão de Publicações e Biblioteca, Agência Geral das Colónias, 1945.

Pelletan, Jean Gabriel. *Mémoire sur la colonie du Sénégal*. Paris: Panckoucke, An IX [1800].

Pereira, Nunes. *A Casa das Minas: Contribuição ao estudo das sobrevivéncias do culto dos Voduns, do Panteão daomeano, no Estado do Maranhão, Brasil*. Petrópolis: Vozes, 1979. 2nd ed. of *A Casa das Minas: Contribuição ao estudo das sobrevivéncias daomeianas no Brasil*. Introduction by Arthur Ramos. Rio de Janeiro, 1947.

Pierson, William D. *Black Yankees: The Development of an Afro-American Subculture in Eighteenth Century New England*. Amherst: University of Massachusetts Press, 1988.

Portuando Zúñiga, Olga. *Entre esclavos y libres de Cuba colonial*. Santiago de Cuba: Editorial Oriental, 2003.

Postma, Johannes Menne. *The Dutch in the Atlantic Slave Trade, 1600–1815*. Cambridge: Cambridge University Press, 1990.

Rashid, Ismail. " 'A Devotion to Liberty at Any Price': Rebellion and Anti-Slavery in the Upper Guinea Coast in the Eighteenth and Nineteenth Centuries." In *Fighting the Slave Trade: West African Strategies*, edited by Sylviane A. Diouf, 132–69. Athens, Ohio: Ohio University Press, 2003.

Reis, João José. "Ethnic Politics among Africans in Nineteenth-Century Bahia." In *Trans-Atlantic Dimensions of Ethnicity in the American Diaspora*, edited by Paul E. Lovejoy and David Trotman, 240–64. London: Continuum, 2003.

Richardson, David. "Shipboard Revolts, African Authority, and the Trans-Atlantic Slave Trade." In *Fighting the Slave Trade: West African Strategies*, edited by Sylviane A. Diouf, 199–218. Athens: Ohio University Press, 2003.

Roberts, Richard. *Warriors, Merchants, and Slaves: The State and the Economy in the Middle Niger Valley, 1700–1914*. Stanford: Stanford University Press, 1987.

Rodney, Walter. *A History of the Upper Guinea Coast, 1545–1800*. Oxford: Oxford University Press, 1970.

———. *How Europe Underdeveloped Africa*. London: Bogle-L'Ouverture Publications, 1972.

Rodrigues, Nina. *Os Africanos no Brasil*. 2nd rev. ed. São Paulo: Companhia Editora Nacional, 1935.

Rout, Leslie B., Jr. *The African Experience in Spanish America: 1502 to the Present Day*. Cambridge: Cambridge University Press, 1976.

Ryder, Alan. *Benin and the Europeans, 1485–1897*. New York: Humanities Press, 1969.

Sandoval, Alonso de. *De instauranda Aethiopum salute: El mundo de la esclavitud negra en América*. Facsimile of 1627 edition. Bogotá: Empresa Nacional de Publicaciones, 1956.

———. *Naturaleza, policia sagrada y profana, costumbres, abusos, y tiros de todos los Etiopes que se conocen en el mundo; y de otras cosas notables, que se cuentan de sus Reinos . . .* Madrid, 1647.

———. *Un tratado sobre la esclavitud*. 1627 edition. Edited by Enriqueta Vila Vilar. Madrid: Aliaza Editorial, S.A., 1987.

Schuler, Monica. *Alas, Alas Kongo: A Social History of Indentured African Immigration into Jamaica, 1841–1865*. Baltimore: Johns Hopkins University Press, 1980.

Schwartz, Stuart B. *Sugar Plantations in the Formation of Brazilian Society: Bahia, 1550–1835*. Cambridge: Cambridge University Press, 1985.

Searing, James F. *West African Slavery and Atlantic Commerce: The Senegal River Valley, 1700–1860*. New York: Cambridge University Press, 1993.

Sevilla a comienzos del siglo XII: El tratado de Ibn Abdūn. Edited and translated by Emilio García Gomez and E. Lévi-Provençal. Madrid: Monedo y Crédito, 1948.

Shakundi, al-Andalus. *Elogio del Islam español*. Translated by Emilio García Gómez. Madrid: Impr. de E. Maestre, 1934.

Soares, Marisa de Carvalho. *Devotos da cor: Identidade étnica, religiosidade e escravidão no Río de Janeiro, século XVIII*. Rio de Janeiro: Civilização Brasileira, 2000.

Studer, Elena F. S. de. *La trata de negros en el Río de la Plata durant el siglo XVIII*. Montevideo: Libros de Hispanoamérica, 1984.

Sundiata, Ibrahim K. *Black Scandal, America and the Liberian Labor Crisis, 1929–1936*. Philadelphia: Institute for the Study of Human Issues, 1980.

———. *From Slaving to Neoslavery: The Bight of Biafra and Fernando Po in the Era of Abolition, 1827–1930*. Madison: University of Wisconsin Press, 1996.

Talbi, M. "The Spread of Civilization in the Maghrib and Its Impact on Western Civilization." In *UNESCO General History of Africa*, vol. 4, *Africa from the Twelfth to the Sixteenth Century*, edited by D. T. Niane, 57–77. Berkeley: University of California Press, 1984.

Tardieu, Jean-Pierre. "Origins of the Slaves in the Lima Region in Peru (Sixteenth and Seventeenth Centuries)." In *From Chains to Bonds: The Slave Trade Revisited*, edited by Doudou Diène, 43–54. Paris: UNESCO Publishing, 2001.

Taylor, Joe G. "The Foreign Slave Trade in Louisiana after 1808." In *Louisiana History* 1, no. 1 (1960): 36–44.

Thomas, Hugh. *The Slave Trade: The Story of the Atlantic Slave Trade, 1440–1870*. New York: Simon and Schuster, 1997.

Thornton, John K. *Africa and Africans in the Making of the Atlantic World*. Rev. ed. Cambridge: Cambridge University Press, 1998.

———. "African Dimensions of the Stono Rebellion," *American Historical Review* 46 (1991): 1101–13.

———. "African Political Ethics and the Slave Trade: Central African Dimensions." Unpublished paper.

———. *The Kingdom of Kongo: Civil War and Transition, 1641–1718*. Madison: University of Wisconsin Press, 1983.

———. *The Kongolese Saint Anthony: Dona Beatriz Kimpa Vita and the Antonian Movement, 1684–1706*. Cambridge: Cambridge University Press, 1998.

———. "Religious and Ceremonial Life in the Kongo and Mbundu Areas, 1500–1700." In *Central Africans and Cultural Transformations in the American Diaspora*, edited by Linda M. Heywood, 71–116. Cambridge: Cambridge University Press, 2002.

———. *Warfare in Atlantic Africa, 1500–1800*. London: University College of London Press, 1999.

"Timeline of Slavery." In *Macmillan Encyclopedia of World Slavery*, edited by Finkelman and Miller, 2:981.

Vanhee, Hein. "Central African Popular Christianity and the Making of Haitian Vodou Religion." In *Central Africans and Cultural Transformations in the American Diaspora*, edited by Linda M. Heywood, 243–66. Cambridge: Cambridge University Press, 2002.

Vansina, Jan. Foreword to *Central Africa and Cultural Formations in the American Diaspora*, edited by Linda M. Heywood, xi–xv. Cambridge: Cambridge University Press, 2002.

———. *Kingdoms of the Savanna*. Madison: University of Wisconsin Press, 1966.

————. *Paths in the Rainforests: Toward a History of Political Tradition in Equatorial Africa.* Madison: University of Wisconsin Press, 1990.

Verger, Pierre. *Flux et reflux de la traite des nègres entrele Golfe de Bénin et Bahia de Todos os Santos du 17e au 19e siècle.* Paris: Mouton, 1968.

————. *Trade Relations between the Bight of Benin and Bahia from the 17th to 19th Century.* Translated by Evelyn Crawford. Ibadan: Ibadan University Press, 1976.

Vila Vilar, Enriqueta. "The Large-Scale Introduction of Africans into Veracruz and Cartagena." In *Comparative Perspectives on Slavery in New World Plantation Societies,* edited by Vera Rubin and Arthur Truden, 267–80. New York: New York Academy of Sciences, 1977.

————. *Hispanoamérica y el comercio de esclavos.* Seville: Escuela de Estudios Hispano-Americanos, 1977.

Vydrine, Valentin. *Manding-English Dictionary (Mandinka/Bamana).* Vol. 1. St. Petersburg, Russia: Dimitry Bulanin Publishing House, 1999.

Walsh, Lorena. "The Chesapeake Slave Trade: Regional Patterns, African Origins, and Some Implications." *William and Mary Quarterly* 58, no. 1 (2001): 139–70.

————. *From Calabar to Carter's Grove: The History of a Virginia Slave Community.* Charlottesville: University Press of Virginia, 1997.

Wax, Darold D. "Preferences for Slaves in Colonial America," *Journal of Negro History* 58, no. 4 (1973): 371–401.

Wondji, C. "The States and Cultures of the Upper Guinea Coast." In *UNESCO General History of Africa,* vol. 5: *Africa from the Sixteenth to the Eighteenth Century,* edited by B. A. Ogot, 368–98. Berkeley: University of California Press, 1992.

Wood, Betty. *The Origins of American Slavery: Freedom and Bondage in the English Colonies.* New York: Hill and Wang, 1997.

Yai, Olabiyi. "Texts of Enslavement: Fon and Yoruba Vocabularies from Eighteenth and Nineteenth-century Brazil." In *Identity in the Shadow of Slavery,* edited by Paul E. Lovejoy, 102–12. (London: Continuum, 2000).

Index

Accra, 115

Adams, Captain John, 127

Addiction: in promoting slave trade in Africa, 18

Affonso, king of Kongo, 15

Afikpo, 127

Africa: European colonization of, xiv, xv; administrators in, 51

African coasts, definitions of, 26

African ethnicities: boundaries and identity formation, xviii; changing meanings and spellings over time and place, xviii; self-identification in Americas, 23, 38–52; multilingualism among, 42; most frequently found in American documents, 57, 175–76

— Agolin, 37

— Aja, 16, 17, 43, 111–14, 123–25, 169. *See also* African ethnicities: Arada; Arara; Dahomeans; Ewe, Fon(d); Gege; Jeje

— Akan, 101, 105, 110–11, 115, 119

— Akus (Yoruba), 133

— Angolans, 36, 46–47

— Anlo, 113. *See also* Ewe

— Arada, 17, 43, 56, 111, 123–25, 169. *See also* African ethnicities: Aja; Arara; Dahomeans; Ewe; Fon(d); Gege; Jeje

— Arara, 36, 112, 115. *See also* African ethnicities: Aja; Arada; Dahomeans; Ewe; Fon(d); Gege; Jeje

— Aro, 129

— Arriatas, 55

— Ashanti, 35, 120

— Bagos, 61. *See also* African ethnicities: Balanta

— Balanta, 61, 80, 88. *See also* African ethnicities: Bagos

— Bamana, 43, 46, 54, 78, 96–100, 119, 176–77. *See also* African ethnicities: Bambara

— Bambara, 22, 53, 96–100; means "barbarian" in Africa, 97; Samba Bambara Conspiracy, 97; meaning of to Europeans in Africa, 98

— Banol, 88

— Banum, 80

— Beafada. *See* African ethnicities: Biafara

— Berbers, 2, 4. *See also* African ethnicities: Sanhaja Berbers

— Berbese. *See* African ethnicities: Berbice

— Berbice, 32, 80, 163, 170. *See also* African ethnicities: Sereer

— Biafada. *See* African ethnicities: Biafara

— Biafara, 80, 84, 88–90

— Bibi. *See* African ethnicities: Ibibio

— Biofo, 80

— Bioho, 88

— Bioko, 130–31, 138

— Birom, 77

— Bissagos, 46, 60–61

— Bran, 80, 84, 88–89

— Bricamo, 36